SCHOOL READINESS: ASSESSMENT AND EDUCATIONAL ISSUES

Gilbert R. Gredler
University of South Carolina

Clinical Psychology Publishing Company, Inc.
4 Conant Square
Brandon, VT 05733

SCHOOL READINESS: ASSESSMENT AND EDUCATIONAL ISSUES

Library of Congress Catalog Card Number: 91-72062
ISBN: 0-88422-112-1

Clinical Psychology Publishing Company, Inc.
4 Conant Square
Brandon, Vermont 05733

Cover Design: Michael F. Gauthier

Printed in the United States of America.

CONTENTS

Section IV   *Related Issues*

ACKNOWLEDGMENTS

In writing this book I would like to state that I owe a great deal to many different individuals. There are many complex issues that revolve around school readiness and entry. Over the last four years I have discussed a number of these topics with parents, educators, and psychologists. I would especially like to thank Helen Schotanus of the New Hampshire State Department of Education who alerted me to many of the problems in the field of early childhood education. I am indebted to the many parents of young children in California, Florida, New Hampshire, South Carolina, Texas, Tennessee, and Pennsylvania who willingly discussed the many problems of early childhood education and shared their perceptions of current educational practices. I have learned that there are many parents throughout the United States who are truly concerned about current school practices and who are making a determined effort to present their reasoned viewpoints to school personnel and boards of education, as well as to the general public.

I have also been impressed with the dedication of school personnel as they attempt to offer appropriate educational programs for young children. These include many teachers, principals, and school psychologists.

The Southern Regional Education Board in Atlanta provided me with grants of financial support, for which I am most grateful. These grants helped me to undertake my interview schedule with parents of children entering school.

Bruce Mallory of the University of New Hampshire, Deborah May of the State University of New York at Albany, and Margaret Gredler of the University of South Carolina all have my appreciation for their helpful comments concerning the manuscript.

I also wish to note that my children, Mark and Judy, now grown, could never have been reduced to a meaningful score on a readiness test.

Gilbert R. Gredler

SECTION I

Introduction

1

SCHOOL READINESS:
AN INTRODUCTION AND OVERVIEW

Over the last several years there has been an increased interest in the topic of school readiness. The latest messages communicated to the public about the learning problems of American children emphasize that lack of social maturity and premature school entrance are major factors in the absence of learning readiness. School readiness is a concept that has long been used in educational circles. However, it is of particular interest today because many controversial beliefs and practices are associated with the topic.

This book is divided into four major sections. This chapter and Chapter 2, "The Concept of School Readiness," comprise Section I, an introduction. Chapter 2 presents four models of school readiness. One view, that readiness is simply a matter of biological maturation, is held by many school personnel. The other three views, in contrast, consider the child's experience when determining the concept of readiness. These views are found in the writings of David Ausubel, the Russian psychologist Lev Vygotsky, and the cumulative skills model developed by Robert Gagné.

For years, educators and psychologists have been discussing the proper age at which a child should enter school. In fact, discussion of the correct entrance age has become an obsession with American educators. Some of the important issues in the entrance age debate and the influence of entrance age on achievement are reviewed in Chapters 2 and 3.

Section II, Assessing Readiness, includes four chapters. The extraordinary increase in the use of assessment measures to screen children as to their "readiness" for school is reflected in Chapters 3 and 4, on screening instruments. Problems associated with screening and assessment procedures that were implemented in the 1940s and 1950s are discussed.

3

Many psychologists and educators, as well as parents, are unaware of the fact that raising the entrance age to school does not reduce the range of age differences found in a first-grade class. That is, the difference between the youngest and oldest child in kindergarten and first grade remains a 12-month range. Teacher perceptions about "youngness" are even more important than the actual entrance age of the child and will be discussed in some detail. Readers will learn that teachers in Great Britain (where children enter school a year earlier than in the United States) speak approvingly of the maturity of their "older" first-grade children. However, these children, if attending American schools, would form the youngest group, and these very same children are often mentioned in negative terms by their American teachers because they make up the youngest group.

Often there is little consideration given as to how to analyze and interpret adequately the results obtained from the administration of a readiness or screening test. Chapter 4 provides such an analysis.

The Gesell School Readiness Test is one of the most frequently used screening measures in American schools today. Chapter 5 presents an overall appraisal of the value of this instrument. The reader will note that the questions raised as to the lack of validity and reliability of this test must be asked about any assessment measure used with young children.

The Gesellians have constantly fought for higher school entrance ages; they state that a majority of children are "overplaced" in school and frequently argue for delayed entrance to school and/or placement in a prekindergarten or transition room for those who are "developmentally unready." The ways that this belief structure affects the organization of educational programs for the young child will be discussed in several chapters of this book.

Many kindergarten and first-grade teachers are concerned about the social and emotional adjustment of the children in their classrooms. A number of teachers insist that many children present symptoms of "immaturity" and social maladjustment. Therefore both the validity and reliability of assessment measures used by educators to diagnose the adjustment status of young children become important issues. This is one of several topics discussed in Chapter 6. Results of important studies of the emotional and social adjustment of children as they enter kindergarten and first grade will also be presented.

Section III of the text, School Practices, describes several solutions for perceived lack of readiness in children. One solution, discussed for years, is that of raising the school entrance age. Some of the important issues in the entrance age debate and the influence of entrance age on achievement are discussed in Chapters 7 and 8.

Discussed also in Chapter 7 are some of the reasons for the steady increase in school entrance age over the last 30 years. Various developmental factors that contribute to the child's state of readiness are also analyzed and summarized. Physiological indicators such as vision and teething status are considered of extraordinary importance by many educators. In this section the reader also will find the latest research described and analyzed as to its significance.

Another important topic concerns sex differences that are found in the reading performance of first-grade children. The beliefs that boys will automatically have more difficulty in the early grades and that entrance of male students to school should be delayed are discussed in Chapter 7. Important research studies that investigate the reading performance of boys and girls are also presented.

Parents are often told that a "young" child entering school is at risk for either failure or low school achievement. Chapter 8 provides an in-depth analysis of the influence of entrance age on school achievement. The reader will learn that entering school at a young age does not necessarily predispose a child either to failure or to poor academic performance.

The transition room is a program commonly found in many American schools today. These programs are discussed in Chapter 9. Although such programs have been a part of American schools for the past 50 years, the transition/readiness room has become particularly popular with educators within the past 15 years. Important research studies about the progress of children in transition-room programs and a thorough analysis and critique are presented.

Pertinent examples of the curriculum for transition programs will be presented. In addition, important research studies comparing transition room–placed children with both "at-risk" children who go directly to first grade and regular first-grade students will be discussed.

Another school practice, that of retention, is discussed in Chapter 10. Few topics bring forth more concern from parents than the possible retention of their children in kindergarten or first grade, or placement of their children in a prekindergarten or prefirst (transition) program. Retention has been a component of established school policy in American schools since the turn of the century. Problems with the use of retention as the main approach to deal with young children who demonstrate learning and/or behavioral problems will be presented. Important investigations that examine the progress of retained versus nonretained students will be reviewed.

Many schools use retention as the major remedial approach for kindergarten and first-grade children who may have either learning and/or behavioral problems. Retention too often involves only a repetition of the same curriculum with which the children had difficulty in the first place. No specific diagnosis and assessment of the child's difficulties are provided; neither is an intervention program tailored to the needs of the child. Discussion of remedial and intervention approaches other than retention that have been shown to be of value in the educational environment will be found in Chapter 11.

Important issues affecting early childhood education are discussed in Chapter 12. Various concepts as to what constitutes appropriate kindergarten objectives and curriculum are reviewed. Once the domain of a few educators, the objectives and goals of the kindergarten year have come under the increased scrutiny and discussion of parent groups, professional early childhood education groups, as well as a few school psychologists.

Parents have become increasingly vocal and concerned about the early childhood programs currently operating in the public schools. An impression often found among school personnel is that the parents' main goal is to "push" their children to engage in more academic tasks at yet an earlier age. Chapter 13 provides the reader with the many concerns of parents of young children and presents some of their anxieties and worries as to how their children will fare as they begin their school experience. Parental advocacy efforts, a new phenomenon, will also be discussed in this chapter.

As has been stated, a number of school systems have organized programs to screen children entering kindergarten and first grade and have developed alternative educational placements for children whom they consider to be at risk. Few questions about the ethical or legal issues involved have been considered. I raised some of these issues at a school psychology institute at Temple University in 1972 in my presentation on ethical and legal issues in school readiness practices (Gredler, 1975). However, it has only been within the last few years that these topics have been addressed more fully by educators, psychologists, and parents. A number of ethical and legal problems are considered in Chapter 14, as well as the ways that state departments of education are coping with the increased use of alternative placement programs for kindergarten and first grade. Specific rulings that have largely escaped notice by the public, but which are of primary importance, are described.

A recap of the major issues facing educators and psychologists today as they attempt to provide suitable educational programs and use proper assessment is provided in Chapter 15.

2

THE CONCEPT OF
SCHOOL READINESS

The term *readiness* is described in Webster's dictionary as (1) mental or physical preparation for some experience or action; (2) being notably dexterous, adroit, or skilled; and (3) immediate availability. These somewhat differing descriptions are reflected in the several views of school readiness that have developed over the years. One view of school readiness is that of chronological age; i.e., physiological and psychosocial growth are age-related. In other words, by a certain age, the majority of children can enter school and progress satisfactorily.

Another view of readiness is that of developmental growth or maturation. The advocates of this perspective believe that an internal timing mechanism determines the child's readiness for school and that it cannot be tampered with. If left alone, the child will automatically show signs of readiness for school at some point in time.

Other views of readiness, in contrast, emphasize the role of the child's experience in becoming able to learn particular tasks or subjects. David Ausubel (1962), for example, describes readiness as a particular state in the child that depends on both growth and maturation *and* the social experiences of the child. Another perspective, that of Lev Vygotsky (1930–35/1978), describes readiness as the level of tasks that can be learned in collaboration with a more knowledgeable peer or adult. Finally, the cumulative skills model developed by Robert M. Gagné (1985) describes readiness as the availability of relevant skills or capabilities in the learner. Assessing readiness, in his view, is a matter of determining that the learner has acquired the prerequisite skills essential for learning a particular subject.

These differing views and theories have each influenced educational practices and programming in the public schools. Acceptance of a particular theory leads to the use of particular kinds of school experiences for children. For example, use of the Reading Recovery Program in Ohio (see Chapter 11) indicates that school personnel have committed themselves to a major intervention effort while the child is in first grade. Such a practice indicates a belief in the role of the classroom environment in developing particular skills. In contrast, educators who accept the maturational model have opted instead for a higher entrance age and the use of prereadiness and transition rooms. Acceptance of the maturational model (and the exclusion of other child development theories) also is accompanied by the use of retention as the remediation approach with young children who show possible learning/behavioral problems.

School Readiness as Maturational Development

The maturational concept of readiness views the child as an organism whose readiness is inextricably linked with biological unfolding, an unfolding that environmental opportunities can do little to alter. Some individuals (e.g., Washburne, 1936) consider maturation and readiness to be essentially synonymous terms. According to this view, as a child matures he or she will automatically show certain signs of readiness. Thus the result is a *wait and see* attitude. Washburne (1936), one of the main advocates of this approach, states that there are many factors that "must be taken into account if we are not to force open a bud not yet ready to bloom" (p. 127).

The concept of maturation as the avenue of *readiness* led to an emphasis in the school on postponement of the introduction of various subjects until the child showed adequate "signs" of being able to learn. However, even at the time that the unfolding concept of readiness was being promulgated, other educators, such as Brownell (1938) and Buswell (1938), were arguing that such an approach to readiness took into account only the kinds of methods and materials in use at that time.

The maturational school of thought has been championed in the United States by educators such as Hymes (1958, 1963) and Washburne (1936); by pediatricians such as Gesell (1954); and later by various psychologists such as Ilg and Ames (1965) and Donofrio (1977). The maturational theory is best described by Ames in her book *Is Your Child in the Wrong Grade?* (1967), in which she emphasizes that up to two thirds of all schoolchildren are *overplaced* in school because of lack of a proper maturational age.

Gesell and his followers attempted to establish a timetable that outlines the correct ages for learning the various tasks of the school curriculum. However, according to Ausubel (1962), Gesellian theory more adequately fits sensorimotor and neuromuscular development of the child that takes place during the prenatal and early infancy periods instead of explaining readiness for kindergarten.

When evidence has been produced that children can learn at earlier ages than the Gesellians indicate is possible, there are cries that educational personnel are tampering with the internal timing sequence and harm will result to the child (Ausubel & Robinson, 1969). The maturationalists also hint that the harm resulting from beginning to read at too early an age might not become evident until the child is a young adult. They predict a number of later dire consequences for the child who begins school at too early an age. The latest example of such beliefs is found in the statement by two Gesellian educators that children beginning school at an early age are more prone to suicide when they reach young adulthood (Uphoff & Gilmore, 1985). This latter comment is addressed in more detail in Chapter 6, on social and emotional adjustment.

Another maturationalist speaks passionately about the hazards of a lowered entrance age and argues that parents are primarily at fault. Halliwell (1968, pp. 55–56) maintains that the trend toward an earlier first-grade entry age has become more pronounced as a result of parental pressure.

Halliwell notes that "in the past, when educators refused to succumb to parental pressure in regard to the early admission of children, they could inure themselves to continued manifestations of parental frustration (in the name of their children), fortified by the assurance that a belated entrance to school could only increase the child's probability of attaining a measure of academic success" (Halliwell, 1968, pp. 55–56).

Altman (Gredler, 1964) believes the problem is a simple one that involves essentially accepting the child's present developmental level. However, if the child hasn't reached certain maturational stages of development the teacher must wait. Altman continues by stating that the immature child has no place in kindergarten or first grade. He or she will become unhappy if pushed; what he or she needs is understanding and love. For Altman, a prefirst or transitional first grade is the answer to the problem of the immature first-grade child. These educators believe the issues are quite clear-cut: Maturation is the important variable; it is easy to identify the "immature" child; and a transitional program will always provide the needed intervention. Additional discussion of the internal ripening hypothesis and the role of various physiological factors in a child's readiness will be found in Chapter 8, on entrance age and achievement.

The Influence of Piaget

One theory that has been cited as supporting the maturationalist view of readiness is the cognitive-development theory of Jean Piaget. A well-known Swiss psychologist, Piaget influenced the development of school curricula that promoted discovery learning in the United States in the 1960s. Believing that children are not "little adults" in their thought processes, Piaget's goal in his studies of children was to trace the specific changes in thinking processes from the illogical conclusions of the young child to the reasoning processes of the adult (Piaget, 1975). For Piaget, understanding intelligence meant understanding the ways that the child's mind constructs reality and the ways the child's beliefs gradually approach logical thinking.

Observation of and research with children led Piaget (1970) to identify four broad periods or stages of thinking that are qualitatively different. The four stages and the appropriate ages associated with each are presented in Table 2–1.

According to Piaget (1970), the infant, and then the child, develops each stage

Table 2–1.
Piagetian Stages of Cognitive Development

Stage	Approximate ages	Major characteristics
Sensorimotor	Birth to 1–2 years	1. Development of strategies to manipulate objects in the environment 2. Separation of self from the environment (occurs at about 12 months) and the concept of objects (an object out of sight still exists)
Preoperational	1–3 years to 7–8 years	1. Language development and representation of events by symbols 2. Ideas related to each other on a perceptual base; based on perceptions (soap floats because it is small and iron sinks because it is thin)
Concrete operational	7–8 to 11 years or older	1. "True" logical thought begins—child separates concepts such as number and length, volume and shape, weight and shape, and so on. 2. Child supports reasoning processes by manipulating concrete objects.
Formal operational	Begins at age 11 or older	1. Hypothetical thought begins—reasoning is not limited to concrete objects; individual can build theories with several interacting ideas and systematically test hypotheses about them.

of thinking through interacting and experimenting with the environment. Furthermore, each stage makes possible the next broad period of development. Although the order of the four stages does not change, the stages may develop at different ages in different cultures. Rural children, for example, were observed to be 1 to 2 years behind the children originally studied by Piaget. Also, not every individual may reach the stage of formal operational thinking, the advanced stage of logical thought. Many American college students, for example, have been found to be in the concrete, rather than formal operational, period (Piaget, 1972).

The purpose of the theory, according to Piaget (1970), is to describe the development of intelligence, defined as logical thinking. The theory does not address the learning of specific items, such as the date America was discovered, or procedures, such as learning to read.

However, the exponents of the internal ripening perspective insist that Piaget's theory of mental development upholds their position (Ausubel & Robinson, 1969). *If* evidence could be found indicating that successful instruction in a subject depends upon the appearance of certain stages of cognitive development, then the school would be justified in postponing formal instruction in that area until that stage appeared.

For example, if conservation of number occurs at age 7 and if understanding fractions depends upon this type of reasoning, then the case might be made that the teaching of fractions should not be taught until the child demonstrates number conservation. However, Ausubel and Robinson (1969) note that ". . . analysis of relevant theoretical issues and available data call into question the argument that the existence of a *particular* Piagetian stage is a prerequisite for a *specific* kind of school learning; in fact it may be just as reasonable to argue that the acquisition of addition and subtraction skills provides readiness for conservation of number, as to assert that the acquisition of number conservation constitutes readiness for addition and subtraction" (p. 201).

Readiness as Growth and Social Experience

In the early 1930s, Arthur Gates, then a professor of educational psychology at Teachers College, Columbia University, undertook a 5-year study on the relationship between mental age and success in reading. His research (Gates, 1937; Gates & Bond, 1936) challenged the findings of Morphett and Washburne (1931) who stated that a mental age of $6\frac{1}{2}$ to 7 years of age was a necessary prerequisite for success in beginning reading. Gates's research dramatically emphasized *what few other studies have done;* namely, the influence of environmental conditions on the success of children in first-grade reading. Gates was convinced that classroom activities, i.e., the use of appropriate instructional methods and curriculum materials, play an important part in a child's progress in reading. To discover some of the specific factors that might be of importance, Gates studied the relationship between teaching conditions in four different first-grade classrooms. The purpose was to ascertain whether such conditions would affect the mental age level at which most children would learn to read.

Specifically, the investigation involved the analysis of reading instruction in those classes that varied on three important dimensions. They were (1) quality of teacher instruction, (2) availability of a wide range of supplementary reading material that was both easy and interesting, and (3) use of diagnostic assessment measures.

The data in Table 2–2 clearly illustrate that the success rate of the first-grade children with lower mental ages is considerably enhanced if they were members of either class A or B. For example, in class A, whereas 77% of the children with mental ages ranging from 4-5 to 5-4 met the first-grade criterion of 1.95 at the end of first grade, only 15% did so in classroom D. Although 95% of the children with mental ages from 6-0 to 6-4 were successful in first-grade reading in classroom A, only 53% with the same mental age in classroom D achieved to the same criterion. It was classroom A which met the three standards Gates had outlined: high quality of teacher instruction, a wide range of supplementary reading materials, and judicious use of diagnostic measures.

Table 2–2.

Percentage of Children Able to Read to Criterion (1.95) in Four Different First-Grade Classrooms Distributed According to Mental Ages

| Mental ages | Classes | | | |
	A	B	C	D
4-5 to 4-11	14%	40%	0%	0%
5-0 to 5-4	63%	63%	29%	15%
5-5 to 5-11	95%	80%	56%	47%
6-0 to 6-4	95%	89%	78%	53%
6-5 to 6-11	100%	88%	86%	64%
7-0 to 7-4	100%	100%	100%	57%
7-5 to 7-11	100%	100%	0%[b]	67%
8-0 to 8-4	c	c	c	100%
8-5 to 8-11	100%[a]	c	c	c

[a]2 children.

[b]1 child.

[c]No children in sample.

Note. Adapted from "The Necessary Mental Age for Beginning Reading" by A. Gates, 1937, *Elementary School Journal, 8*, pp. 497–508. Copyright 1937 by *Elementary School Journal,* University of Chicago, Publisher. Adapted by permission.

It must be remembered that the Morphett and Washburne study (1931) had received an extraordinary amount of publicity when published. At that time many educators were quite convinced that a mental age level of $6\frac{1}{2}$ years was absolutely necessary for a child to be able to learn to read successfully.

The concept of readiness as composed of both growth and social experience was formally developed by David Ausubel (1962), a contemporary educational psychologist. A cognitive theorist, Ausubel also is well known for the concept of linking instruction to the student's store of learned information. According to Ausubel, "readiness signifies that the current development of the organism is such that a reasonably economical increment in capacity may be anticipated in response to adequate stimulation—irrespective of how this state is achieved or the type of stimulation that is applied" (Ausubel, 1962, p. 82).

Therefore, a child who is categorized as "not ready" may be deficient because of a lack of sufficient *learning* as well as lack of a sufficient maturational level. Stott (1967) concurs, indicating that "an alternative view of the matter, which is more in line with the current conceptions of the nature of human development, regards learning readiness as something more than a result of biological maturation alone" (p. 276).

Equating the principles of readiness and maturation is a major error because lack of readiness in the child may reflect lack of cognitive maturity that may in turn be the result of an unstimulating or inadequate educational environment (Ausubel & Sullivan, 1970, p. 92). Ausubel and Sullivan (1970) also point out that ascribing a lack of maturation to the child can "become a conveniently available scapegoat whenever children manifest insufficient developmental readiness to learn" (p. 92). School personnel then believe they are absolved of all responsibilities for the child's education, and the school "consequently fails to subject its instructional practices to the degree of self-critical scrutiny necessary for continued educational progress" (p. 92). Specifically, Ausubel (1962) describes readiness as the state at which (1) the child can learn easily and without emotional strain, (2) the child will show adequate motivation because efforts at teaching provide adequate results, and (3) instructional approaches that build on prior learning are carefully implemented.

Because most developmental patterns consist of and reflect both maturational and learning facets, identification of the factor responsible for a particular behavior is difficult at best (Ausubel, 1962). Thus, the "internal ripening" theory has been highly detrimental in its effects on pupils and teachers because of "far fetched and uncritical extrapolation of developmental generalizations that either have not been adequately validated, or which apply only to a very restricted age segment of the total span of children's development" (Ausubel & Sullivan, 1970, p. 95). As Ausubel and Sullivan point out, many educators view a child's readiness for school in absolute terms. They fail "to appreciate that, except for such traits as walking and grasping, the mean age of readiness can never be specified apart from relevant environmental conditions" (p. 93).

Another prominent cognitive theorist and educational psychologist, Jerome S. Bruner, specifically questions the postponement of education for the child. "We begin with the hypothesis that any subject can be taught effectively in some intellectually honest form to any child at any stage of development" (Bruner, 1966, p. 33). Director of the Harvard Center for Cognitive Studies in the 1960s, Bruner (1966) recommended that the subject matter should be represented in terms of the child's way of viewing the world. The fundamental structure of the subject matter should be identified and used as the basis for curriculum development. Referred to as a "spiral curriculum," such an organization allows the child to master essential skills from which more powerful skills may be developed.

The Influence of Lev S. Vygotsky

Lev S. Vygotsky, a Russian psychologist and theoretician, developed a socio-cultural theory of learning in the early 1930s. The basic premise of the theory is that the development of complex mental functions such as categorical perception, conceptual thinking, and logical memory are a product of the child's social interactions with other members of his or her culture. Recently discovered by American educators, Vygotsky's theory includes a view of readiness that assigns a primary role to the child's culture and the nature of the interaction between the child and knowledgeable members of the culture (M. Gredler, 1992).

The child's developmental level, Vygotsky (1930–35/1978; 1934/1962) noted, typically is assessed as those tasks that the child can complete without assistance. However, such an assessment indicates only the developmental level that the child has attained up to the present time. That is, such information does not measure the child's potential for learning or for further development.

Vygotsky (1930–35/1978; 1934/1962) posed the situation in which, using traditional mental tests, two children are found to be the same mental age. However, if both children are provided the opportunity to work on the problems with adult assistance, important differences are likely to emerge. That is, one child at the mental age of 8 (according to traditional mental tests) may be able to solve problems at the level of a 12-year-old with adult assistance. In contrast, the other may only be able, with assistance, to solve problems up to the 9-year-old level.

According to Vygotsky, the two children differ considerably in their potential for learning. The differences between 12 and 8 and between 9 and 8 are examples of the *zone of next or proximal development* (Vygotsky, 1930–35/1978). Specifically, it is the difference between the developmental level reflected by the child's independent problem solving and the problem solving accomplished with guidance (Vygotsky, 1930–35/1978, p. 86). In other words, the tasks that the child can accomplish in collaboration today, he or she can accomplish alone tomorrow (Vygotsky, 1934/1962, p. 104).

Planning instruction, therefore, includes determining the lowest threshold at which instruction may begin (Vygotsky, 1934/1962, p. 104). In the teaching situation, adult guidance leads the child first to solve problems collaboratively and then moves these partial skills toward independent problem solving. The teacher first models the appropriate behaviors and then structures the learning tasks so that the student undertakes only those aspects that he or she is capable of completing. Under the teacher's guidance, the student undertakes additional parts of the task. As the child gains proficiency, task demands are raised until the child is functioning independently and the teacher functions as a supportive observer (M. Gredler, 1992).

A current example of Vygotsky's principles is the method referred to as *reciprocal teaching* (Palincsar & Brown, 1984). Students who participated in the pilot study and those who were taught later by classroom teachers initially averaged 2 years below grade level in reading comprehension. With small groups of five or six students, teachers first modeled the tasks of summarizing, questioning, clarifying, and predicting. The goal was understanding and remembering text. The teachers then provided support and guidance as the students attempted the four skills already named. Techniques used by the teachers included prompting, instruction, modifying the task, specific feedback related to the student's action, and modeling any activity that continued to need improvement. At the end of 15 days of instruction, performance on comprehension questions had increased from 40% to 80%.

Of primary importance in Vygotsky's theory is the concept that readiness is not a static entity. Instead, readiness is the learner's ability to benefit from collaborative problem solving with a tutor or more knowledgeable peer. More important, the zone of proximal development, which is the manifestation of readiness, is created in the interaction between the adult and the child. Thus, the child's "readiness" depends to a great extent on the sensitivity, diagnostic skills, and teaching skills of the adult.

The Cumulative-Skills Model

The maturationalists identify growth as the primary factor in human behavioral development. Several cognitive theorists and educators, in contrast, emphasize the role of the environment and/or the curriculum in human behavioral development. Robert Gagné, an educational psychologist who has applied his theory to the design of classroom instruction for over 40 years, extends the latter view even further.

Gagné's early research on military training problems indicated that three principles contributed to successful learning. They are (1) providing instruction on the set of component tasks that build toward the final task, (2) ensuring that each component task is mastered, and (3) sequencing the component tasks to ensure optimal transfer to the final task (Gagné, 1962). Continued observation of students in a variety of public school classroom settings indicated that the lack of success experienced by many students was the result of apparent gaps in their knowledge (Gagné, 1987). In other words, a primary factor in human behavioral development is the child's prior learning.

According to Gagné (1977; 1985) human learning is cumulative. That is, many skills that are learned contribute to the learning of more complex skills. Once a child has learned to add, for example, he or she does not need to learn this skill all over again when learning long division.

The importance of the cumulative learning model is that education should identify the sequences of skills that build on each other and proceed to teach those skills. Therefore, developmental readiness, according to Gagné (1968, 1977), is composed of the relevant skills identified as essential prerequisites for the new learning. The skill of addition is prerequisite to learning long division. Therefore, regardless of the chronological or mental age of the child, once addition is learned, long division may be taught.

Given that learned skills are the basis for future learning, society has the responsibility to design and implement effective instruction. Only through well-designed instruction that takes into account motivational states, the learner's skills in processing information, and the nature of the skill to be learned can individuals acquire the skills to become competently functioning members of society (Gagné, 1977).

Implications

Some psychologists and educators emphasize that school readiness is a relative rather than an absolute concept. That is, readiness depends, to a great extent, on the demands made by school personnel on the first-grade children. Specifically, readiness is related to the form of instruction and to the methods utilized by the teacher in the classroom (Johansson, 1965).

Ausubel and Sullivan (1970) pointed out that the "age of reading readiness is always influenced by cultural, subcultural, and individual differences in background experience, and, in any case, varies with the method of instruction employed and the child's IQ" (p. 93). They specifically emphasize that the quality of education a student receives is a "significant determinant of [the child's] *developmental* readiness, as well as of his subject matter readiness, for further learning" (p. 93).

The conclusions of a Swedish school committee report reiterate this important point by mentioning that the school-readiness concepts of Swedish teachers have tended to preserve the traditional school environment, traditional forms of classroom instruction, and traditional curricula. "The adaptation of a child to school is primarily an adaptation to the instructions and the guidelines the children are given there" (Johansson, 1965, p. 25). The report warns that "if a child fails in one beginner's class it need not be on account of characteristics of the child; a child who's not ready for school in one class may well succeed in another, when the teacher applies different methods" (Johansson, 1965, p. 25).

The same point is made by Husén, who states: "The concept of school readiness should be viewed in relation to the demands made by the first grade of the school" (in Johansson, 1965, p. 26). These views lend further support to the growth/social experience, sociocultural, and cumulative-skills views of readiness.

The differing viewpoints on defining readiness would be of minor importance if the arguments were confined to the printed page or to presentations at conventions of psychologists and educators. However, the advocates of various readiness theories often translate their theoretical perspectives into guidelines for public school programs. Jerome Bruner advocated a spiral curriculum, and Lev Vygotsky recommended adjusting instruction to the child's zone of proximal development. Robert Gagné developed guidelines for analyzing learning tasks and providing instruction on prerequisite skills.

All of these perspectives are essentially adaptive in that they view the responsibility of the school as that of accommodating individual differences. In contrast, the maturationalist view is one of the child adapting to the school curriculum. Thus the emphasis of educators and psychologists who hold this view is frequently placed on (1) changing the school entrance age, (2) deferring children's entry to school by requesting they stay home an extra year, or (3) suggesting placement in some type of alternative educational program other than a regular kindergarten or first-grade classroom.

The controversy has become more intense as the reality of the current educational scene has become more apparent: A large percentage of children are now attending preschool educational programs before they enter kindergarten. How should the curriculum of those programs be constituted? Should these young children be introduced to a program that is partly academic in nature? Operation Headstart is a popular preschool program that has been in existence for several years. Some of the Headstart programs also have introduced disadvantaged children to academic material at an early age. The controversy over the proper educational program for preschoolers is as heated as is the controversy concerning the "readiness" of the kindergarten child (Glazer, 1988).

At the same time, many middle-class families have accepted tenets of the Gesellian philosophy and have decided that entrance to public school kindergarten and/or first grade should be deferred, especially if their child is a boy. Thus, in the schools in one Ohio county (Hodapp, 1988) a large proportion of parents of *older* children have either kept their children out of school an extra year or placed them in a prekindergarten program. The reason is to ensure that the child is "ready" to negotiate what is obviously perceived as a hazardous passage to completion of kindergarten and first grade. The message in these schools has been so taken to heart that in addition to the 484 younger children kept out of school, parents of 700 older children also have delayed their children's entrance to school.

Summary

Four different perspectives on the issue of school readiness were discussed in this chapter. They are the maturational view, the growth and social experience view, the sociocultural theory of Lev Vygotsky, and the cumulative-skills model of Robert Gagné. Of these four, only the maturational view advocates a biological moment when the child can learn the curriculum.

In contrast, the other three perspectives emphasize the role of the environment in learning. David Ausubel, for example, describes readiness as an interaction between growth and the child's social experiences. Flexibility of curriculum is stressed by Jerome Bruner, who believed that the essential concepts in any subject matter could be successfully taught to the child if presented in terms of the child's way of viewing the world.

Reacting against the use of assessment tools to determine readiness, Lev Vygotsky maintained that such tests do not measure learning potential. Instead, learning potential consists of those tasks that the child can accomplish in collaboration with an adult or more knowledgeable peer. Planning instruction, therefore, includes determining the lowest threshold at which instruction may begin.

Finally, the cumulative-skills model developed by Robert Gagné describes readiness as the attainment of essential prerequisite skills. Learning long division, for example, cannot proceed until the child has learned to add. In other words, learned skills are the basis for future learning, rather than physical growth or mental age. Society, therefore, is responsible for designing and implementing effective instruction.

Implications of adopting the maturational view are that the child must wait until deemed ready to be taught the curriculum. Transition rooms and prekindergarten placements are two administrative mechanisms used when school entrance is delayed. Implications of the other models, however, consist of planning and implementing instruction that adapts to individual differences. In other words, in one view the child adapts to the curriculum, while in the other perspectives the curriculum adapts to the child.

SECTION II

Assessing Readiness

3

ISSUES IN EARLY CHILDHOOD SCREENING AND ASSESSMENT

The use of screening tests of one type or another has been a common practice in American schools for over 50 years. Such tests originally were used at the beginning of first grade to identify children who were likely to have difficulty in learning to read.

Since the 1940s, however, interest in the child's readiness to begin formal schooling has increased. The advent of educational programs for the disadvantaged child as well as political demands for increased accountability in the schools have been accompanied by an increased emphasis on screening young children.

A recent survey of 48 states concerning entrance/retention practices in early childhood education indicates that mandated evaluation measures have proliferated within the last 10 years (Cannella & Reiff, 1989). For example, in 7 states, over 50% of the school districts require kindergarten screening at the time of school entrance. Also, 5 states require the administration of a kindergarten exit exam or first-grade entrance exam.

Discussed in this chapter are some important issues related to the measurement of potential problems of young children. Part one discusses the rationale for screening, the instability of behavior, use of inappropriate measures, defining the "at-risk" population, and problems in prediction.

Part two of the chapter presents a method for calculating the predictive validity of a screening measure. Computation is derived from the four possible outcomes of the administration of a screening measure: (a) number of children identified as at risk who later perform poorly, (b) number identified as not at risk who later perform poorly, (c) number identified as at risk who later perform adequately, and (d) number identified as not at risk whose later performance is adequate.

Measurement Issues in Screening Procedures

Discussed in this section are the rationale for early screening, the instability of behavior, inappropriate measures, and problems in prediction.

Rationale for Early Screening

The practice of early screening of children by the educational system was derived from the practice of early medical screening (Potton, 1983). Medical screening is used to detect disorders that then can be certified and a treatment program instituted. Such a course of action can produce major benefits.

An example is the screening of newborns for PKU. Prior to legislation mandating such testing, this condition typically was not diagnosed until the child was 4 years of age. However, when treatment for PKU is not begun in the early weeks of life, mental retardation soon will become evident. Thus, early screening and treatment have effectively reduced the problem (Frankenburg, 1985).

The rationale for early identification of children who may be at risk for developing learning/behavioral problems later in school is that outcomes similar to those due to a lack of early medical screening may result. Barnes (1982) states that "the human ramifications of a child not having a serious reading disability detected until the second or third grade may be such that the child never does learn to read adequately" (p. 97).

The assumptions of early educational screening, summarized by Reynolds (1979), are as follows:

(1) "early identification can accurately pinpoint the child's difficulties and a program can then be tailored to help ameliorate these difficulties";

(2) if early detection is not undertaken, the child is likely to remain behind during most of his or her school years;

(3) preschool screening will, in some cases, lead "to total or near total remediation of . . . problems prior to the beginning of first grade" (p. 277)

Reasons such as those stated by Barnes and Reynolds, however, reflect the assumptions that learning and behavioral problems can be predicted accurately from early childhood assessment and that children's potential problems are being measured accurately and reliably. However, problems with accurate prediction do exist; these are discussed in the following sections.

At present, screening instruments and readiness tests are used to identify potential problems in children. The purpose of a screening instrument is to assess an individual who might be considered to be at risk for developing various learning and/or behavioral problems (Taylor, 1984). The Denver Developmental Screening test (Frankenburg, Dodds, Fandal, Kazuk, & Cohrs, 1975) is one such instrument. It contains items that attempt to measure personal-social adjustment, fine motor and gross motor competence, and language ability. Readiness tests, on the other hand, are considered by some to be similar to screening tests, but narrower in scope (Meisels, 1989a). The major difference between screening tests and readiness tests, however, is that readiness tests attempt to link the measurement of the child's abilities to early school performance (Taylor, 1984). An example is the Metropolitan Readiness Test (Nurss & McGauvran, 1976), which samples a number of different skill areas. The Boehm Test of Basic Concepts (Boehm, 1971), however, is a readiness test that measures only a child's mastery of concepts.

An analysis of screening practices in 177 school districts in New York state demonstrated that many school districts indiscriminately mix developmental screening tests and readiness tests in their early identification programs (Joiner, 1977). Some psychologists consider that developmental screening tests should identify children who need early intervention for developmental lags such as possible mental retardation. However, the objective of a readiness test should be to facilitate curriculum planning for the child and to assess the child's ability to benefit from an academic program (Meisels, 1989a). In reality, however, both kinds of tests are used to make judgments about the child's ability to begin a formal learning program.

Instability of Behavior

One of the problems in testing young children is that of unstable behavioral patterns. Testing that is conducted too early in the school year, for example, is likely to reflect behavioral problems that may not be present a few months later. In one study of over 11,000 young children, teachers indicated that 76% had effectively "settled down" or adjusted to school at the end of 1 month. However, 18% of the children required 3 months to adjust to the school environment and the demands placed on them. The remaining 6% of the children continued to exhibit maladaptive behavior after 3 months (Pringle, Butler, & Davie, 1966).

The implications for screening programs derived from that study are that an initial time period should be allowed for the child to adjust to the school and to permit the building of a positive teacher–student relationship. After at least 3 months of schooling, the use of screening measures may be considered.

In addition to month-by-month changes early in the school year, some conditions identified as deficits or delays at a young age may not be present at a later age. A study by Silva and Ross (1980) of the gross motor development of 800 children at age 3 and again at age 5 indicates the ephemeral nature of some deficits.

Of the 800 children tested, 31 demonstrated poor motor performance at age 3. However, at age 5, only 10 of the 31 children continued to exhibit poor motor performance. The other 21 children did not differ from the total sample on motor ability, language, or IQ.

The 10 children who continued to perform poorly on motor tests at age 5 also were deficient in language and IQ at that age. However, the other 21 children who performed poorly at age 3 had caught up by age 5. Had the results of the tests of the 3-year-olds been used to identify potential learning problems, 2 out of 3 children would have been misclassified.

The results of the Silva and Ross study indicate that motor delays observed in many children at age 3 tend to be unstable and often may not be associated with other areas of the child's development. The researchers conclude that "these results do not suggest that delayed motor development, at least at the preschool level, deserves identification and intervention efforts" (Silva & Ross, 1980, p. 224).

An example of a screening program that tests at an early age is the program used by the New Jersey State Department of Education (1975). In this program, screening of various abilities is begun at age 2. Children are referred on the basis of failure on one to three items when they are tested at ages 2 through 5. However, according to the data presented by Silva and Ross, such a program for motor delays lacks adequate evidence to identify accurately children who will have later problems in motor development.

As noted by Lindsay (1984), "Children not only develop at different rates, they change position relative to each other on different dimensions, and also their own profiles of abilities over time" (p. 175). In other words, for early identification to make sense, there must be sufficient consistency over time between a child's early functioning and what is educationally significant for the child in later years (Lichtenstein & Ireton, 1984, p. 65).

Motor skill development is not the only area in which changes occur in young children. In a comparison of the IQ scores of 84 children from 6 months to 17 years of age, several shifts in ability levels were found (Hindley & Owen, 1978). Between the ages of 5 and 11 years, 25% of the IQs changed by more than 16 points and 3% changed by more than 30 points. The change was even greater in the younger children. Fifty percent of the children between 6 months and 5 years demonstrated IQ changes of more than 19 points and 25% by more than 30 points.

It is important to note that these examples of the difficulties in accurately identifying children at risk impinge directly on the efforts of educational and psychological personnel who are involved in designing an early screening and intervention program for children up to age 6. Before any identification program is developed for children in this age range through P.L. 99–457, the hazards of providing valid and reliable assessments must be addressed. As noted by the Silva and Ross study, accurate assessment of the motor development of 3- to 5-year-olds is almost impossible to achieve.

The efficacy of early identification procedures for kindergarten and first-grade children has been questioned by professionals in education and psychology in recent years. Sparrow, Blackman, and Chauncey (1983) note that a screening program implemented in the spring before children enter kindergarten will result in an excessive number of children being categorized as at risk who subsequently will be found to have no learning problems. Leach (1980) states that attempting to identify the at-risk child early in the elementary school program involves an error rate of 33%. In other words, approximately 330 out of 1,000 children said to be at risk will be wrongly classified. And, as mentioned previously, the younger the child is at the time of screening, the more questions will be raised because a definitive diagnosis is more difficult (Joiner, 1977). At best, a screening decision in the months before kindergarten can be considered only tentative because the child has not yet been introduced to a formal learning environment and the demands of that environment.

Potton (1983) notes that psychologists and educators often attempt to identify children at an early age who are likely to have reading problems because of a delay in language or speech development or because of emotional problems or cognitive deficits. However, he indicates that such personnel are engaging in speculation that the child will be vulnerable to learning problems as a result of these specific factors. According to Potton, the process should be labeled "speculative screening" because the poor performance has not yet appeared and it is not certain that the child will indeed have learning problems.

Lindsay (1984) arrives at the same conclusion and states: "A child's status at any time is seen to be a result of the interaction between intrinsic and extrinsic strengths and weaknesses. In addition, there is a third dimension of time: the pattern may change from month to month, or even more quickly" (p. 176). Lindsay continues by mentioning that children at the extremes (of a distribution) are more predictable, but this evidence applies to *groups* of children. The performance of *individuals* within these groups may be quite variable, but the performance of the majority of children who are not at the extremes and who are not subject to extensive influences will be more variable (Lindsay, 1984, p. 176).

Inappropriate Measures

Instruments used to identify or predict learning problems should undergo stringent development procedures to ensure accuracy. However, in one small-town school system in Tennessee, a rating scale was devised by the school psychologist and elementary teachers to make decisions about promotions to first grade and transition room placement. The scale was heavily weighted with motor items, including such items as "ability of the child to tie his shoes." No evidence was provided as to the effectiveness of the scale or the relationship of shoe-tying success to success in reading.

Indicators other than tests or scales often are used to make decisions about placement. One practice involves the inspection of the children's teeth. If the second molars have not yet appeared, it is purported that the child is not sufficiently mature to be successful in first grade (Ames, 1967).

Other dubious practices used to make decisions about children are described below:

(1) A kindergarten child is placed in pre-first because the teacher states that during a test period the child required a long time to learn letters. A decision is made after working a few minutes with the child because the teacher spent what is believed to be an inordinate amount of time working with the child.

(2) A kindergarten child is promoted to first grade because he is larger than the other children. Although the teacher doubts the child's ability to undertake first-grade work, the teacher states that the child is too large to remain in kindergarten and thinks behavior problems might result.

(3) An 8-year-old child is promoted to first grade on the basis of his age. Although his kindergarten performance does not differ from three other children who were retained, the teacher concluded that he was "too old" to remain in kindergarten.

(4) In another school, a child who went rapidly from one activity to another without finishing the first was labeled "immature." In one case of a child who acted in this manner, the teacher also checked the child's birthdate and then labeled him "immature." (Leiter, 1974)

There is no question about the good intentions of those who make use of such practices. However, as Potton (1983) has indicated, the educational concept of "at risk" is of an abstract nature, is composed of complicated concepts, and is difficult to explain by a single score from a screening test. In order to rely on the score obtained from a screening test, the test must have adequate validity and reliability. The concept of validity refers to the degree to which the test being used actually measures the characteristic of behavior in which we are interested (Walsh & Betz, 1990, p. 58). The concept of reliability refers to the degree that the results of measuring an attribute of the child will be consistent. In other words, repeating the measurement should bring similar results (Walsh & Betz, 1990, p. 49).

It is unfortunate that drastic intervention methods (i.e., delay of entrance to school; denial of entrance to kindergarten or first grade) currently are associated with brief screening batteries and that speculative screening is now found to be commonplace in many school systems. The remainder of this chapter reviews ways of defining the at-risk population, the many problems in prediction, and methods to determine the forecasting efficiency of a screening measure.

Defining the "At-Risk" Population

Difficulty in reaching agreement about which child is truly at risk for later learning problems is widespread. Estimates of those likely to have learning problems later in school have varied from 7% to 50% of the school population (Leach, 1980). Often the definition of a potential learning problem is derived from the particular philosophy of the school. For example, schools that expect a high level of reading readiness skills or knowledge of words and letters in those children entering first grade will define learning problems differently from schools that do not hold these expectations for the children.

Because schools define success in school in different ways, the concept of who is at risk will therefore also vary. For example, an analysis of the Boulder, Colorado, schools indicated that kindergarten retention rates varied from 0–25%. The children who were labeled as failures in one school (and who were retained) had counterparts of similar kindergarten performance in another school who were promoted to first grade and succeeded (Shepard & Smith, 1985).

Different expectations for entering abilities and different definitions of success therefore constitute one problem in defining the at-risk population. Another problem is that no screening instrument can assess the quality of teaching that the child will receive. In other words, accurately defining who is at risk requires an analysis of the subsequent teaching environment. Consider the study of 954 children conducted by Silva, McGee, and Williams (1983). They found that 168 children had a low IQ (i.e., 89 or below) or reading problems. However, of the 168 children, only 37 had both a low IQ and reading problems. Sixty-eight children had a low IQ, but no reading problems. Furthermore, 61 of the children with reading difficulties were those who also had a normal IQ. As found in the earlier study conducted by Gates (1937) (discussed in Chapter 2), a variety of environmental factors can influence success rates in schools.

Problems in Prediction

Perhaps the most important objection to early screening programs is that they are not very accurate. If prediction were highly accurate, then the case might be made for mandatory assessment of all children as they enter school (Adelman & Fishbach, 1975).

Often only a correlation coefficient between a group's scores on a preschool screening instrument and a later achievement measure is provided in the literature as evidence of the test's effectiveness. Such data, although important, provide information only on the similarity of the group's performance on both tests. A correlation coefficient provides no information as to the specific identification of the at-risk and not-at-risk children and the relationship between such status and the projected outcome of a good or poor reader (Satz & Fletcher, 1988).

Further, "[The] correlation coefficient is . . . an inadequate and simplistic statistic on which to base decisions about the comparative utility of [such] devices" (Leach, 1980, p. 185). Moreover, most of the correlations cited as evidence of predictive validity range only from .30 to .60 (Satz & Fletcher, 1988). Such correlations account for only a small amount of the variability of performance on the two measures. For example, in one study, a correlation of .73 was obtained between the readiness instrument and the criterion test. However, such a correlation only accounts for 53% of the variability of the children's performance. In other words, the relationships between single, specific preschool tests and later school achievement are too low to permit definitive decisions about individual children (Keogh & Becker, 1973).

Psychological tests predict best for those who are at the extremes of the performance range. Such is also the case with existing readiness tests. Jansky (1978), in commenting on the predictive efficiency of an early identification battery devised by Satz et al. (1978), pointed out that the predictors were effective in identifying poor readers in only two of the five studies. Moreover, she stated, in the best of cases, Satz's tests would fail to identify 15% to 25% of the high-risk children.

The following comments by Jansky (1978) about the effectiveness of predictive test batteries administered in kindergarten indicate the magnitude of the problems associated with early screening:

> I believe that no kindergarten test battery, regardless of its makeup, is going to predict failing readers in prospective samples at better than the 75 percent level. Obviously, variables that intervene between prediction and outcome account for some predictive failures. (p. 383)

Jansky mentions that these variables include such factors as the skill of the teacher, the instructional methods he or she utilizes, frequency of school changes, frequency of attendance of the child, differences in attitudes toward learning as well as the experiential background of the child. These are factors that are difficult to control and that combine with the developmental changes within the child to make for difficulty in predicting the child's academic and behavioral performance (Jansky, 1978, p. 383). In addition, Jansky notes that reading is such a complex task that accurate prediction of academic studies would be difficult *even if an ideal set of kindergarten predictors could be assembled.*

A Method for Calculating the Predictive Validity of a Screening Measure

The decision that a child is at risk and should be placed in a transition room often is made on the basis of a test score. The child's score on the test is functioning as a "prediction score." That is, if placed in the regular first grade, the child is predicted to experience problems in learning.

A test or screening measure that identifies those children with potential learning problems and does not misclassify other children is said to have predictive validity. Determining the predictive validity of an instrument requires two sets of data. One is the children's scores on the screening measure. Then, 1 or more years later, data are collected again on the children to determine which children actually developed problems. Typically, some type of achievement measure or rating scale is used at that time. This assessment is referred to as the criterion measure.

Calculating Predictive Validity

Two types of information are determined from the scores on the screening measure. They are the number of children identified as at risk and the number identified as not at risk. Two types of information also are determined from the scores on the criterion measure. They are the number of children who developed learning problems and the number who did not (as indicated by adequate performance in school).

In other words, the data from administration of the screening test and the criterion measure yield four possible outcomes. Organization of the data into a 2 × 2 matrix provides a basis for the analysis of the screening measure. (See Table 3–1.)

In the matrix, the numbers of children accurately identified by the screening measure are represented by Cells a and d. That is, the number of children predicted to have learning problems *and* who subsequently performed poorly are found in Cell a. This group is referred to as the *valid positives.* Cell d reflects the number who were identified as not at risk and who later performed adequately. They are the *valid negatives.* These two groups then are the number of children identified accurately by the screening measure.

Table 3–1.
Possible Outcomes of Screening

Subsequent performance on the criterion measure	Decision on the screening or diagnostic test	
	At risk	Not at risk
Poor performance	(a) Number identified as at risk and there is a poor outcome; *Valid positive* (VP)	(b) Number identified as *not* at risk who later perform poorly; *False negative* (FN)
Adequate performance	(c) Number identified as at risk but there is a "good" outcome, i.e., child performs adequately; *False positive* (FP)	(d) Number identified as *not* at risk and subsequent performance is adequate; *Valid negative* (VN)

In contrast, Cells b and c reflect the numbers of children who have not been identified correctly. The number indicated by the screening measure as not at risk and who subsequently perform inadequately are the *false negatives* (Cell b). The *false positive* group (Cell c) is the number of children identified originally as at risk who later demonstrated adequate performance on the criterion.

Table 3–2 illustrates a hypothetical data set of 491 children who were administered a readiness test at the end of kindergarten and then a standardized reading test at the end of first grade. For this data set, the number of valid positives is 61 and the number of valid negatives is 321. The former number predicts the accurate identification of children said to be at risk. The latter number reflects the accurate identification of children predicted to be *not* at risk. However, 80 children

Table 3–2.
Relationship Between Readiness Level and First-Grade Reading: A Hypothetical Case

Performance on the criterion measure (1st-grade reading test)	Performance on the screening measure (Readiness test)		
	Poor performance (at risk)	Good performance (not at risk)	Totals *N*
Poor performance	(a) 61 (VP)	(b) 29 (FN)	90
Good performance	(c) 80 (FP)	(d) 321 (VN)	401
Totals	141	350	491

who were predicted to perform poorly were later found to be successful in first-grade reading (false positives) and 29 children predicted to be not at risk performed poorly on the criterion reading test (false negatives).

The data obtained from such a prediction matrix may be used to compare screening instruments in various ways. One comparison is the overall effectiveness of the instrument, which is the percentage of the total group correctly identified by the instrument. In other words, the valid positives (Cell a) plus the valid negatives (Cell d) are what percentage of the total class? The formula for computing this index is $(a+d)/(a+b+c+d)$. For the hypothetical data set ($N = 491$), the overall effectiveness index is 78%. (See Tables 3–3 and 3–4.)

The total ratio, however, often is a misrepresentation of the true effectiveness of a screening instrument. The reason is that Cell d (the valid negatives) usually contains a large number. That is, the instrument identifies a large number of children who will not be at risk and who later do perform adequately in school. Thus, a high effectiveness ratio reported for an instrument frequently reflects the ability of the screening instrument to predict (accurately) the academic performance of the children *who were considered originally not to be at risk* (Leach, 1981). In the hypothetical example given (e.g., Tables 3–2 and 3–4), 350 students were predicted to perform adequately on academic tasks and 321 (or 92%) did in fact do so.

Several indices must be calculated to determine the effectiveness of a screening measure, according to Leach (1981). One is the percentage of poor performers on the criterion measure who were earlier correctly identified by the screening instrument, $a/(a+b)$. In other words, of the total number of children who are not performing adequately in school, how many were correctly identified *originally* by the screening test? This index (referred to as the population validated positive rate by Leach, 1981) is typically referred to as the *index of sensitivity*. For the data in Table 3–2 (further illustrated in Tables 3–3 and 3–4), 61 of 90 children, or 68% of those performing poorly on the reading test at the end of the first grade, were correctly identified by the screening test.

Also of importance is the percentage of adequate performers on the criterion measure who were correctly identified originally by the screening test, $d/(c+d)$. This index (referred to as the population validated negative rate by Leach, 1981), is typically referred to as the *index of specificity*. In the example in Table 3–2, 321 of 401 or 80% of the adequate performers were originally predicted to be successful readers by the readiness test. (See also Table 3–4.)

It is important to remember that the indices of sensitivity and specificity report the percentages of the total number of poor performers and adequate performers on the criterion who were identified *originally* by the screening test.

Two other indices of importance, in contrast, report (1) the percentage of children identified as at risk who in fact did later perform poorly, $a/(a+c)$, and (2)

Table 3–3.
Indices of Predictability for a Screening Measure

Index	Components	Formula
Overall effectiveness	Number of successes and failures correctly identified / Total class	$\dfrac{a+d}{a+b+c+d}$
Index of sensitivity (percentage of poor performers correctly identified originally by the screening test)	Number of poor performers correctly identified originally by the screening test / Total number of poor performers at criterion	$\dfrac{a}{a+b}$
Index of specificity (percentage of adequate performers correctly identified originally by the screening test)	Number of adequate performers correctly identified originally by the screening test / Total number of adequate performers at criterion	$\dfrac{d}{c+d}$
Percentage of children identified as at risk who later failed	Number of at risk identifications who later performed poorly / Total number originally identified as at risk	$\dfrac{a}{a+c}$
Percentage of children identified as *not* at risk who later performed adequately	Number of not-at-risk identifications who later performed adequately / Total number originally identified as not at risk	$\dfrac{d}{b+d}$

the percentage of children labeled as *not* at risk who later performed adequately, $d/(b+d)$. These indices reflect the percentage of correct identifications of at-risk and not-at-risk status made by the screening instrument.

As will be noted from the data in Tables 3–2 and 3–4, the screening test was much less effective in predicting the number of children labeled at risk who actually were poor performers on the criterion (i.e., reading) test administered at the end of the first grade, $a/(a+c)$. Only 61 of 141 children (or 43%) who were considered to be at risk actually performed poorly by the end of first grade.

Special note also should be made of the effectiveness of the prediction of not-at-risk status, $d/(b+d)$. In the example, 321 of 350 children (or 92%) who were labeled as being not at risk performed adequately on the academic test at the end of first grade.

The Interpretation of Matrix Data

Once the ratios as outlined in Tables 3–3 and 3–4 have been calculated, the obvious question to be raised is what should be considered the minimum level of accuracy for a screening measure to be acceptable for use in the schools? To answer this question, the conceptual framework that Kingslake (1981, 1983) proposes is important in interpreting a screening measure.

First, Kingslake indicates that portraying the four types of outcomes in a 2×2 matrix is essential. Then the matrix data should be examined from a retrospective point of view. This means the question to be considered is: Of all the children who actually fail, what percentage were originally identified as being at risk by the screening measure? The reader should refer to the data in Table 3–4 for an answer to this question. As illustrated, 68% of all children who failed a grade were originally designated at risk on the screening measure, (a/a+b). Thus 32% of all children who failed were missed by the readiness test. How acceptable is the miss

Table 3–4.
Indices of Predictability for a Hypothetical Screening Instrument

Index	Formula	Values	Percentage
(a) Overall effectiveness	$\dfrac{a+d}{a+b+c+d}$	$\dfrac{382}{491} =$	78%
(b) Index of sensitivity	$\dfrac{a}{a+b}$	$\dfrac{61}{90} =$	68%
(c) Index of specificity	$\dfrac{d}{c+d}$	$\dfrac{321}{401} =$	80%
(d) Percentage of children identified as at risk who later failed	$\dfrac{a}{a+c}$	$\dfrac{61}{141} =$	43%
(e) Percentage of children identified as *not* at risk who later performed adequately	$\dfrac{d}{b+d}$	$\dfrac{321}{350} =$	92%

rate of 32%? Kingslake (1981, 1983) states that at least 75% of the failing population must be originally identified by a screening measure. Because the screening only identified 68% of the group of children who failed, the screening measure "fails" on this standard.

Kingslake states that the second question to be addressed involves a *prospective* judgment about the accuracy of the original label of "at risk." Do all the children designated as being at risk by the readiness test *actually* fail? The results from Table 3–4 indicate quite definitely that a large percentage of the children labeled at risk in fact did not perform poorly in reading at the end of the first grade, a /(a+c). The predictive accuracy of the at risk classification indicates that only 43% of the children originally labeled as being possible learning problems actually did perform poorly in reading at the end of first grade. Once again the screening measure fails to meet Jansky's (1978) and Kingslake's (1981, 1983) criterion that the accuracy of detection should be 75% or higher. (See Table 3–4.)

If 57% of the group of children who are considered to be at risk for school learning problems can succeed without any intervention program, how can such a screening measure be used as a baseline if an attempt is made to validate a program of intervention using the results of such an instrument (Kingslake, 1983, pp. 25–26)?

Both retrospective and prospective accuracy are interrelated and *both* must be considered in any analysis of the value of a screening measure. More emphasis has been placed in this book on the prospective use of predictive data because school personnel make program and placement decisions based mainly on the fact that the child has been labeled as at risk or immature.

A Longitudinal Predictability Study

Stevenson, Parker, Wilkinson, Hegion, and Fish (1976) analyzed the effectiveness of a prekindergarten battery of cognitive and psychometric tasks and teacher ratings administered in preschool to predict reading and arithmetic achievement in third grade. Correlation coefficients were computed between performance on the preschool tasks and later achievement and the teacher rating-scale scores and later achievement. For example, the correlation of prekindergarten measures with third-grade reading performance was .71, and correlation of teacher ratings with third-grade reading was .41.

In their review of the data, performance was analyzed in two ways. First, the sample was divided into lowest 10% and upper 90% of the population on both the preschool tasks and third-grade test performance. Success predictions then were analyzed when the sample was divided into lower 25% and upper 75% on both measures. These data, placed in 2 × 2 matrices, are illustrated in Tables 3–5 and 3–6.

Table 3–5.

Relation of Preschool Performance to Third-Grade Reading

Reading performance in third grade	Screening measure: Performance on preschool tasks		
	Lowest 10% of student distribution	Upper 90% of student distribution	N
Lowest 10% of student distribution	4 a|b	8	12
Upper 90% of student distribution	5 c|d	117	122
Total	9	125	134

Note. Data from "Longitudinal Study of Individual Differences in Cognitive Development and Scholastic Achievement" by H. W. Stevenson et al., 1976, *Journal of Educational Psychology, 68*(4), 377–400. Copyright 1976 by the American Psychological Association. Adapted by permission.

As indicated in Table 3–7, the index of sensitivity is low for both cutoffs, i.e., 33% and 39%. That is, the percentage of poor readers actually found at the end of third grade and who were originally identified by the preschool measures is less than 40%. Similarly, the percentages of children identified as at risk who later failed are, respectively, 44% and 59%. That is, between 56% and 41% of the children predicted to be low achievers performed satisfactorily (i.e., above the cutoff).

Table 3–6.

Relation of Preschool Performance to Third-Grade Reading

Reading performance in third grade	Performance on preschool tasks		
	Lowest 25%	Upper 75%	N
Lowest 25% of student distribution	13 a|b	20	33
Upper 75% of student distribution	9 c|d	92	101
Total	22	112	134

Note. Data from "Longitudinal Study of Individual Differences in Cognitive Development and Scholastic Achievement" by H. W. Stevenson et al., 1976, *Journal of Educational Psychology, 68*(4), 377–400. Copyright 1976 by the American Psychological Association. Adapted by permission.

Tables 3–8 and 3–9 illustrate the results of the teacher rating scales when the sample is divided into (a) 10% and 90% on the criterion and (b) 25% and 75% on third-grade reading achievement. Table 3–10 illustrates the indices of predictability for these ratings for third-grade reading performance. Although 15% of the third-grade students below the 25% cutoff were identified originally by the teachers, 85% of the poor readers were not identified (index of sensitivity). Further, only 50% of those children who were earlier identified by the teachers as being at risk subsequently became poor readers (i.e., performed below the 25th percentile on the criterion measure).

This lack of success is reinforced by the results of the analysis of 33 early identification predictive validity studies by Lichtenstein and Ireton (1984). The

Table 3–7.
Comparison of the Predictability Indices of Preschool Tasks for Third-Grade Reading

Index	Formula	Values 10%/90% cutoff	Values 25%/75% cutoff	Percentages 10%/90% cutoff	Percentages 25%/75% cutoff
(a) Overall effectiveness	$\dfrac{a+d}{a+b+c+d}$	$\dfrac{121}{134}$	$\dfrac{105}{134}$	90%	78%
(b) Index of sensitivity	$\dfrac{a}{a+b}$	$\dfrac{4}{12}$	$\dfrac{13}{33}$	33%	39%
(c) Index of specificity	$\dfrac{d}{c+d}$	$\dfrac{117}{122}$	$\dfrac{92}{101}$	96%	91%
(d) Percentage of children identified as at risk who later failed	$\dfrac{a}{a+c}$	$\dfrac{4}{9}$	$\dfrac{13}{22}$	44%	59%
(e) Percentage of children identified as *not* at risk who later performed adequately	$\dfrac{d}{b+d}$	$\dfrac{117}{125}$	$\dfrac{92}{112}$	94%	82%

Note. Data from "Longitudinal Study of Individual Differences in Cognitive Development and Scholastic Achievement" by H. W. Stevenson et al., 1976, *Journal of Educational Psychology, 68*(4), 377–400. Copyright 1976 by the American Psychological Association. Adapted by permission.

Table 3–8.
Relation of Kindergarten Teacher Ratings to Third-Grade Reading with Cutoffs of 10% and 90% on the Criterion

	Kindergarten teacher ratings		
Reading performance in third grade	Predicted to be a learning problem	Predicted to have no learning problem	
Lower 10% of student distribution	3 a | b	11	14
Upper 90% of student distribution	9 c | d	129	138
Total	12	140	152

Note. Data from "Longitudinal Study of Individual Differences in Cognitive Development and Scholastic Achievement" by H. W. Stevenson et al., 1976, *Journal of Educational Psychology, 68*(4), 377–400. Copyright 1976 by the American Psychological Association. Adapted by permission.

Table 3–9.
Relation of Kindergarten Teacher Ratings to Third-Grade Reading with Cutoffs of 25% and 75% on the Criterion

	Kindergarten teacher ratings		
Reading performance in third grade	Predicted to be a learning problem	Predicted to have no learning problem	
Lower 25% of student distribution	6 a | b	33	39
Upper 75% of student distribution	6 c | d	107	113
Total	12	140	152

Note. Data from "Longitudinal Study of Individual Differences in Cognitive Development and Scholastic Achievement" by H. W. Stevenson et al., 1976, *Journal of Educational Psychology, 68*(4), 377–400. Copyright 1976 by the American Psychological Association. Adapted by permission.

average percentage of children identified as being at risk who actually failed (i.e., effectiveness of referral) was 49%. In other words, 51% of the children labeled at risk later performed successfully in school. As can be easily seen, the percentage of 49 is considerably below the minimum level of 75% considered optimal by Jansky (1978), Leach (1981), and Kingslake (1983).

Stevenson et al. correctly concluded in 1976 that "batteries of prekindergarten tasks can be used only cautiously in identifying children who need help" (p. 398). This conclusion remains the same today. These authors also mention that the most reasonable use of predictive measures, such as a psychometric screening battery and teacher ratings, is to identify children who should be considered for further

Table 3–10.
Indices of Predictability for Preschool Teacher Ratings of Third-Grade Reading Performance

Index	Formula	Values		Percentages	
		10%/90% cutoff	25%/75% cutoff	10%/90% cutoff	25%/75% cutoff
(a) Overall effectiveness	$\dfrac{a+d}{a+b+c+d}$	$\dfrac{132}{152}$	$\dfrac{113}{152}$	87%	74%
(b) Index of sensitivity	$\dfrac{a}{a+b}$	$\dfrac{3}{14}$	$\dfrac{6}{39}$	21%	15%
(c) Index of specificity	$\dfrac{d}{c+d}$	$\dfrac{129}{138}$	$\dfrac{107}{113}$	93%	95%
(d) Percentage of children identified as at risk who later failed	$\dfrac{a}{a+c}$	$\dfrac{3}{12}$	$\dfrac{6}{12}$	25%	50%
(e) Percentage of children identified as *not* at risk who later performed adequately	$\dfrac{d}{b+d}$	$\dfrac{129}{140}$	$\dfrac{107}{140}$	92%	76%

Note. Data from "Longitudinal Study of Individual Differences in Cognitive Development and Scholastic Achievement" by H. W. Stevenson et al., 1976, *Journal of Educational Psychology, 68*(4), 377–400. Copyright 1976 by the American Psychological Association. Adapted by permission.

observation and evaluation rather than using the results for assigning children to special groups or classes.

Summary

Screening programs for kindergarten and first grade have proliferated over the past several years. A number of factors exist that limit the effectiveness of any screening program and such factors need to be considered more carefully by educators and psychologists.

A number of inappropriate screening practices have been described. In addition, there has been an in-depth analysis of how to evaluate correctly the effectiveness of predictive measures that are used in kindergarten and first grade. It is important to realize that the error rate in the use of predictive measures at this age level is considerably higher than is generally understood. The high error rate in predicting who really is at risk suggests that the use of screening measures with kindergarten and first-grade children should be restricted.

4

ANALYSES OF SOME
READINESS/SCREENING TESTS

The predictive indices described in Chapter 3 are applied in this chapter to several readiness/screening tests. First, data are given about the school outcome for several readiness tests. Then there is an analysis of data obtained from the use of the Metropolitan Readiness Test. Following that discussion, the middle range of performance of children is described, and the implications of the results for the classroom teacher are given. Finally, research studies of two well-known screening tests are analyzed and discussed.

A Comparison of Several Current Readiness Tests

Table 4–1 illustrates the predictability indices computed from data reported by different researchers on several readiness tests. In the Table, the author of the particular study for the test is listed first, followed by the test name. Column 1 is the percentage of correct predictions made by the test or the overall effectiveness for the reported data. Column 2 is the index of sensitivity, that is, the percentage of poor performers on the criterion measure who were correctly identified earlier by the screening test. Column 3 indicates the percentage of adequate performers who were correctly identified by the screening test originally (the index of specificity). Column 4 indicates the percentage of children identified as at risk who later failed, and Column 5 indicates the percentage of children identified as *not* at risk who later succeeded. Finally, Column 6 reports the percentage of the total number of children who actually are failing.

In nine of the screening situations, the overall effectiveness index ranges from 80% to 92%. However, a number of these screening procedures report low indices

Table 4–1.
Reanalysis of a Sample of Screening Procedures

Author(s) of research study	Screening measure (Predictor of at-risk status)	Criterion measure	1 % of total group correctly identified $\frac{a+d}{a+b+c+d}$	2 Index of sensitivity $\frac{a}{a+b}$	3 Index of specificity $\frac{d}{c+d}$	4 % of children identified as at risk who failed later $\frac{a}{a+c}$	5 % of children identified as *not* at risk who later succeeded $\frac{d}{b+d}$	6 % of children who are actually failing $\frac{a+b}{a+b+c+d}$
Lichtenstein, 1981	Minneapolis Preschool Screening Instrument (refer/pass)	Teacher ratings: Mild to severe problems/no problems	89%	63%	93%	62%	93%	15%
Lichtenstein, 1981	DIAL (refer/OK)	Teacher ratings: Mild to severe problems/no problems	87%	54%	93%	59%	92%	15%
Hainsworth & Siqueland, 1969	MSSST (high risk/average, and low risk)	End of year reading level (failing/passing)	81%	71%	87%	40%	95%	15%
Hase, 1977	First Grade Screening Test (FGST)	Teacher rating: Fair and good school performance/poor performance	90%	91%	89%	78%	96%	30%

Study	Test	Criterion						
Badian, 1982	Holbrook Kindergarten Screening Battery	Good/poor academic achievement at end of 3rd grade	92%	91%	89%	57%	99%	10%
Jansky & deHirsch, 1972	Perceptual Motor & Language Measures	Reading test at end of 2nd grade	77%	77%	66%	58%	82%	38%
Funk, Sturner, & Green, 1986	McCarthy GCI	California Achievement Test (1st grade)	83%	76%	85%	66%	90%	27%
Funk, Sturner, & Green, 1986	McCarthy GCI	California Achievement Test (2nd grade)	79%	80%	91%	50%	91%	27%
Lindeman, Goodstein, Sachs, & Young, 1984	Yellow Brick Road Test (using cutoff score recommended by test authors)	Metropolitan Achievement Test: poor achievement (0–33), average and significant achievement (34–100 percentile)	28%	100%	17%	15%	100%	13%
Eaves, Kendall, & Crichton, 1974	Modified deHirsch Index	Academic performance in grade 3	85%	60%	92%	63%	90%	20%
Satz & Friel, 1974	Developmental/Neuropsychological test battery	Reading performance at end of 1st grade	84%	78%	85%	49%	95%	15%
Chase, 1970	Metropolitan Readiness Test	First grade failure	86%	78%	89%	65%	84%	25%

of sensitivity, i.e., 63%, 54%, 71%, and 60% (Column 2). The high overall effectiveness index of several of the instruments results from the accuracy in identifying the children not at risk who later perform adequately. As indicated in Column 5, with two exceptions of 82% and 84%, these percentages range from 90% to 100%.

The data also indicate that the percentages of children identified as at risk who later failed (Column 4), with one exception, range from 15% to 66%. In other words, 34% to 85% of the children predicted to fail did *not* develop learning problems. In only one study did the instrument meet the minimum level of acceptability of 75% correct identified by Jansky (1978) for the use of the instrument.

The Metropolitan Readiness Test

The Metropolitan Readiness Test is a measure for use with children either in kindergarten or first grade. This readiness test was first published in 1933 and subsequently revised in 1949, 1965, 1976, and 1986 (Bieger, 1985; Hughes, 1987). The items used in the following example measured perceptual factors, word meaning, sentences, numbers, and copying (Hildreth & Griffiths, 1949).

The use of the Metropolitan reported here was undertaken in 1970 by Chase. This example is used because of the difficulty in finding Metropolitan data reported in sufficient detail so that 2 × 2 matrices can be constructed.

In her research, Chase studied 309 children who were attending first grade in a large midwestern school system for the first time. In February of the school year, the children were administered several different measures of their first-grade experience.

Children's readiness scores were compared with the teachers' ratings of the children after five of six grading periods had been completed. Promotional decisions were made in June based on the information obtained from those grading periods. It is important to note that whereas Chase used a number of different measures, the results reported here only deal with the relationship of the Metropolitan scores to teacher promotion decisions.

Table 4–2 illustrates the data obtained when classified with a 2 × 2 matrix. Table 4–3 shows the indices of predictability for the promotion status of the children and readiness status as determined in February by the Metropolitan.

Although the overall effectiveness index and the indices of sensitivity and specificity are acceptably high, the percentage of children who were originally identified as being at risk and who actually failed later (i.e., readiness score of below 39) is unacceptably low. The percentage of 65 indicates that over one-third (35%) of the children with a poor Metropolitan score were able to perform adequately in first grade, according to criteria set forth by the classroom teachers. The percentage of error allowable should not be greater than 25%. That is, the

Table 4–2.
Outcomes for Promotion Decisions (Based on Teachers' Grades) in Relation to Metropolitan Readiness Scores of First-Grade Children

Criterion	Decision on the MRT[a]		Totals
	Low readiness score (≥ 39)	Average and above-average readiness score (39+)	
Nonpromoted	51 $\quad$ a $\mid$ b	14	65
Promoted	c $\mid$ d $\quad$ 28	216	244
Totals	79	230	309

[a]A correlation of .53 was obtained between the readiness test scores and school failure.
Note. Data from *Differential Behavioral Characteristics of Nonpromoted Children* by J. A. Chase, 1970. Request for use approved by Graduate School, University of Maine.

Table 4–3.
Indices of Predictability of the Metropolitan for Promotion Decisions of First-Grade Children

Index

(a) Overall effectiveness

$$\frac{a+d}{a+b+c+d} \qquad \frac{267}{309} = 86\%$$

(b) Index of sensitivity

$$\frac{a}{a+b} \qquad \frac{51}{65} = 78\%$$

(c) Index of specificity

$$\frac{d}{c+d} \qquad \frac{216}{244} = 89\%$$

(d) Percentage of children identified as at risk who later failed

$$\frac{a}{a+c} \qquad \frac{51}{79} = 65\%$$

(e) Percentage of children identified as *not* at risk who later performed adequately

$$\frac{d}{b+d} \qquad \frac{216}{230} = 94\%$$

Note. Data from *Differential Behavioral Characteristics of Nonpromoted Children* by J. A. Chase, 1970. Request for use approved by Graduate School, University of Maine.

percentage of children predicted to be at risk by the readiness/screening measure (and who then performed inadequately by the end of the first grade) should not be lower than 75%.

Analysis of a Screening Measure

An important study that compared children's varying levels of readiness with later school achievement was undertaken by Butler, Marsh, Sheppard, and Sheppard (1982). A screening measure was administered in kindergarten to 320 students, and the scores were then compared to reading performance in grades 1, 2, and 3.

Butler et al. also provided a classification table that shows the actual and predicted reading placement for third-grade students. The students were divided into 20 groups, with each group containing 5% of the sample. The results of this study are similar to many other predictive studies with many more errors found within the middle range. For example, of the lowest 5% of children in the predicted group (i.e., very low score on the readiness test), 88% also performed in the lowest 20% of the group on achievement tests. However, as the predicted classification group becomes larger, more errors in prediction are found. When the lowest 25% of the predicted group is compared to their actual performance in third grade, only 59% of the predicted group remain in the lowest quartile at the end of third grade. (See Table 4–4.)

Most predictive studies do not provide information about the later reading performance of the middle group of students in a class. Fortunately, the Butler et al. study does include such data. In Table 4–5, note that 18% of this middle group of students fall in the lowest quartile in third-grade reading while 28% are performing in the upper quartile. (See Table 4–5.)

The results of Butler et al.'s study indicate that a substantial percentage of children (18%) who were *not* predicted to be problem readers when screened in kindergarten do in fact now demonstrate poor reading performance in the third grade. Also, a considerable number ($N = 45$) actually demonstrated superior reading performance, as indicated by their scoring in the upper quartile of the third-grade class. The data from this study thus reflect a wide range of reading performance for the middle 50% of the student group on the original kindergarten screening test. Such findings indicate once again the considerable fragility of the prediction process when used with educational data.

The Denver Developmental Screening Test

The Denver Developmental Screening Test (DDST) is a measure for use with children up to 6 years of age. It consists of 105 items that test four areas of

Table 4–4.
Predicted Group Performance on a Kindergarten Screening Test and Achievement Level in Third Grade

Criterion	Score on kindergarten screening test		
	Lowest 25%	Upper 75%	Totals
Lowest 25% on achievement test in third grade	47 a	b 33	80
Upper 75% on achievement test in third grade	c 33	d 207	240
Totals	80	240	320

$$\frac{a}{a+c} = \frac{47}{80} = 59\%$$

Note. Data summarized from "Early Prediction of Reading Achievement with the Sheppard School Entry Screening Test: A Four Year Longitudinal Study," by S. R. Butler et al., 1982, *Journal of Educational Psychology, 74,* 286. Used by permission.

Table 4–5.
Performance in Third Grade of Students Within the Middle 50% of the Group on the Screening Test Given in Kindergarten

Grade placement score on reading test administered in third grade	Middle 50% of group on kindergarten screening test	
	N	*%*
Lowest quartile	28	18%
Middle quartile	87	54%
Upper quartile	45	28%
N =	160	100%

Note. Data summarized from "Early Prediction of Reading Achievement with the Sheppard School Entry Screening Test: A Four Year Longitudinal Study," by S. R. Butler et al., 1982, *Journal of Educational Psychology, 74,* 286. Used by permission.

functioning: language, motor, adaptive, and personal/social. This test has been particularly popular with medical personnel when screening preschool populations. The Denver also has been used frequently as a screening/readiness test with children about to enter kindergarten. Meisels (1985) considers the Denver to be a valid screening measure; however, questions are raised in this chapter as to its effectiveness as an early identification instrument.

According to Meisels (1985), the DDST is "the best known and most widely-used developmental screening instrument available. With its wide age range, a child can be screened with the same test across a period of several years" (p. 33). He also notes that interobserver reliability is adequate (.96) as is test-retest reliability (.78). Meisels comments that the test is more accurate when used with infants and severely impaired children than it is when used with preschool or mildly handicapped children. However, he also states that the false negative rate for the Denver is low. That is, "very few children who are *not* at risk are incorrectly referred by the DDST" (p. 33).

A most important study of the Denver and its usefulness for kindergarten screening was undertaken recently by Cadman et al. (1984) wherein over 2,500 children were screened in the province of Ontario, Canada. The test was administered by public health nurses 5 to 7 months prior to the children's fall 1980 entry to kindergarten. Then, at the end of the school year, kindergarten teachers were asked to rate the children on four dimensions of behavior. These included learning abilities, classroom behavior, amount of special attention required, and referrals to special education. The teachers rated the children an average of 14 months after the original DDST screening on (1) incidence of learning problems, (2) incidence of behavioral problems, and (3) referrals for special class placement. The cell numbers for the three possible outcomes are presented in Tables 4–6 through 4–8.

Table 4–9 illustrates the indices of predictability for the behavioral and learning problems identified by the teachers. Both the overall effectiveness index and the index of specificity are high. However, these indices are influenced by the large numbers in Cell d for each problem. Also, the percentage of children identified as not at risk who later do not develop problems varies from 78.8% to 89.2%.

The effectiveness of the instrument to predict learning and behavioral problems, however, is quite different. That is, only 55% of the children who were predicted to be at risk developed learning problems; only 31% of the at-risk group developed behavioral problems, whereas 62% required special class placement. That is, from 38% to 69% of the group labeled as at risk did *not* experience learning or behavioral problems.

As previously stated, Jansky (1978) has mentioned that the percentage of error allowable should not be greater than 25%. That is, the percentage of children predicted to be at risk by the screening measure and who actually turn out to perform poorly should not be lower than 75%.

Table 4–6.
Relationship of Teacher-Reported Learning Problems and the DDST with Kindergarten Children

Criterion Teacher-reported learning problems	Decision on the DDST		
	At risk	Not at risk	Totals
Yes	23 $\quad$ a $\mid$ b	381	404
No	19 $\quad$ c $\mid$ d	2,020	2,039
Totals	42	2,401	2,443

Overall effectiveness $\qquad \dfrac{a+d}{N} = \dfrac{2,043}{2,443} = 83.6\%$

Percentage of children with learning problems originally identified by the screening test $\qquad \dfrac{23}{404} = 5.7\%$

Percentage of children originally identified as at risk who later developed problems $\qquad \dfrac{a}{a+c} = \dfrac{23}{42} = 55.0\%$

Percentage identified as *not* at risk who later performed adequately $\qquad \dfrac{d}{b+d} = \dfrac{2,020}{2,401} = 84.1\%$

Note. Data summarized from "The Usefulness of the Denver Developmental Screening Test to Predict Kindergarten Problems in a General Community Population," by D. Cadman et al., 1984, *American Journal of Public Health, 74,* 1093, 1096. Used by permission. Copyright 1984 by American Public Health Association. Adapted by permission.

A screening test is administered primarily to identify children who are likely to be at risk in developing learning problems. However, the sensitivity index for the Denver also indicates that it was not effective for this population. Only 23 (or 5.7%) of the children reported as having learning problems were previously identified by the Denver. Similarly, only 4.8% of behavior problems reported by the teachers and only 4.9% of the children reported by the teachers as needing special attention for learning/behavior problems were originally identified by the test. On the basis of similar findings, Cadman et al. (1984) properly conclude that the Denver screening test is neither an effective nor efficient screening measure for use in the schools.

Table 4–7.
Relationship of Teacher-Reported Behavior Problems and the DDST with Kindergarten Children

Criterion	DDST results		
Teacher-reported behavior problems	Column 1, at risk	Column 2, not at risk	Totals
Yes	13 $\quad$ a	b $\quad$ 260	273
No	29 $\quad$ c	d $\quad$ 2,141	2,170
Totals	42	2,401	2,443

Note. Data summarized from "The Usefulness of the Denver Developmental Screening Test to Predict Kindergarten Problems in a General Community Population," by D. Cadman et al., 1984, *American Journal of Public Health, 74,* 1093, 1096. Copyright 1984 by American Public Health Association. Adapted by permission.

Table 4–8.
Relationship of Teacher-Reported Special Attention for Learning/Behavior Problems and the DDST with Kindergarten Children

Criterion	DDST results		
Special attention needed for learning/behavioral problems (i.e., special class placement)	At risk	Not at risk	Totals
Yes	26 $\quad$ a	b $\quad$ 507	533
No	16 $\quad$ c	d $\quad$ 1,889	1,905
Totals	42	2,396	2,438

Note. Data summarized from "The Usefulness of the Denver Developmental Screening Test to Predict Kindergarten Problems in a General Community Population," by D. Cadman et al., 1984, *American Journal of Public Health, 74,* 1093, 1096. Copyright 1984 by American Public Health Association. Adapted by permission.

Table 4–9.
Indices of Predictability of the DDST for Teacher-Reported Problems of Kindergarten Children

Index	Learning problems	Behavioral problems	Special class placement
(a) Overall effectiveness $\dfrac{a+d}{a+b+c+d}$	$\dfrac{2,043}{2,443} = 83.6\%$	$\dfrac{2,154}{2,443} = 88.1\%$	$\dfrac{1,915}{2,438} = 78.5\%$
(b) Index of sensitivity $\dfrac{a}{a+b}$	$\dfrac{23}{404} = 5.7\%$	$\dfrac{13}{273} = 4.8\%$	$\dfrac{26}{533} = 4.9\%$
(c) Index of specificity $\dfrac{d}{c+d}$	$\dfrac{2,020}{2,039} = 99.1\%$	$\dfrac{2,141}{2,170} = 98.7\%$	$\dfrac{1,889}{1,905} = 99.2\%$
(d) Percentage of children originally identified as at risk who later failed $\dfrac{a}{a+c}$	$\dfrac{23}{42} = 55.0\%$	$\dfrac{13}{42} = 31.0\%$	$\dfrac{26}{42} = 62.0\%$
(e) Percentage of children identified as not at risk who later performed adequately $\dfrac{d}{b+d}$	$\dfrac{2,020}{2,401} = 84.1\%$	$\dfrac{2,141}{2,401} = 89.2\%$	$\dfrac{1,889}{2,396} = 78.8\%$

Note. Data summarized from "The Usefulness of the Denver Developmental Screening Test to Predict Kindergarten Problems in a General Community Population," by D. Cadman et al., 1984, *American Journal of Public Health, 74,* 1093, 1096. Copyright 1984 by American Public Health Association. Adapted by permission.

Revised Denver Developmental Screening Test

Results of the use of the Revised Denver Developmental Screening Test (RDDST) have been reported by Diamond (1990). Ninety-two children were screened prior to kindergarten entrance using the RDDST. Children could receive a rating of normal, questionable, or abnormal. No students in this sample received a rating so low as to be classified as abnormal or high risk. Seventy-eight children remained in the school system during the 5-year follow-up period. Follow-up data included school grades, number of children retained, special class placement, and remedial help offered in reading and math. Although Diamond states that the RDDST was able to predict academic performance in reading accurately, a further analysis of the progress of those children originally labeled as at risk on the revised Denver raises doubts as to the efficacy of this instrument. Of 17 children in grade 2 who had received a questionable rating, 16 obtained either an A or B in reading at the end of first grade. Only one child with a low screening score earned either a C or D in reading. Thus only 6% of the children labeled as possible risks for learning subsequently received a poor school grade. The same low percentages also were found in grades 3 and 4 (range 18% to 27%). That is, a large percentage of children with questionable readiness scores performed satisfactorily in school subjects.

However, as has been demonstrated for many other readiness tests, many of the children originally labeled as not at risk later performed quite adequately in school. Of 66 second-grade children with a normal screening score on the RDDST, 64 (or 97%) obtained an A or B in reading. However since very few children who received a low DDST score received a poor reading grade it is obvious that the revised version of the Denver also does not meet the guidelines of an effective screening measure as outlined by Kingslake (1981, 1983) and Jansky (1978).

Analysis of the Meeting Street School Screening Test

The Meeting Street School Screening Test was developed by Hainsworth and Siqueland in 1969. The theoretical assumption on which the instrument is based is that the test will identify deficiencies in psychoneurological skills. The test is used with children in kindergarten and first grade. It is individually administered and requires about 20 minutes to complete. The three subtests consist of the visual-perceptual motor scale, a motor patterning scale, and a language scale. The standardization sample consisted of students from the East Providence, Rhode Island, schools. Scores below 39 points for kindergarten children and below 55 points for first-grade children are considered appropriate cutoff points for indicating a high risk for learning problems (Rafoth, 1984). Two important studies investigating use of the test with age samples of schoolchildren are briefly discussed.

Hodge (1981) investigated the predictive efficiency of the Meeting Street as it related to children's academic achievement 1 to 5 years after assessment. Hodge's sample consisted of 535 first-grade students attending school in a southeastern state. He investigated a number of factors including sex, race, and kindergarten experience. However, the emphasis in this analysis is on the congruency of decisions made about children who were below the cutoff score of 55 recommended by the manual and their subsequent remedial placement in school. Remedial placement is defined as including Title One, resource room, or self-contained class.

Table 4–10 illustrates the relationship between the at risk and not at risk decisions on the MSSST and remedial-program placement in the second grade. Table 4–11 illustrates these same four outcomes for children in the sixth grade. Similar to the other readiness tests analyzed in this text, the MSSST also identifies a large number of not-at-risk children who later are successful in school (Cell d).

Table 4–12 illustrates the indices of predictability for the four outcomes from the MSSST. Of the adequate performers in grades 2 and 6, the MSSST identified 86% and 87%, respectively. However, the overall effectiveness indices are lower, i.e., 61.7% and 65%. The problem with the instrument is that a large number of children identified as at risk did not require remedial room placement (Cell c). Table 4–12 indicates that only 37% (grade 2) and 43% (grade 6) of the at-risk groups actually were placed in a remedial-room program. In other words, 63% and 57% of the at-risk group remained in the regular classroom. In addition, of the children placed in a remedial program in grades 2 and 6, the MSSST originally identified 72.7% and 78.1% of this group. That is, 26.3% and 21.9% of the subsequent remedial program placements were not identified by the MSSST.

The results of an investigation of the predictive power of this measure in a Georgia school system are quite similar (Rafoth, 1984). Over 1,300 children in a Georgia school district were administered the Meeting Street School Screening Test in 1979 and 1980. In 1983, children who had been placed in a learning disability program were identified, and their MSSST scores were tabulated using a 2 × 2 matrix. (See Table 4–13.)

Table 4–10.
Relationship of MSSST Decisions and Remedial Placement in Grade 2

| Criterion | MSSST | | |
	At risk	Not at risk	Total
Placement in a remedial program	128 a	b 48	176
No remedial program placement	c 219	d 303	522
Totals	347	351	698

Note. Data summarized from *Predictive Study of the MSSST and Academic Achievement from Grades 2 Through 6 by Race, Sex and Kindergarten Experience* by C. C. Hodge, 1981, unpublished doctoral dissertation, University of South Carolina. Used by permission.

Table 4–11.
Relationship of MSSST Decisions and Remedial Placement in Grade 6

Criterion	MSSST		
	At risk	Not at risk	Total
Placement in a remedial program	118 a	b 33	151
No remedial program placement	c 154	d 227	381
Totals	272	260	532

Note. Data summarized from *Predictive Study of the MSSST and Academic Achievement from Grades 2 Through 6 by Race, Sex and Kindergarten Experience* by C. C. Hodge, 1981, unpublished doctoral dissertation, University of South Carolina. Used by permission.

Table 4–12.
Indices of Predictability of the MSSST for Remedial Placement in Grades 2 and 6

Index	Grade 2	Grade 6
(a) Overall effectiveness $$\frac{a+d}{a+b+c+d}$$	$\frac{431}{698} = 61.7\%$	$\frac{345}{532} = 65\%$
(b) Index of sensitivity $$\frac{a}{a+b}$$	$\frac{128}{176} = 72.7\%$	$\frac{118}{151} = 78.1\%$
(c) Index of specificity $$\frac{d}{c+d}$$	$\frac{303}{522} = 58\%$	$\frac{227}{381} = 59.6\%$
(d) Percentage of children originally identified as at risk who later were placed in a remedial program $$\frac{a}{a+c}$$	$\frac{128}{347} = 37\%$	$\frac{118}{272} = 43\%$
(e) Percentage of children originally identified as *not* at risk who later performed adequately $$\frac{d}{b+d}$$	$\frac{303}{351} = 86\%$	$\frac{227}{260} = 87\%$

Note. Data summarized from *Predictive Study of the MSSST and Academic Achievement from Grades 2 Through 6 by Race, Sex and Kindergarten Experience* by C. C. Hodge, 1981, unpublished doctoral dissertation, University of South Carolina. Used by permission.

Rafoth also investigated the value of the Meeting Street as a screening measure of readiness for first grade. To do this she compared the cutoff scores of students with actual placement in special education programs (Table 4–14).

Again, the results indicate that the instrument is highly accurate in identifying children who later perform adequately. (See Table 4–15, index e.) However, of the children originally identified as at risk, only 8% and 19%, respectively, received special placement. (See Table 4–15, index d.)

The results of both studies should give educators pause when considering continued use of such instruments for screening. However, certain other limitations of these studies should be mentioned. Whether special education placement should be the main criterion of judging the efficacy of a screening instrument is debatable. In the real world of the public school, there are never enough placement slots available for all the children who could probably be so assigned. In Rafoth's study, remediation was defined as including only children placed in special education classes. Hodge's study also included children placed in a Title One program. However, many schools do not have any remediation programs available for students who are low performers, with the exception of actual retention in grade. Also, it would have been helpful if achievement test performance of all the students had been compared to levels of readiness as determined by the screening test.

Discussion

Predicting the outcomes of a young child's performance on either academic or behavioral measures is obviously subject to a substantial rate of error. At-risk

Table 4–13.
Relationship of Predictions of MSSST and Learning-Disabled Placement

	MSSST		
Criterion	At risk	Not at risk	Total
Placement in a learning disability program	71 a	b 10	81
Not placed in a learning disability program	c 787	d 509	1,296
Totals	858	519	1,377

Note. Data summarized from *Early Identification of Learning Disabilities: The Predictive Validity of the Meeting Street School Screening Test* by M. K. Rafoth, 1984. Unpublished doctoral dissertation, University of Georgia. Used by permission.

Table 4–14.

Relatonship of Predictions of the MSSST and Special Education Placement

	MSSST		
Criterion	Below cutoff score of 55	Above cutoff score	Total
Placement in a special education program	161 a	b 17	178
No placement	679 c	d 502	1,181
Totals	840	519	1,359

Note. Data summarized from *Early Identification of Learning Disabilities: The Predictive Validity of the Meeting Street School Screening Test* by M. K. Rafoth, 1984. Unpublished doctoral dissertation, University of Georgia. Used by permission.

groups formed on the basis of a score from a screening procedure will exclude a number of vulnerable children (false negatives) and will also include many children who will turn out not to be really at risk (false positives). Misidentifying children as false positives, and placing them in an intervention program that is unnecessary for them, will obviously distort the seemingly beneficial effects of the particular intervention program (Kingslake, 1981).

Many American educators and psychologists support the use of screening and readiness tests to such an extent that alternative approaches that could be used to monitor performance of the students and to improve academic functioning often are not attempted. In discussing this problem, Bookbinder (1978) argues for the simple use of a base line in evaluating the effectiveness of instructional methods. In his school district, the results of a survey reading test showed that 25% of all second-graders were labeled nonreaders in 1969. In 1978 this percentage had dropped to 6%. Kingslake (1981) cites this example to demonstrate that it is possible to reduce significantly the number of poor achievers without using screening procedures.

Kingslake (1981) also mentions another example of the use of a base line against which to measure improvement in basic skills. Citing a study by Bailey and Rogers (1979) she points out how, following appropriate in-service training and increased remedial support, there was a definite improvement in the teaching of reading in the elementary schools. (See Table 4–16.)

No reorganization of the school structure was undertaken, nor were there any known demographic changes in the student population. Kingslake points out that

Table 4–15.
Indices of Predictability of the MSSST for Learning-Disabled and Special Education Placement

Index	Learning-disabled placement	Special education placement
(a) Overall effectiveness $$\frac{a+d}{a+b+c+d}$$	$\frac{580}{1,377} = 42\%$	$\frac{663}{1,359} = 49\%$
(b) Index of sensitivity $$\frac{a}{a+b}$$	$\frac{71}{81} = 87.6\%$	$\frac{161}{178} = 90.1\%$
(c) Index of specificity $$\frac{d}{c+d}$$	$\frac{509}{1,296} = 31.6\%$	$\frac{502}{1,181} = 42.5\%$
(d) Percentage of children originally identified as at risk who later received special placement $$\frac{a}{a+c}$$	$\frac{71}{858} = 8\%$	$\frac{161}{840} = 19\%$
(e) Percentage of children originally identified as *not* at risk who later performed adequately $$\frac{d}{b+d}$$	$\frac{509}{519} = 98\%$	$\frac{502}{519} = 97\%$

Note. Data summarized from *Early Identification of Learning Disabilities: The Predictive Validity of the Meeting Street School Screening Test* by M. K. Rafoth, 1984. Unpublished doctoral dissertation, University of Georgia. Used by permission.

the upward shift in the mean score could have occurred just from the very good readers now reading even better, *without* any improvement in the reading performance of the poor readers. The most important information in Table 4–16 is the data indicating that the number of children with standard scores below 85 was reduced by over 50% (from 6.3% to 3.3%) over the 3-year time period.

It can be legitimately concluded that there is no screening procedure sufficiently accurate to be used as a base line in implementing an instructional program. Both Kingslake and Bookbinder (Kingslake, 1981) emphasize that today's screening procedures are often expensive, time consuming and "possibly dangerous." "Even if a screening procedure is quick and inexpensive, if it is inaccurate it is useless

Table 4–16.
Young Reading Test at Age 7 over a 3-Year Time Period

	1976	1977	1978
Mean score on Young Reading Test	105.35	107.88	108.15
Number scoring below a standard score of 85	119 (6.3%)	78 (4.19%)	62 (3.3%)
Total N =	1,875	1,860	1,877

Note. Adapted from *An Experimental Examination of On-Entry to School Screening* by
B. J. Kingslake, 1981. Unpublished doctoral dissertation, City of Birmingham Polytechnic.
Used by permission.

and even dangerous in that it may mislead the educator" (Kingslake, 1991).
Moreover, as has been previously noted, in American schools screening procedures
are used to deny children entrance into a regular kindergarten or first-grade
program. When such a judgment is made, the gravity of the educational decision
is compounded. Because of the known errors in prediction, denying a child an
opportunity to begin a regular educational program is obviously a risky decision
and should be avoided.

5

ANALYSIS OF THE GESELL SCHOOL READINESS TEST: SOME FACTORS TO CONSIDER

Educational personnel in many school districts are sophisticated in their use of readiness tests and utilize the results in a positive way to assist in the planning of instructional strategies for the child during the school year. However, others insist that a readiness test alone can provide answers about the child's level of academic, social, emotional, and physical maturity. The readiness test that purports to address all these issues is the Gesell School Readiness Test. Proponents of the test state that the administration of the Gesell results in a "behavioral age" that predicts success and failure in school more effectively than any other measure. However, several researchers and educators have expressed grave reservations about the effectiveness of the test, and this chapter discusses those issues.

Overview of the Test

The Gesell School Readiness Test was developed in the 1950s by two associates of Arnold Gesell, Frances Ilg and Louise Bate Ames. Gesell was a faculty member at Yale University, and he was both a psychologist and physician. He believed that many children failed in school because they were not "ready" to learn.

Ilg and Ames were interested primarily in the patterns of behavior that children demonstrate at different age levels. They believed that the various patterns of children's behavioral and personality characteristics could be identified accurately by a psychometric instrument. Use of their test gives a developmental age that is considered by some to be a truer measure of the child's capabilities to master school tasks than simply the child's chronological age (Kaufman, 1971a). Therefore, chronological age should not be used as the sole indicator as to the child's readiness to enter school.

Ilg and Ames also founded the Gesell Institute in New Haven, Connecticut. The institute emphasizes the use of readiness tests, administered by developmental examiners, to assess children's developmental progress.

The Gesell test attempts to assess the child's "developmental age." The concept includes a composite of tasks that reflect the child's social, emotional, intellectual, and physical functioning (Shepard & Smith, 1985). Two versions of the test presently exist. One is the Preschool Test, which is used with children $2\frac{1}{2}$ to 6 years of age. The other is the Gesell School Readiness Test (GSRT), which is administered to children ages $4\frac{1}{2}$ to 9 years of age. The latter test is the one that is used by schools for several purposes. That is, the test is used (1) to determine the child's readiness to begin kindergarten, (2) to assess developmental readiness at the end of kindergarten, and (3) to determine whether the child should be allowed to begin first grade (Carlson, 1985; Shepard & Smith, 1985).

Ilg and Ames express high expectations for their test: ". . . a child could be seven-years-old and could have an IQ of say 120, but if he were behaving like a six-year-old, we would like to see him placed in first, not second, grade" (Ilg, Ames, & Baker, 1981, p. 237). They consider that the use of the GSRT can be the major determiner of whether or not a child is "behaving" at an appropriate age for school.

Therefore, a main concern about the use of the Gesell is whether sufficient evidence exists that the GSRT can validly classify a 7-year-old child as developmentally at the level of a 6-year-old. Or, whether a 6-year-old child is behaving as a 5- or $4\frac{1}{2}$-year-old. That this is an important question is indicated by the fact that a number of school districts do place children either in a prekindergarten or a pre-first grade based only on the developmental age determined for the child by the GSRT.

Critique of the GSRT

Concerns about the GSRT include several issues. They are problems with test validity and reliability, the norming sample, the scoring system, and the extensive training required for test administrators.

Test Validity and Reliability

Concerns about test validity center on three issues. One is the lack of definitive information about the effectiveness of the test for "developmental placement" (Bradley, 1985; N. L. Kaufman, 1985). Nadine Kaufman (1985) notes that test effectiveness rests largely on testimonial statements.

Alan Kaufman (1971a) provides a predictive validity coefficient of .64 for the GSRT. However, because he *essentially rebuilt the test,* the data in his 1971 study do not provide any information on the version of the GSRT currently in use in the schools. Predictive validity coefficients cited by him would not necessarily apply to the version used in the school with its *subjective* system of scoring.

A second concern about test validity relates to the nature of the test items. Naglieri (1985) challenges the authors' claims that the test is a behavioral evaluation and that there are no similarities to intelligence tests. Instead, many of the items are similar to those found in the Stanford-Binet and McCarthy tests (Naglieri, 1985). Other researchers note that some of the test vocabulary is out-of-date (Bradley, 1985; Waters, 1985). For example, words such as "palm" and "ring-finger" are included, words which Bradley states were more common in conversation 20 years ago.

Further, Waters (1985) states that the test items emphasize cognitive, language, and motor tasks, although the test authors emphasize the role of social maturity in school readiness. Thus the rating of a child as "immature" can be quite misleading.

A third concern relates to the range and nature of the behaviors viewed as important in determining "developmental age." For example, the Gesell manual states that the child's tongue "barely protrudes at $5\frac{1}{2}$ years, but at age 6, the tongue pushes against the cheek or lower lip." Shepard and Smith (1985) note that for most of the process observations obtained using the instrument, "there is no evidence at all as to how valid these behaviors are as indicators of developmental maturity or how reliable is their assessment" (p. 57).

Also related to validity are the differences in performance between the norming sample of the 1940s and unpublished normative data from a 1970s sample of children. On 23 of the 52 tasks (44%) of the total number of tasks a more recent population sample scored 6 months or more *above* the 1940s norms (Shepard & Smith, 1985, p. 45). Such data indicate clearly that "the tests do not measure enduring biological traits for which it is immaterial where and when the normative data were obtained" (p. 45).

The lack of test reliability also is a problem (N. Kaufman, 1985; Shepard & Smith, 1985). Furthermore, Shepard and Smith note the large standard error of measurement reported by Alan Kaufman (1971b) in his study. They do not consider that the instrument is accurate enough to differentiate between children who are at a "developmental" age of 4 (and supposedly not ready for kindergarten) and those at a "developmental age of five who are acceptable for kindergarten" (Shepard & Smith, 1985, p. 44).

Norming Samples

One of the concerns about the norming sample expressed by Alan Kaufman (1971a) is that the children all lived in one geographical area, i.e., North Haven,

Connecticut. They also were above average in both intelligence and socioeconomic status. Nadine Kaufman (1985) also notes that the sample basically is Caucasian and therefore unrepresentative of the current school population. Shepard and Smith (1985, p. 44) note that no new normative data have been collected and published for 5-year-olds since 1960. Bradley (1985) concurs that the norms are outdated and do not adequately represent various ethnic groups and the different geographical areas in the United States.

In addition, in the standardization sample, children ranged in age from 5 years to 10 years. However, Alan Kaufman (1971a) points out that a number of tables provide norms for children aged $4\frac{1}{2}$. He also mentions that, at each of the seven age levels, the age range of the children was 5 to 8 months, which he considered too wide. Also, he noted that the average age of the child at each level was too high (e.g., 5 years 2 months instead of 5-0 and 6 years 4 months instead of 6-0, Kaufman, 1971a, p. 33).

Scoring System

A recent study of the psychometric characteristics of the Gesell is provided by Lichtenstein (1990). The Gesell was administered twice during the last 2 months of the school year to a sample of 46 kindergarten children of average mental ability. Lichtenstein reports that "reliability data" contradict using the GSRT as a sole, or even primary basis for grade placement decisions (p. 374). Test-retest agreement pertaining to placement decisions occurred in 78% of the cases. Test-retest reliability was .73, which is below acceptable standards. It should be noted that the test-retest time period ranged from only 1 to 5 weeks. Interrater reliability of .71 indicates, as Lichtenstein states, substantial differences among the trained examiners when interpreting the test performance of the same child. Lichtenstein concedes that the nonstandard scoring system used with the Gesell is the major contributor to the lower correlation coefficient obtained in his study and the resultant inconsistency between examiners (Lichtenstein, 1990, p. 374).

Discussions of the test frequently note the lack of a systematic scoring procedure for the Gesell. Alan Kaufman (1971a) notes that this problem makes scoring of the test a real challenge even for those who have been trained as developmental examiners. Shepard and Smith (1985) also comment that too much is left to the examiners to "sense" 5-year-old behavior from the clustering of various subtests. They also conclude that the distribution of age levels overlaps to a great extent (p. 46).

Another problem is that the Gesell School Readiness Test lacks a composite score or index (Carlson, 1985). Although a developmental age for each task is indicated, the examiner is faced with the problem of adequately summarizing and integrating the results of an examination. "Developmental age is, in the end, subjectively determined as the basis of a clustering of successes" (Carlson, 1985, p. 317).

Concern also has been expressed about both the vague directions for the test as well as the scoring system (Kaufman, 1985). Such conditions can lead to inconsistency of evaluations from different examiners. Because many school systems use the Gesell test as a basic determiner of placement in prekindergarten or pre-first classes, the lack of a systematic scoring system alone will result in many placement errors.

In addition, examiners who use the Gesell in testing the child are urged to pay close attention to the specific behaviors of the child during the examination. An example is the way that the child sits while writing. Another example is that the size, placement on the paper, starting point, and directionality of the child's drawing of a circle is considered in addition to "roundness" in assessing the child's developmental levels (Kaufman, 1971a, p. 32).

The resulting interpretation of the child's state of maturity, therefore, is based on the child's performance (the product) *and* the accompanying behaviors that the child engages in while reaching the solution to each task (Kaufman, 1971a; Shepard & Smith, 1985). Interpretation of such behaviors obviously leads to considerable diversity of opinion because the decisions are subjective.

Training

The extensive training practice and experience required to administer and summarize adequately the two Gesell tests are stressed by Carlson (1985). He mentions that one school system requires 70–75 hours of training for teachers who are to be Gesell examiners. Bradley (1985) also is concerned about the level of clinical expertise required to administer the GSRT.

The reality in most school systems, however, is that many teachers receive only a few hours of training. The problems resulting from inadequate training in the administration and interpretation of the tests are discussed by Leiter (1974) and are presented in Chapter 3, on assessment.

Problems in Screening Children

The screening program in one Florida county illustrates one use of the GSRT for the placement of children. The test is administered to children during the kindergarten year and is used to select first-grade students.

In a discussion of this program, Sincere (1987) noted that on a Saturday in March, 1987, 247 kindergarten children were assembled at an elementary school for a screening program. The aim was to ascertain if they were "ready" for entrance to first grade. In addition to testing the children's vision and hearing, the Gesell School Readiness Test was administered. After the 20-minute examination was completed the test was scored and the child recommended either for pre-first or regular first-grade placement.

"Bredekamp questions taking children into a foreign environment to be ordered to perform tasks by people they have never seen before" (Sincere, 1987, p. 28). However, school personnel insist that the Gesell is used only as a verification of teacher observations made in the classroom.

The defense of the Gesell by school personnel in this county in Florida rests on two major points. One is that the research department in the school system indicates that the Gesell is a "fine" instrument (Sincere, 1987, p. 28). However, no data are given. Second, county personnel state that pre-first children were more successful in school; however, they refused to release the research study because it had not been translated into "layman's" terms (Sincere, 1987, p. 29).

Furthermore, county educators state that the first-grade curriculum is difficult; however, they see no role as educators in changing it. Instead, the book companies are cited as the source of the difficulty of the curriculum. School personnel also resort to the use of sociometric measures as evidence of the success of their transition room program. (The problems with use of sociometric data are discussed in Chapter 6.)

In summary, the major problems with the screening procedure are, first, that it relies on the use of one test administered in a strange environment for the child. Second, valid data on the success of the procedure in that system are not available.

Analysis of the Predictive Validity of the GSRT

One of the few predictive validity studies undertaken on the GSRT was conducted by Wood, Powell, and Knight (1984). In this study, the child's developmental status as determined by the GSRT was related to kindergarten outcomes. The criterion variable was the "special needs" status that was assigned by the school to children who experienced difficulty in adjusting to the kindergarten program. The GSRT was administered 1 to 4 months later to all the children in the study ($N = 84$).

Wood et al. then chose three different developmental ages derived from a previous statistical analysis of the data to be used as possible cutoff points and considered by them to be possible "critical ages." The three possible critical ages were 55.6 months, 57.6 months, and 58.1 months. Critical age was defined by the authors as a point on the developmental age continuum below which the children would be recommended to delay school entry until they were more developmentally mature. Using the overall effectiveness index, Wood et al. stated that the predictive accuracy of these three critical ages ranged from 69% to 78.6%.

For Wood et al. the most effective cutoff age would be 57.6 months. They believe that such a cutoff age identifies a large number of children who actually fail, without including too many children predicted to fail but who actually succeeded. The authors cite the high agreement rate between the Gesell and teacher assessment of children's performance, i.e., the overall effectiveness index.

However, the decision accuracy of the different cutoff ages can best be determined through the construction of 2 × 2 matrices and analyses of the data. As already discussed, the information from such a table indicates the number of false positive and false negative cases. Tables 5–1, 5–2, and 5–3 have been constructed from the data provided by Wood et al. in their article and provide a more precise interpretation of test effectiveness.

Table 5–4 illustrates the indices described in Chapter 3 computed for the cutoff ages of 55.6, 57.6, and 58.1 months. As indicated (Row a), the overall effectiveness indices are 79%, 77%, and 69%, respectively. For all three developmental ages the instrument identified a high percentage of children who later would be judged successful (Line e). These percentages are 87%, 93%, and 96%, respectively. However, of particular interest are Lines b and d in Table 5–4. The indices of sensitivity, the percentages of later failures originally identified by the instrument, are 47%, 76.5%, and 88%, respectively. In other words, 13 and 15 of the total 17 failures were predicted by the developmental ages of 57.6 and 58.1. However, and most important, the instrument also predicted a large number of children to fail *who in fact later succeeded.* Line d of the Table indicates that only 47%, 46%, and 38%

Table 5–1.
Relation of Gesell DA to Success and Failure in Kindergarten for 55.6 Months Developmental Age

Kindergarten outcome	Developmental age as indicated by the Gesell				Totals
	< 55.6 months (Unready)		> 55.6 months (Ready)		
Failure	8	a	b	9	17
		c	d		
Success	9			58	67
Total	17			67	84

Note. Data summarized from "Predicting School Readiness: The Validity of Developmental Age," by C. Wood et al., 1984, *Journal of Learning Disabilities, 17,* 8–11. Copyright 1984 by the Donald D. Hammill Foundation. Reprinted by permission.

Table 5–2.
Relation of Gesell DA to Success and Failure in Kindergarten for 57.6 Months Developmental Age

Kindergarten outcome	Developmental age as indicated by the Gesell		Totals
	< 57.6 months (Unready)	> 57.6 months (Ready)	
Failure	13 a	b 4	17
	c	d	
Success	15	52	67
Total	28	56	84

Note. Data summarized from "Predicting School Readiness: The Validity of Developmental Age," by C. Wood et al., 1984, *Journal of Learning Disabilities, 17,* 8–11. Copyright 1984 by the Donald D. Hammill Foundation. Reprinted by permission.

of the children predicted to fail actually failed. In other words, of those predicted to fail, 53%, 54%, and 62% succeeded in kindergarten.

Wood et al. considered that the developmental age of 57.6 months is the optimal cutoff to use. They state that accurate detection of potential failure "is the main objective of a developmental screening program." Using 57.6 months as the critical age, one-third of all kindergarten children would be recommended to delay entry into kindergarten. However, the data in Table 5–4 indicate that of the children who would be recommended to be retained, only 46% were actually kindergarten "failures." Thus 54% of the children recommended to delay kindergarten entry had a successful kindergarten outcome. In other words, more *incorrect* classifications of unreadiness are thus made than correct decisions. Any instrument that produces such a high error rate is of dubious value for use in making placement decisions. The conclusion to be drawn from this analysis is that a low developmental age as determined by the Gesell is unrelated to success or failure in kindergarten.

Shepard and Smith (1985) note that the 55.6 months critical age (Table 5–1) produces the fewest classification errors. Although the percentage of children originally identified as at risk but who later failed is 47%, a/(a+c) (and thus the error rate is 53%), the actual number of children labeled unready but who did succeed is reduced from 24 (Table 5–3) to 9 (Table 5–1). However, the reader should note that in all three tables the percentages of children labeled as immature and unready, who end up demonstrating poor achievement, range from only 38% to 47%. Such percentages obviously do not meet the criterion percentage of 75% minimum considered to be acceptable (Jansky, 1978).

Table 5–3.
Relation of Gesell DA to Success and Failure in Kindergarten for 58.1 Months Develop-mental Age

Kindergarten outcome	Developmental age as indicated by the Gesell		Totals
	< 58.1 months (Unready)	> 58.1 months (Ready)	
Failure	15 a	b 2	17
	c	d	
Success	24	43	67
Total	39	45	84

Note. Data summarized from "Predicting School Readiness: The Validity of Develop-mental Age," by C. Wood et al., 1984, *Journal of Learning Disabilities, 17,* 8–11. Copyright 1984 by the Donald D. Hammill Foundation. Reprinted by permission.

Of major importance is that the overall effectiveness ratio of the data in Table 5–1 is inflated by the large number of successful children predicted by the instrument, i.e., 58. That is, of 67 children who were predicted to be not at risk, 58 or 87% subsequently were considered successful in kindergarten.

Two other limitations of the study also may be identified. One is that the investigation should probably be considered a concurrent measurement study (Shepard & Smith, 1985). However, the predictive aspect was emphasized by the investigators.

Second, the criterion was based on teacher referral. This procedure raises the issue of possible teacher bias. Use of standardized assessment measures at the end of the kindergarten year may have produced more definitive conclusions (Shepard & Smith, 1985). Nevertheless, the data in the study are useful in examining the accuracy of the decision process if the GSRT is to be used to predict kindergarten failure (Shepard & Smith, 1985).

The Kaufman Revision of the GSRT

In the early 1970s, Alan Kaufman initiated an investigation of the psychometric properties of the GSRT. However, in the process he eliminated both individual test items and subtests and changed the scoring system (Kaufman, 1971a). Thus, the conclusions reached by Kaufman may only be applied to his version of the test because it was a major revision.

Table 5–4.
Indices of Predictability for Three Developmental Ages on the Gesell

Index	Developmental age		
	55.6 months	57.6 months	58.1 months
(a) Overall effectiveness $$\frac{a+d}{a+b+c+d}$$	$\frac{66}{84} = 79\%$	$\frac{65}{84} = 77\%$	$\frac{58}{84} = 69\%$
(b) Index of sensitivity $$\frac{a}{a+b}$$	$\frac{8}{17} = 47\%$	$\frac{13}{17} = 76.5\%$	$\frac{15}{17} = 88\%$
(c) Index of specificity $$\frac{d}{c+d}$$	$\frac{58}{67} = 87\%$	$\frac{52}{67} = 78\%$	$\frac{43}{67} = 64\%$
(d) Percentage of children originally identified as at risk who later failed $$\frac{a}{a+c}$$	$\frac{8}{17} = 47\%$	$\frac{13}{28} = 46\%$	$\frac{15}{39} = 38\%$
(e) Percentage of children originally identified as *not* at risk who later performed adequately $$\frac{d}{b+d}$$	$\frac{58}{67} = 87\%$	$\frac{52}{56} = 93\%$	$\frac{43}{45} = 96\%$

Note. Data summarized from "Predicting School Readiness: The Validity of Developmental Age," by C. Wood et al., 1984, *Journal of Learning Disabilities, 17,* 8–11. Copyright 1984 by the Donald D. Hammill Foundation. Reprinted by permission.

Three complete subtests were removed from the GSRT (in addition to individual items from the subtests). Only one test, Animals, was administered exactly as found in the original GSRT. Table 5–5 illustrates the similarities and differences between the two forms of the test.

Kaufman also extensively revised the scoring system. Originally the developmental age was "estimated by the developmental examiner from all the formal and informal evidence obtained in the test situation" (Kaufman, 1971a, p. 52).

Examples of "informal" evidence (noted in the prior section) are aspects of behavior such as whether the child held the examiner's hand when walking to the test room and the type of comments the child made during a drawing task.

In order to objectify the administration and scoring system, Kaufman developed specific guidelines for administration of the tests and a scoring system that includes illustrative material as to whether a test item was correct. Also, a range of score points was assigned to the variety of responses that might be expected from the children.

Table 5–5.
Test Items Found on Two Versions of the Gesell

Gesell School Readiness Test	Kaufman Revision[a]
1. *Initial interview*—answering questions about siblings, birthdate, father's occupation	1. question about birthday party left out; item dealing with posture deleted
2. *Writing*—writing name, address, date, and numbers from 1–20	2. ability to write name with nondominant hand deleted; not asked to write address or date
3. *Copy forms*—copying printed two-dimensional geometrical forms (i.e., circle, diamond) and three-dimensional forms (i.e., cylinder)	3. order of copying the lines of most of the geometric forms changed; copying three-dimensional forms deleted because given only to one-half of the children in the study
4. *Incomplete man*—completing a partially drawn man and answering questions about his emotions	4. two advanced questions about emotions of incomplete man eliminated
5. *Right and left*—identifying parts of the body and discriminating between right and left in numerous ways	5. *complete test deleted*
6. *Monroe visual tests*—making designs and reproducing designs from memory	6. *complete test deleted*
7. *Animals*—naming as many animals as possible in one minute	7. *only test given in original form*
8. *Home and school preferences*—states favorite indoor and outdoor activities at home and school	8. *all items eliminated*

[a]Adapted from *Comparison of Tests Built from Piaget's and Gesell's Tasks: An Analysis of Their Psychometric Properties and Psychological Meaning,* by A. S. Kaufman, 1971a. Unpublished doctoral dissertation, Columbia University. Used by permission.

Kaufman stated that he obtained a reliability coefficient of .84 for his sample of kindergarten children, a coefficient which he considered to be "adequate." It is important to note that these results were based on the use of the previously included test items and objective scoring system.

A predictive validity correlation coefficient of .64 was obtained by Kaufman and Kaufman (1972) between the Kaufman version of the GSRT administered in kindergarten and the Stanford Achievement Test administered at the end of first grade. The mean IQ of the group was 108, and 67% of the children came from families who ranked in the highest three categories of an occupational status scale (i.e., lawyer, high school teacher, optometrist, etc.) It should be emphasized again that the Gesell test used here was the Kaufman version.

The coefficient of .64 is a respectable correlation coefficient. However, the data in a predictive matrix also are important. Table 5–6 was constructed using the developmental age of 5 years as a cutoff and correlated with subsequent performance on the Stanford Achievement Test administered at the end of first grade.

Table 5–7 illustrates the various effectiveness indices constructed from the data in Table 5–6. As indicated, the overall effectiveness index is 90.78%. Also of interest is that the children who performed in the lowest quartile of the Stanford Achievement Test (poor performers) were effectively identified earlier by Kaufman's test (sensitivity index = 100%). In addition, all of the children identified as "mature" by Kaufman's test later performed adequately on the Stanford. (See Line e, Table 5–7.)

Table 5–6.

Relation of Gesell Developmental Age to Academic Performance at the End of First Grade Using the Kaufman Revision

Criterion	Developmental age		
Stanford Achievement Test	Immature (DA below 5)	Mature (DA of 5 or greater)	Totals
Poor performance (lower quartile)	14 a	b 0	14
Adequate performance (middle & upper quartile)	c 7	d 55	62
Totals	21	55	76

Note. Constructed from data in "Tests Built from Piaget's and Gesell's Tasks as Predictors of First Grade Achievement," by. A. S. & N. L. Kaufman, 1972, *Child Development, 32,* 530. Copyright 1972. Used by permission.

Table 5–7.

Indices of Predictability on the Stanford Achievement Test for the Developmental Age of 5.0 on Kaufman's Revision of the Gesell

Index	Value
(a) Overall effectiveness $\dfrac{a+d}{a+b+c+d}$	$\dfrac{69}{76} = 90.78\%$
(b) Index of sensitivity $\dfrac{a}{a+b}$	$\dfrac{14}{14} = 100\%$
(c) Index of specificity $\dfrac{d}{c+d}$	$\dfrac{55}{62} = 88.7\%$
(d) Percentage of children originally identified as at risk who later failed $\dfrac{a}{a+c}$	$\dfrac{14}{21} = 66.7\%$
(e) Percentage of children originally identified as *not* at risk who later performed adequately $\dfrac{d}{b+d}$	$\dfrac{55}{55} = 100\%$

Note. Constructed from data in "Tests Built from Piaget's and Gesell's Tasks as Predictors of First Grade Achievement," by A. S. & N. L. Kaufman, 1972, *Child Development, 32*, 530. Used by permission.

However, of the children identified as "immature," 66.7% later performed poorly on the Stanford. That is, 33.3%, or one third of those labeled as immature, did in fact perform adequately on the achievement test at the end of the first grade. In other words, transition room placement, if based on the immature rating of this objective form of the Gesell, would have been in error in one out of three cases.

Summary

The developers of the GSRT maintain that the administration of the test results in a "behavioral age" that effectively predicts school success and failure. Information as to the lack of effectiveness of the instrument, however, comes from two sources. One includes the analyses and comments of both researchers and educators on the nature of the instrument. First, the test fails to meet two criteria essential for psychological and educational tests—validity and reliability. Other concerns include the restricted nature of the norming sample and the lack of an objective scoring system. These weaknesses call into question two other characteristics essential for tests—generalizability and objectivity.

The second major source of information about the ineffectiveness of the instrument is found in detailed analyses of the predictions made through use of the test. Predictive studies reported to date indicate that the percentage of error in labeling children as immature who in fact succeed is too large to continue use of the test in making placement decisions. Errors in the identification of "unready" children ranged from 53% to 62% (Wood et al., 1984).

Although the Gesell Institute announced a major effort to "revise, renorm, and validate" the Gesell readiness tests, the revision has not been completed to date (Cohen, 1989). In view of this fact, educational personnel would be well advised to use the Kaufman version of the Gesell, which provides an objective scoring system. In any case, judgment concerning the type of placement or intervention should not be made based only on the results of a readiness test. However, the main question that should be considered is whether any test should play such an important part in a child's educational career, especially when used with children so young. Carlson (1985) asks the most important question of all: "Might we re-examine what might be done to change the schools, rather than to assess the child's propensity to adapt to the system and prescribe alterations in the child's life in order to make such an adaptation?" (p. 318).

6

SOCIAL AND EMOTIONAL ADJUSTMENT OF "YOUNG"-FOR-AGE CHILDREN

A concern that is continually expressed about children entering school is the question of the adequacy of their social and emotional adjustment. Some educators and psychologists insist that children are entering school too early and as a result are too immature and inattentive. Gesellians insist that the main contribution of the Gesell School Readiness Test is that it identifies "developmentally immature" children, that is, children who are not ready to begin schooling because they are not emotionally ready for the demands of school. The important question is, How can a child's social and emotional status be properly appraised? And, when this is accomplished, can a link between school adjustment problems and the child who enters at a younger age be established?

Types of Data

A host of specific questions must be addressed in order to ascertain adequately the adjustment status of children entering kindergarten or first grade. What constitutes adequate evidence that younger-aged children do in fact have more emotional problems in school? Are ratings of children obtained from kindergarten or first-grade teachers at the end of the school year sufficient proof that certain children indeed do have emotional problems? Are "testimonials" from either parents or teachers sufficient proof that a child is better or more poorly adjusted? Or is it necessary to look at adjustment status 3 or 4 years after children have begun their elementary schooling? Can we, in fact, link an individual's adjustment as an adult to the age when the child entered school as is the thesis of some educators (Uphoff & Gilmore, 1984)?

Four types of evidence have frequently been utilized in studies evaluating the social and emotional adjustment status of children entering kindergarten or first grade. They are (1) anecdotal evidence, (2) number of particular events taken from school or public records, (3) teacher ratings of behavior, and (4) sociometric data. Anecdotal evidence typically includes statements of teachers and/or parents. Generally, little attempt is made to quantify the data; thus the reader is left with only impressionistic statements about various children.

In contrast, certain types of events, such as the number of times a child is involved in disciplinary difficulties or the number of referrals made to psychological services, are taken as evidence of poor adjustment. Positive indicators, such as the number of elected positions held by students as they progress through school, have been cited as evidence of leadership ability and linked to positive social growth.

Two methods of classroom data collection involve evaluations of children's behavior using behavior rating scales made out by teachers and sociometric data. Briefly summarized, sociometric data provide some information about the child's popularity and acceptance by the peer group. The use of sociometric data is discussed in part two of this chapter.

Anecdotal Evidence

Decisions as to the placement or retention of a child often are made by school personnel based on observation of the child's activities within the classroom. Recently a kindergarten teacher in a central Florida elementary school pointed out a child in her class who she said was too immature to be passed to first grade. Although she readily acknowledged that the child would be able to handle the academic demands of first grade, the teacher was convinced that this student's emotional adjustment was not sufficient to handle the overall demands of the first-grade environment. The main emphasis by the teacher was concern for the "immaturity" of this child. The teacher was planning to make this decision either by herself or with the aid of a primary supervisor. However, no referral to a school psychologist had ever been suggested. The teacher ended her discussion with the plea: "I just don't know how I can convince her parents that she should stay back."

Currently school psychologists and special education personnel must proceed cautiously in labeling and classifying children for possible special education placement. However, kindergarten and primary-grade teachers are often allowed to make a decision about kindergarten retention or first-grade placement by themselves without any additional input from other educational personnel or from parents. For example, in the above case the teacher was convinced that the child's "immaturity" doomed her to a failure experience if she were to be allowed to go on to first grade.

School officials do concede that it is difficult for teachers to determine the difference between a so-called "immature" child and a child with a learning disability. Nevertheless, in one school district, they also state that it is their aim to have pre-first classes that are "pure," i.e., free of children with learning and emotional problems (Sincere, 1987, p. 21).

One study by Dennler (1987) found that teacher perceptions of immature behaviors vary considerably in different school systems. She noted that while educational personnel talked of retaining immature children, teacher judgment about retained children centered instead around perceptual motor problems in one school district and academic problems in another district. In view of the fact that teachers have difficulty in making accurate global predictions as to who will succeed in the primary grades (Stevenson et al., 1976), it would appear presumptuous to expect teachers to be able to make a distinction between a child who is immature and one who has a learning or behavioral problem at such an early age.

The Use of Psychological Referral Data

Psychological referral is sometimes used as an indicator of social or emotional adjustment status. One study of referrals to psychological services in York County, Canada, schools indicated that boys who were early entrants to school in the primary grades were referred more frequently than were older entrants (DiPasquale, Moule, & Flewelling, 1980). Youngest entrants in this study refers to children with a November or December birthdate, because the entrance-age cutoff for the school district was December 31.

This study has been cited in the literature as evidence that young entrants have more adjustment problems than do older school entrants (Braymen & Piersel, 1987). However, the majority of referrals in this school system were for academic problems rather than emotional or social adjustment problems ($N = 434$ vs. 118). Of the social/emotional/behavioral referrals, roughly 23% of the youngest entrants (i.e., November/December birthdates) were referred. However, an equal percentage of older children (i.e., March/April birthdates) also were referred for these reasons (24%).

A number of children born late in the year were referred for psychological services for learning problems in the primary grades (i.e., K–3rd grade). Therefore, DiPasquale et al. concluded that these children were encountering more difficulties within the classroom. Although this statement may be accurate, it is incomplete as it stands because it says nothing about the etiology of such difficulties.

DiPasquale et al. automatically consider that the difficulties lie within the child. However, it is possible that other factors, such as quality of teaching and appropriateness of curriculum, might also be involved. In Chapter 7, on entrance age, it is emphasized that educational personnel tend to be very aware of calendar-age differences of children entering school. Because of such sensitivity, it would seem logical that younger children might be referred more frequently for psychological services because of teachers' beliefs that children entering at a young age are almost always at risk for problems. Thus, the teachers' expectation that young children automatically will have difficulty in school may be an important factor that leads to an increase in referrals to psychological services of this age group.

Also of importance is that DiPasquale et al. analyze the data on psychological referrals as though age were the only variable influencing the frequency of referrals. In the study, age is treated as an independent variable, and number (frequency) of referrals is treated as a dependent variable. However, the differences in the frequency of referrals may be the result of socioeconomic status (SES) and home environment. Other contaminating influences include all of the reasons that lead school personnel to make referrals in the first place—teacher expectancy for performance as previously mentioned, degree of disruptive student behavior, etc.

Furthermore, these researchers do not cite data as to the number of younger children versus older children who achieved satisfactorily at the end of the first grade in their school system. No analysis is provided about the number of referrals to psychological services of young children from different schools within the total system. It is quite possible that some schools in York County, which the authors serve, were providing a satisfactory educational program for their young children. Thus, it is a serious error not to determine which schools contribute the most psychological referrals.

A study of referrals in one large school system showed many differences in incidence of diagnostic and assessment activities and referrals from school to school. In other words, what was considered a problem in one school was not so considered in another (Carson, 1969).

That the rate of psychological referrals can be considered an important index of possible adjustment problems in young children is thrown further in doubt in a study of young entrants in an Ohio school system. Wonderly (1981) examined the rate of psychological referrals in the primary grades of two schools in northeastern Ohio. Referrals from kindergarten through grade 6 were analyzed to determine whether a higher number of young males were referred for psychological services. In Wonderly's study young entrants were defined as children whose birthdates fell between April 1 and September 30—the cutoff date in Ohio for school entrance to kindergarten or first grade. Wonderly found no relationship between number of referrals and age of the male students; 54% of the male referrals were younger-age children and 46% were older males, which resulted in a nonsignificant difference. What was significant was the percentage of male referrals as compared to female: 76% of all referrals within these two schools were male children.

The Use of Suicide Data

Information in school records is not the only data source for events hypothesized to indicate poor emotional/social adjustment. Since 1985 several statements have appeared in both the press and professional journals concerning a possible connection between youth suicide and the age that children entered school. The belief is that children who are early entrants to school (young for age) are at risk for possible suicide before age 26.

A typical description of the suicide study by Uphoff and Gilmore (1985) is found in an article by Brocato (1988). Brocato mentions that 45% of male youth suicides in Uphoff and Gilmore's study were summer children and early entrants to school. This percentage increased to 55% when males born in October and November (who had begun school even earlier) were added to the figures. Brocato is astounded at the rate of female suicides which showed that 83% had summer birthdates.

To "combat" this suicide risk, Uphoff and Gilmore (1985) proposed a number of possible actions. They include (1) changing the cutoff date for school entrance from late fall to late summer, (2) using a thorough developmental evaluation to determine the child's readiness for kindergarten, (3) keeping "too young" children out of school for one year, (4) reducing pressure in the early grades, and (5) placing "developmentally unready" children in prekindergarten (Brocato, 1988).

The belief that suicides can be linked to the age when the children enter school must be examined very carefully. To accept such an argument means that the children's entrance age is the most overwhelming event in their lives. In order to conclude that there is a possible link between the child's suicide and age of entrance, the school history of each child who committed suicide would have to be examined carefully. If each of the children involved had been evaluated by school personnel as under severe stress about school, had a poor or failing academic record during the kindergarten and first-grade years, and had been referred to school support personnel for possible emotional problems, then a more complete picture of the actual role of the school environment would emerge.

The Uphoff and Gilmore data are suspicious for several reasons. First, the sample of children was very small ($N = 28$). It is risky to attempt to arrive at any meaningful conclusion on the basis of a study that involved only 28 youths. Second, suicides were tabulated in Montgomery County, Ohio, for only $1\frac{1}{2}$ years, a relatively brief span. Third, a greater percentage of young female entrants were found to have committed suicide than male entrants. However, the maturationalist argument is that boys are more at risk for school problems than girls. If so, how can the large percentage of female suicides be explained? Also, it should be noted that the number of females in this study was extremely small ($N = 6$).

A more complete review of youth suicides was undertaken by the author in an attempt to respond to some of the weaknesses of the Uphoff and Gilmore study. Youth suicides were calculated for the five largest population centers in South

Carolina for a period of 5 years. Using the same definition of "youth" as the Uphoff and Gilmore study (i.e., all those under age 26), the number of suicides for each of the 5 years was tabulated and related to the individual's entrance age to school. (See Table 6-1.)

No significant differences in incidence of suicide and entrance age were found. The obtained chi-square value (.754) was nonsignificant. That is, the suicide rate for those who were youngest or oldest when they entered school did not differ from the expected (random) frequency.

Also of importance is the variation in suicide rate from one year to the next. The total number of suicides for 1985 was almost double that for 1984. Two and one half times as many of the oldest individuals committed suicide in 1985 as in 1984, while the rate for the youngest was only 1.4 times as many. In 1981 only 16% of the total number of suicides came from the oldest group, while 27% were from the youngest group. But in 1985 27% of the total number of suicides were from the oldest group of entrants, while only 18.9% were from the youngest entrants.

Table 6–1.
Suicide Deaths of Individuals 25 Years and Younger by Entrance Age for Five South Carolina Urban Areas (Charleston, Greenville, Lexington County, Richland County, Spartanburg)[a]

Year	"Oldest"	Next oldest	Younger	"Youngest"	Totals
1980	5	5	6	10	26
1981	6	9	12	10	37
1982	7	11	6	5	29
1983	7	6	5	7	25
1984	4	4	6	5	19
1985	10	8	12	7	37
Totals					
Actual rate of occurrence	39.00	43.00	47.00	44.00	173
Expected rate of occurrence	43.25	43.25	43.25	43.25	

Males   = 136
Females =   37   Chi square = .754 (n.s.)
             173

[a]Data provided in personal communication by personnel from the Department of Health and Environmental Control, Columbia, S.C., 1987, June.

As previously mentioned it is difficult to accept the idea that age of entrance could be closely linked to student suicides because so many other important events have intervened in the students' lives since entering school. Only by recapitulating the psychological factors, i.e., undertaking a psychological autopsy, could it be ascertained whether school events were an overwhelming factor in youth suicides.

Analysis of the suicide question has been discussed extensively in this chapter because the data from the study by Uphoff and Gilmore (1984) have been repeated so frequently by educators and accepted as factual. Thus, it is important to (1) emphasize the falsity of the argument and (2) present data from a sample of suitable size indicating there is no relationship between entrance age and risk of suicide.

Use of Behavior Rating Scales

Frequently teachers are asked to report their observations of the emotional and social behavior of children in school. Some school districts use a rating measure devised by local school personnel that often asks for general descriptions of behavior. Examples would be: "Is this child ( ) socially mature or ( ) immature? Is s(he) ( ) passive in nature or ( ) acting out in nature?"

Such items are too broad in scope and, as a result, the rater will find it difficult to make a valid generalization. Such items are also easily subject to distortion. A teacher may remember two or three incidents about a child that reflect immature behavior. However, she may forget the number of times the child demonstrated appropriate behaviors. Indeed, a number of locally constructed as well as some published behavior scales list only negative behaviors, and, as a result, proper interpretation of the child's behavior is difficult. Informal scales, locally constructed, often emphasize to an unwarranted degree negative behavior on the part of the child and thus result in a biased view of the child's behavior.

Using a properly constructed and standardized rating scale will afford the rater the opportunity to evaluate a broad sampling of different behaviors of the child. Specific information is included about the attribute or behavior to be rated which, in turn, provides the rater with a common frame of reference. The degree of frequency of the observed behavior also is often requested.

A standardized behavior rating scale should provide information that will be of greater value because a large variety of behaviors will be sampled. The responses checked by the teacher about the child can then be compared with the scores obtained by children in the normative sample. Such a comparison can indicate the relative standing of the child on the specific factor being measured (Helton, Workman, & Matuszek, 1982).

Because the rating scale samples a wide variety of behaviors, the school psychologist can then compare the teacher's responses to those from a regular class as well as from specific subgroups of children who have demonstrated deviant behavior.

There are several behavior rating scales that provide helpful data about the child in question. These include the Child Behavior Checklist (Achenbach & Edelbrock, 1983), the Louisville Behavior Checklist (Miller, 1984) (for parents to rate the child), and the Bristol Social Adjustment Guides (Stott, 1970a,b).

A good example of a behavior rating scale that not only asks the teacher to rate possible deviate behaviors but also positive behaviors of the child is the Bristol Social Adjustment Guides (BSAG)(Stott, 1970a,b). The revised BSAG (Stott, 1970a,b; McDermott, 1980) contains 110 verbal phrases which describe the behavior problems of children as seen in the school environment.

Each of the scale's phrases is linked to a specific social or learning event in which the child's adjustment in reference to peers, self, or adults may be observed and evaluated. One example of a phrase used in this scale is "talking with teacher." The BSAG asks the teacher to underline what she or he thinks is the behavior appropriate for the child being rated: "can't get a word out of the child"; "overtalkative, tires teachers with constant chatter"; "chats only alone with teacher," etc. The indicators are couched in teacher terminology, are focused on behavioral observations, do not use clinical language, and thus reduce the need for the teacher to make inferences as to the meaning of the behavior being observed (McDermott, 1981, pp. 310-311).

The Use of Sociometric Data

Sociometry is a method of acquiring information about peer relationships. Basically, the technique identifies the most and least popular individuals in a group. In recent years, some psychologists and educators have attempted to make predictions about the social and emotional adjustment of children using this technique. The problems with such a procedure are discussed in this section.

Description of the Method

Sociometry originally was developed for use by the U.S. Navy. The purpose was to identify accurately the enlisted men who were good candidates for officer training. Sociometry was used to determine which enlisted men were viewed by their peers as leaders.

The technique subsequently has been applied in school settings to acquire information about children's social relationships. Children are asked a question such as "Whom would you like to work with on a project?" or "Whom do you wish to sit next to?" The children are asked to name three or four choices on a slip of paper and turn it in to the teacher.

The choices are then compiled in a graphic display referred to as a sociogram. A circle is used to represent each child and an arrow is drawn from that circle to any other circles that represent a choice made by the child.

Three types of categories are determined from the sociogram. They are the star, the neglectee, and the isolate. The star is the student who is selected by a large number of other students and, therefore, is popular. The neglectee is the child who is chosen relatively few times by his or her classmates. Children who receive fewer sociometric choices than could be expected by chance would fall into the neglectee category (Gronlund, 1959). The isolate is the child who is not chosen by any of the others.

Some texts suggest that, in implementing the sociometric technique, children also should be asked to make negative choices. That is, "whom would you *not* want to work with on a project?" (The child who received a preponderance of negative choices would then be classified as a rejectee.) However, this practice is not recommended for use in the classroom setting because good friends often later discuss their choices. The information becomes public, and feelings can be hurt in the process.

Also of importance is that (1) the technique be used in conjunction with a school activity, such as a group project, *and* (2) that the data be used in placing students in the activity. One sophisticated approach to measuring peer relationships in a group is that of nominating children for parts in a proposed class play. Byrd (1951) emphasized that he found a high degree of correspondence (.80) between stated choices made by students as to preferred fellow actors and actual choices made when given an opportunity to present impromptu plays. Wonderly (1981) also used a class play format with one hundred sixty-seven 3rd- and 6th-graders. The instrument used was one devised by Lambert and Bower (1961) that required children to make choices from their peer group for 20 acting roles. The acting roles reflected both positive social behavior and negative behavior. It is important to note that Wonderly found no significant differences between younger children and older children for chosen roles. In other words, the younger children were as popular as older children and were nominated as frequently for positive acting roles in the class play.

Sociometric data indicate to the elementary or middle-school teacher two types of information. One is the class leaders whom the other students tend to emulate. The other is the child who is on the fringe of the social relationships in the classroom. Thus, in arranging children for group projects, the teacher can avoid assigning two class leaders to the same group. Children who have few social relationships with others also can be assigned to different groups. In other words, group activities provide an opportunity for the shy child or the newcomer to the class to interact directly with others.

A revision of the sociometric procedure was developed by Asher, Singleton, Tinsley, and Hymel (1979) for use with young children. Each child first is shown a large felt board on which photographs of all of the children in the class are displayed. After the child correctly identifies each peer, the pictures are removed from the board in random order. Following instructions and practice, the child then sorts the pictures into one of three boxes that are visually and verbally labeled. They are "like a lot" (smiling face), "kinda like" (neutral face), and "don't like" (sad face). Pictures in each box are assigned a rating of 3, 2, or 1 with 3 indicating the greatest liking.

Cautions in Using Sociometry

Although sociometry provides some information about the popularity of students in the class, the data are accompanied by limitations. First, to be realistic, the children can be asked only to name three or four choices. Thus, children who are not chosen might have been selected had six or seven choices been made. The inference cannot be made that all isolates or neglectees are necessarily rejected by their classmates.

Second, children's choices are not stable over time. A sociogram constructed in April of the school year, for example, will differ from one constructed the previous October. In one study of constancy of the child's choices, Northway (1952) investigated the number of *actual* preferences given on the first sociometric test that were repeated at a later time. Northway investigated the sociometric choice of elementary school children attending camp. She found that whereas 66% of the children's first choices on the original test were the same 3 weeks later, only 50% of the children's second nominations were chosen again. Further, only 35% of the third nominations were chosen a second time. The overall correlation coefficient between scores on the two sociometric tests was .96. However, reporting only the correlation coefficient masks the dramatic decline that occurred in the consistency pattern of the child's second and third friendship choices.

Third, the children who are not selected by their peers (neglectees and isolates) are primarily those that have low interaction patterns with others in the class. Some researchers, however, have attempted to identify relationships between nomination patterns (sociometry) and particular prosocial and antisocial behaviors. Ladd and Mars (1986), for example, correlated the peer nominations of 4- and 5-year-olds in two day care centers with their ratings of their classmates on aggressive and prosocial behaviors. They found only low to moderate correlations between these two sets of data; also there were differences between the two day care centers. In addition, the correlations between cooperative play and nomination status ranged from .54 to .56. Thus, 69% and 71% of the variability (variance) in the children's nominations is accounted for by other factors. In addition, the correlations between social conversation ("laugh, talk, and say nice things") and nomination status were .05 and .17. For this relationship, 99% to 97% of the variability in the children's nominations is accounted for by factors other than social conversation.

The results are similar for aggressive behaviors. The correlations between physical aggression and nomination status are $-.07$ and $-.40$, and the relationships between verbal aggression and nomination status are $-.01$ and $-.41$. Thus, these behaviors account for only between 1% and 17% of the variability in children's nominations. In other words, sociometric data cannot be used alone as indicators of "acceptable" or "unacceptable" behavior in the classroom.

Although neglected children have been shown to spend more time in solitary play and do not converse as frequently as accepted children, they were found to engage in as much sharing behavior as accepted children (Dodge, 1983). The assumption has often been made that if social interaction is considered to be quite important for normal psychological development, then children who are found to interact rarely with their peers are possibly at risk for psychological problems at a later age.

However, although rejected status has shown a pattern of stability from elementary school to high school, neglected status has not demonstrated such a pattern (Coie & Dodge, 1983). It is questionable whether psychological referrals of kindergarten and first-grade children should be based primarily on negative choices made by peers. Rather, teacher behavior rating scales should probably be used initially as a screening device. (See Li's, 1986, study described in the following pages.) Intervention strategies could then be based on the results from the rating scales with follow-up in first and second grades if necessary.

Young children whose low rate of interaction with others in kindergarten was of concern to their teachers were studied intensively by Li (1986). Low rate of interaction range was defined as children whose peer interaction role was at least one standard deviation below the mean of the children's group and was obtained through observing a child at three different times during free play time in the classroom. Teacher and parent ratings of the child's behavioral and social adjustment also were collected. Although the parent perceived these children as presenting some behavioral problems, the teacher did not target these children who were socially isolated as being socially maladjusted. The lack of significant findings from the teacher rating scales suggests that low peer interaction is not necessarily associated with severe social maladjustment.

Analysis of the Peer Relations of Neglected Children

Important to our understanding of the behavior of elementary grade children is the finding that the behavioral characteristics of neglected children (i.e., those who are chosen very seldom by their classmates) are surprisingly quite similar to the behavioral patterns of accepted children (Cantrell & Prinz, 1985). Teachers did *not* see the children as socially withdrawn, anxious, unpopular, or inattentive (Cantrell & Prinz, 1985).

In order to provide more information on the teacher's perceptions of these neglected children, Gredler analyzed the teacher rating-scale scores obtained by Li (1986) on the neglected children and classified their symptoms on a typology of behavioral disturbance as outlined by McDermott (1983). This analysis is found in Table 6-4. The classificatory system developed by McDermott attempts to accurately portray a child's adjustment status by assessing the child's behavior on a number of dimensions. The analysis incorporates 16 different syndromic profile types of children's social behavior and is described more fully in Table 6-2. This approach is helpful in describing children's behavior because it examines more than one dimension of behavior such as aggression or anxiety.

Using factor analysis and a hierarchical cluster analysis, 16 classifications were produced. The tightness of fit among the profiles of children within each type was tested by a homogeneity coefficient. A mean coefficient of .66 was obtained that "indicated a substantial within profile type cohesion of variance for the typology" (McDermott, 1983). McDermott divides these 16 groupings into one of four different general behavioral categories. The four categories, illustrated in Table 6-3, are healthy reactions, adjustment reactions, disturbances of emotion, and disturbances of conduct.

When Li's data are further categorized using McDermott's classification system, it is found that 16 of the 23 children studied (70%) who interacted to a low degree with peers can be considered adequately adjusted. (See Table 6-4.) Analysis of the normal and maladjusted groups mirrored the percentage of males and females in the total sample. That is, 61% of the total group were female children, and 63% of the "good" adjustment group were female.

The results of such studies indicate that educators and psychologists must be cautious in concluding that a child is unpopular and possibly maladjusted based on sociometric data. Li's data, along with Gredler's additional analysis, indicate that children can demonstrate a low rate of peer interactions yet be socially well adjusted as perceived by the classroom teacher.

In reviewing a number of sociometric studies, Cantrell and Prinz (1985) also conclude that neglected children in the classroom are neither clinically deviant nor in need of special intervention strategies. Once again it must be remembered that peer choices of young children have low stability; therefore, not too much faith can be placed in them as a primary referral tool or as evidence of the efficacy of a particular intervention strategy such as a transition room program.

School Entrance Age and Social Adjustment

One Florida school district collected sociometric data from first- and second-graders in the 1983–1984 and 1984–1985 school years. The purpose was to

Table 6-2
McDermott's Classification Scheme of Typology

Classification	Type	Description
Good adjustment	1	Teachers observe few, if any, behaviors in this group of children that are considered to be maladaptive.
Adequate adjustment with mild impulsivity	2	Children demonstrate a detectable but mild tendency to engage in impulse-ridden behavior. Such behavior is carried out in absence of preplanning or consideration of the adverse consequences of the behavior; attributed more often to boys than girls (two out of three times); behavior pattern is frequently tolerated and does not elicit social disdain from peers or adults.
Adequate adjustment with mild peer conflict	3	A mild but noticeable degree of difficulty in getting along with some peers. Relationships with adults continue to be generally positive. More often found as adjustment reaction with preadolescents than adolescents. May be frequently associated with academic and social competition found in the school environment.
Avoidant disorder of childhood or adolescence	4	A definite unwillingness and/or inability to demonstrate social assertiveness and extend oneself in learning and/or social situations found more often among girls than boys (two out of three times). Seen more frequently among girls in early elementary school and in early adolescence. Probably reflects child's efforts to cope with the demands of new and changing social roles.
Adequate adjustment with mild emancipatory traits	5	Behaviors shown and composed of both attacking and avoiding actions. These operate to sever the child's relationship because of proactive and unfriendly actions. These behaviors are directed toward adults and those in authority rather than to the child's peers. Seen predominantly in children of early and middle adolescence; can be considered to be adaptive to the degree it reflects emancipatory needs of the child.
Attention deficit disorder	6	Behavioral characteristics are marked by erratic, unplanned, physical interventions typified by aggressiveness, attention seeking, and disruptive and domineering actions. More often found with boys than girls at all age levels. While such behavior is frequently tolerated by peers and adults and is considered to be reflective of "boyish" qualities, those children are definitely maladjusted and/or in need of therapeutic intervention. Diagnostic assessment must clearly differentiate between simple overactivity and true hyperactivity.

(continued)

Table 6–2 *(continued)*

Classification	Type	Description
Adjustment disorder with withdrawal	7	Child demonstrates a definite indifference toward and/or aversion to associate with other children and adults. Unwilling to enter into interpersonal relationships within the social context of the classroom such as engaging in a cooperative academic performance, games, playground activities.
Adequate adjustment with moderate motivational deficit	8	Child demonstrates a motivational deficit which shows itself by a failure to respond to, or to seek out, stimulating aspects in the school environment. More often found in boys than girls. Is sometimes labeled as laziness or lethargy. Not considered a significant maladaptive behavior and is amenable to planned intervention actions.
Adjustment disorder with disturbance of conduct	9	Significant acting out behavior accompanied by poor relationships with peers. May be found to be associated with similar behavior modeled by parents and/or guardians outside of school environment.
Socialized aggressive conduct disorder of childhood or adolescence	10	Provocative behaviors engaged in to test limitations imposed by those in authority. While sometimes viewed as predelinquent behavior, can be considered as more defiant than antisocial. Incidence of this type of behavior increases from early childhood through middle-adolescent age period.
Adjustment disorder with depressed mood	11	Behavior is marked by a serious lack of motivation to cope with academic and social requirements of school. Child is inclined to avoid individuals who are in a position to impose performance demands. McDermott states that this disorder is found predominantly among young teen boys; can be considered transient. It is not considered to be "clinical depression."
Undersocialized aggressive conduct disorder with attention deficit	12	Severe overactive behavior which includes thoughtless aggressive behavior. Vicious cycle often seen which combines child's initial lack of foresight, and subsequent rejection by classmates and teacher, which in turn creates hostility on the part of the child.
Dysthymic disorder	13	Very serious underactive maladjustment. Child shows behavior usually considered reflective of "clinical depression." More frequently found among adolescents who are academic or social failures.

Classification	Type	Description
Schizoid disorder of childhood or adolescence	14	Indifference toward human relationships. More frequently found among early elementary and middle school children.
Oppositional disorder, or passive-aggressive disorder	15	Profound resistance to formal school, often accompanied by various aggressive behaviors such as continual argumentative behavior toward both classmates and teachers; more often found in boys than girls.
Undersocialized aggressive conduct disorder or antisocial disorder of childhood or adolescence	16	Severe conduct-disordered behavior. Child demonstrates provocative behavior, contempt for authority, and general acting-out behavior. Predominantly antisocial, rather than delinquent-oriented actions.

Note. Adapted from "A Syndromic Typology for Analyzing School Children's Disturbed Social Behavior," by P. A. McDermott, 1983, *School Psychology Review, 12,* 256-257. Copyright 1983. Used by permission.

contrast those pupils recommended for pre-first whose parents accepted the decision with those pupils whose parents rejected the decision and had them placed directly in first grade. The hypothesis for the study was that "developmentally immature pupils would find it easier to make friends if they were not prematurely pushed into a regular classroom situation" (p. 1, Broward County Public Schools, 1987, Early Childhood Report).

Percentages in the three categories of 0–1 nominations, 2–3 nominations, and 4 or more nominations are reported. However, of major importance is that the sociometric procedure as developed by researchers was *not* implemented. That is, instead of being asked to name three or four children with whom they would like to play, "each pupil was asked to name the child in their [sic] class with whom they would like to play" (p. 1, Broward County Public Schools, 1987). Thus, the analysis of number of nominations is based on an incomplete data set. When an assessment procedure is not implemented correctly, the data cannot be considered valid.

Second, research indicates that children's choices are not stable and typically vary within the same school year. Thus, relating nomination status (particularly when each child makes only one nomination) to the type of classroom in which the child spent his or her first school year is highly questionable.

Table 6–3.
McDermott's Behavioral Classification Categories

A. Healthy reactions
   Type 1   Good adjustment
   Type 2   Adequate adjustment with mild impulsivity
   Type 3   Adequate adjustment with mild peer conflict
   Type 5   Adequate adjustment with mild emancipatory traits
   Type 8   Adequate adjustment with moderate motivational deficit

B. Adjustment reactions
   Type 7   Adjustment disorder with withdrawal
   Type 9   Adjustment disorder with disturbance of conduct
   Type 11   Adjustment disorder with depressed mood

C. Disturbances of emotion
   Type 4   Avoidant disorder of childhood or adolescence
   Type 13   Dysthymic disorder
   Type 14   Schizoid disorder of childhood or adolescence
   Type 15   Oppositional disorder or passive-aggressive disorder

D. Disturbances of conduct
   Type 6   Attention deficit disorder
   Type 10   Socialized aggressive conduct disorder of childhood or adolescence
   Type 12   Undersocialized aggressive conduct disorder with attention deficit
   Type 16   Undersocialized aggressive conduct disorder or antisocial disorder of
             childhood or adolescence

Note. Adapted from "A Syndromic Typology for Analyzing School Children's Disturbed Social Behavior," by P. A. McDermott, 1983, *School Psychology Review, 12,* 256-257. Copyright 1983. Used by permission.

Third, any efforts to make predictions about the effects of early or late entrance to first grade should be based on valid and reliable research that indicates differences in maturity between these two groups. As the following studies indicate, these differences have not been found.

One study, conducted by Pain (1981), investigated the academic and social adjustment of children who entered at a young age, middle age, and at an older age. Her results on the academic performance of these children are reported in Chapter 7, on entrance age. Her findings concerning the emotional and social functioning of these three groups of children are discussed in this chapter.

Pain used a self-concept inventory, a teacher rating scale, and a sociogram in her study of the emotional adjustment of the students. These particular measures were administered to students in grades 2, 6, 8, and 10. No differences in self-concept were found in grades 2, 8, and 10. Only in grade 6 was the difference significant. Further, the results of the teacher ratings of the children on emotional and social adjustment indicated no differences in adjustment status among the groups in any of the grades.

Finally a sociogram was administered to the students. Each student was asked to choose three classmates (1) to plan a party; (2) to work on a class project; (3) to be members of a ball team; and (4) to go away with on a summer holiday. Out of 20 comparisons, only 3 were found to be statistically significant. Pain concluded that younger children were not at a disadvantage with older students as to their popularity with their classmates.

Pain also reports that as a final, global assessment of development, teachers were asked to name students whom they considered to be doing very well or very poorly in the personal/social adjustment area. No significant differences among the different age groups were noted for students nominated by the teachers as having good or poor personal or social adjustment.

However, despite the lack of significant findings as to either emotional/social adjustment status and academic status in comparison of younger and older

Table 6–4.
Typology of Behavior Disturbance on Kindergarten Children with Low Peer Interaction

Classification		Number	
Healthy reactions			
Type 1	Good adjustment	12	
Type 2	Adequate adjustment with mild impulsivity	2	16 (70%)
Type 5	Adequate adjustment with mild emancipatory traits	2	
Disturbances of emotion			
Type 4	Avoidant disorder of childhood	3	3 (13%)
Disturbances of conduct			
Type 6	Attention deficit disorder	1	
Type 10	Socialized aggressive conduct disorder of childhood	1	4 (17%)
Type 12	Undersocialized aggressive conduct disorder with attention deficit	2	
		$N = 23$	

Note. Original data from A. F. K. Li (1986). Personal Communication. Used by permission. Reader should also consult: "Low Peer Interaction in Kindergarten Children: An Ecological Perspective" by A. F. K. Li, 1986, *Journal of Clinical Child Psychology, 15,* pp. 26–29.

students, considerably more young children were retained by teachers in grades 2, 6, and 8. This fact in and of itself would tend to indicate the reliance on retention as a school practice and the possible need for careful review of retention cases by the school psychologist and/or administrator.

In a study by Loughlin (1966), the first-grade adjustment of young and older entrants was compared using a number of measures devised by Lambert and Bower (1961). The picture game that was used is a self-perception measure administered to the students by the classroom teacher. The student is asked to sort 66 pictures that illustrate home and school situations and then to categorize each picture as happy or sad. Students also were asked to respond to a sociometric-type instrument indicating which of the child's classmates were similar to children in 20 classroom situation pictures. Last, the teacher was asked to rate each student on a behavior rating scale.

Results of Loughlin's investigation indicated no significant differences between the two age groups on these three measures of emotional/social adjustment. An outstanding aspect of this study was the careful delineation and measurement of the social and emotional adjustment status of the children.

Braymen (1988) investigated the social adjustment of high school seniors and attempted to relate their adjustment status to their age of entry to kindergarten. Questions that she sought to answer were: Is it true that younger children are at a disadvantage socially? How accepted are they by their peers? Do they show adequate self-esteem? and, Are they considered emotionally stable? Braymen attempted to answer these questions by using two criteria: (1) a self-report inventory and (2) a social competence measure. No significant differences were found between young entrants and older entrants as to the number of memberships and leadership positions held in extracurricular activities. In addition, results of the administration of the youth self-report measure indicated no differences in behavior problems in several different areas: depression/unpopular, sociometric concerns, thought disorder, delinquency, and aggression.

In a recent study, Carrington (1982) investigated the effect of school entrance age on both achievement and the social adjustment of the children. The Bristol Social Adjustment Guide was the rating scale used by the teachers. This instrument is the same scale used by Li (1986) in her study of kindergarten children with a low peer interaction rate, previously discussed in this chapter.

The subjects in Carrington's study were children from a predominantly White, middle-class, suburban school district in New Jersey. The purpose of the investigation was to determine if differences in school entrance age were a factor in both the academic performance and the social adjustment of children in the first, third, and sixth grades.

Carrington found that differences in entrance age had no effect on either the academic performance or the social adjustment of the children. Scores on the Bristol scale completed by the teachers reflected normal adjustment status for all age groups. Carrington's study is notable for the large sample of children rated on social adjustment (e.g., N = 300+).

In Raygor's (1972) study of the comparison progress of children (1) retained in kindergarten, (2) placed in a transition room, or (3) sent to regular first grade, no significant differences among the groups were found in the areas of social and emotional adjustment. (See Chapter 9, on the transition room experience, for a discussion of academic progress.) In this study the ratings were provided by the teachers. However, these findings are limited in value because the rating instrument was devised by the district's school psychologists, and no validity or reliability information was provided.

Summary

Four types of evidence frequently used in studies of the social and emotional adjustment status of children entering kindergarten or first grade were discussed in this chapter. They are anecdotal evidence, incidence of particular events in school or public records, teacher ratings of behavior, and sociometric data.

Anecdotal evidence, i.e., global teacher or parent perceptions, is not a reliable indicator of social or emotional adjustment status. School record information, such as number of psychological referrals, also is suspect because age is not the only variable influencing frequency of referrals. Other factors include socioeconomic status, home environment, and teacher expectancy, to name a few. Suicide data, which also have been cited to indicate poor adjustment, were found not to vary for different age categories.

It is important to remember that young-for-age children are frequently labeled as immature or emotionally maladjusted without adequate evidence for that assumption. Although a careful assessment of the child's adjustment status is usually undertaken for children classified as having special needs, no such examination is completed for children tagged by the school as not ready for regular kindergarten or first grade. A decision for retention or readiness room placement is often made by the teacher him- or herself based only on personal observations or on the results of a brief screening test such as the Gesell.

Results of several studies described in this chapter indicate that, contrary to what has been assumed, young-for-age children often demonstrate satisfactory emotional and social adjustment in the classroom. These findings are of particular importance because they are based on evidence obtained from assessment measures with known validity and reliability. School personnel and parents should be reassured that many young-for-age children can and do make an acceptable adjustment when they enter school.

Before any child is labeled immature or lacking in adjustment, a careful and complete appraisal of that child should be undertaken. Such an appraisal will include consideration of the child's classroom activities, input from the parents, as well as the child's attitudes and perceptions.

Concerns about the misinterpretation of sociometric data also have been discussed. Although sociometry does provide important information about the popularity of students in the classroom, there are definite limitations in the conclusions from such data and these have been described in this chapter. Important research also has been presented indicating that just because kindergarten children may interact with a low frequency with other children it does not mean they are at risk for further emotional problems. Teachers, using a carefully devised rating scale, judged a substantial majority to demonstrate adequate emotional and social adjustment.

SECTION III

School Practices

7

ISSUES IN THE
ENTRANCE AGE DEBATE

Citizens of the United States have prided themselves for years on the opportunities the public education system has offered to their children. In addition to 12 years of public education, American society has supported an enlarged responsibility to its handicapped children through the passage of federal legislation such as P.L. 94-142 in 1974. The introduction of Operation Headstart in the 1960s is an example of efforts to improve education for children from disadvantaged backgrounds.

Amid all of these developments, a continuing issue in educational policy is the age at which children should begin formal education. The school entry age in the public school system has varied across countries and within the United States. In addition, entrance ages for U.S. schools have risen slowly over the years.

In general, children have entered school when they were old enough to be able to walk to school and be away from home. However, climatic conditions in some countries contributed to the variability in the entrance age of children. Because of severe winters, Swedish and Russian children began school at age 7, while in milder climates, such as the United States, 6 became the adopted norm (Devault, Ellis, Vodicka, & Otto, 1957; Downing, 1973). In the United Kingdom 5 was accepted as the customary age of entrance. However, in some areas of Wales, children could begin formal schooling as early as $4\frac{1}{2}$ years of age (Palmer, 1971).

In the United States, school entrance ages have varied considerably since Colonial times. In the 1700s, children entered reading and writing schools by age 5. By 1890, however, children were allowed to enter primary school at age 6 after completing kindergarten. Entry to kindergarten was permitted at age $4\frac{1}{2}$ (Devault et al., 1957).

Table 7–1.

Entrance Age Dates for a Child to Enter First Grade, for 1966 Through 1986

Entrance age		% of school systems reporting age cutoff to first grade				
	Date	1963	1968	1978	1983	1986
6-1 (August)		0	0	0	3.9	5.9
6-0		13.9	7.5	29.3	27.2	45.0
5-11		10.8	20.0	19.6	17.6	13.8
5-10		14.4	17.1	11.8	7.9	5.9
5-9		34.9	26.5	19.6	11.8	11.8
5-8 (January)		24.9	21.1	11.8	5.9	3.9
Requirements set by locality. In a few localities, entrance age is below 5 years 8 months.		1.1	7.8	7.9	15.7	13.7
		100%	100%	100%	100%	100%

Note. Data from "Ethical and Legal Dilemmas in Assessment of Readiness of Children for School," by G. R. Gredler, 1975, pp. 196-221, in *Ethical and Legal Factors in the Practice of School Psychology,* G. R. Gredler (Ed.). Harrisburg, PA: Pennsylvania State Department of Education.

Entrance to Kindergarten: What Is the Best Age? by J. M. Wolf and A. L.Kessler, 1987. Arlington, VA: Educational Research Service. Copyright 1987. Used by permission.

Since the early 1960s, in particular, a steady rise has occurred in the required entrance age for first grade. In 1963, for example, 25% of the schools allowed children to enter at 5 years 8 months. (See Table 7-1.) However, by 1986, that percentage had dropped to 3.9. Further, only 13.9% of public schools required an entrance age of 6-0 in 1963. However, 23 years later, that percentage had increased over three times to 45%. In addition, approximately 6% of the schools now require an entry age higher than 6-0 years.

Some states, over the years, have implemented a flexible entrance age policy. In the 1960s, Pennsylvania had the distinction of being a state with one of the most liberal entry age policies. Children who would be 6 years old by February 1 were admitted to first grade in the preceding September.

Even today, Pennsylvania stands out as a state with a flexible entrance age policy. As of January, 1988, entrance age policy for Pennsylvania schools was as follows:

> The board of school directors shall establish the district's
> minimum age for beginners which may not be less than a

> chronological age of 5 years and 7 months before September 1
> nor more than 6 years no months before the first day of the school
> term of the district. (Chapter 11, Section 11.5, Admission of
> beginners)

Although states and districts establish policies for school entrance age, schools within districts sometimes set even higher entrance ages. For example, despite the Pennsylvania regulations, one school district restricts boys to a higher entrance age. The policy of the district states:

> Children who are five years old by January 31 are eligible for
> admission to school. All girls who are five years of age by
> January 31 and all boys who are five years old before September
> 1 will be enrolled in a kindergarten program. All boys whose
> date of birth is from September 1 to January 31 will be enrolled
> in a Pre-Kindergarten Program. This policy was brought about
> by the many research studies in child growth and development
> which indicate that boys age six to twelve months behind girls
> when entering kindergarten. (Springfield, Pa. Township
> Schools, 1988)

This policy changes the minimum first-grade entrance age for boys with birthdates after September. In effect, a male child with a December birthdate will enter first grade when he is chronologically 6 years 9 months of age. According to Commonwealth law, this policy is in violation of the State Department of Education regulations.

A similar situation also occurred in Michigan. In that state, the age set in the 1960s for entrance to kindergarten was 5 years by December 1 of the same year. However, a survey of educational practices (Johnson, 1967) indicated that approximately 32% of the districts set earlier cutoff dates of either October or November.

One Michigan district set September 10 as the cutoff date for first-graders to be 6 years old. A younger child who would be 6 by December 1 could *only* be admitted if his or her IQ was above 115. However, the district further stipulated that (a) the intelligence tests had to be administered before the child was enrolled in kindergarten and (b) the parent was to assume all responsibility for the child's success in school in addition to formally requesting the early admission (Johnson, 1967).

In addition to increased entry age requirements, many school districts have now added prekindergarten and/or transition grades for the child referred to as at risk. Such policies further delay entrance to regular first grade for some students for a year or more (Gredler, 1984). In New Hampshire and Florida schools, for example, it is possible for a child to not enter first grade until the age of 8. Such a situation can occur if the child initially is placed in a pre-kindergarten class, then progresses to kindergarten, then to pre-first, and then to first grade. School practices, in other words, are contributing to higher entrance ages for first grade.

Important issues in discussions of entrance age are the various physical and mental characteristics proposed to support a higher entrance age, the policy implications of different entrance ages, and the research on the performance of younger and older children. These topics are discussed in this chapter.

Rationale for Higher Entrance Age

The rationale for raising the school entrance age includes two aspects. They are that the younger child (1) cannot benefit from school and (2) may experience long-term undesirable consequences of such placement. Included in the differences between older and younger learners are mental age factors; developmental, visual, and physiological differences; and differences between the sexes.

Mental Age Differences

Learning to read is described as dependent on attaining a particular mental age. That is, when the entrance age is set too low, many children lack the requisite mental age to learn to read (Jones, 1968). However, a mental age of $6\frac{1}{2}$ has been selected by some as "sufficient" for most children to learn to read (Devault et al., 1957; Hedges, 1977).

The rationale for the mental age of $6\frac{1}{2}$ for beginning reading is derived from a 1931 study by Morphett and Washburne. The uncritical acceptance of the findings led to the conclusion by Betts that the Morphett and Washburne study is the most widely *quoted* and *misquoted* study of reading in existence (Downing, 1973).

Morphett and Washburne studied 141 first-grade children in the Winnetka, Illinois, schools for one semester and then tested them on their progress in reading. The following year 100 children were studied for two semesters. Children were administered a group intelligence test (Detroit) and also an individual intelligence test (Stanford Binet). Reading performance was evaluated by the administration of a sight word test and an oral reading test as well as by the amount of reading material the children had satisfactorily completed. The results indicated that the majority of children who had acceptable scores in reading had a mental age of at least 6 years 6 months.

However, the study includes at least three limitations. First, Winnetka is an upper-middle-class community, and results obtained from such a system cannot be generalized to all schools within the United States.

Second, the sample of children was a fairly restricted one wherein 66% of the children who attended first grade had a mental age of 6 years 6 months or higher and another 14% had a mental age of 6-0 to 6-5. Only 20% of the sample were below a mental age of 5-11. With classes consisting of such a large percentage of children with a high mental age, it was obvious that advanced materials could be used in the classroom program.

However, even within this favored group, a substantial percentage of children did *not* make adequate progress. Of the 68 children with a mental age between 6-6 to 7-11, more than 22% failed to demonstrate adequate progress in the reading program. Furthermore, over one half (53%) of the children with a mental age between 6-0 to 6-5 failed to make adequate progress. As stated previously, the authors' definition of adequate reading progress was completion of a specific number of reading books and responding satisfactorily to comprehension questions about the subject matter.

The majority of the children older than 6 years 6 months did demonstrate suitable reading skills. However, a failure rate of 22%, or one in five children, for this mental age group raises questions about the validity of a mental age of 6-6 as a satisfactory age level for teaching reading to first-graders in Winnetka. The 22% failure rate was obtained when the scores from the Detroit ability test were analyzed. When the Stanford Binet test was used as the IQ criterion, about one third (29%) of the children with mental ages between 6-6 and 7-11 were found to have made poor progress in reading.

Morphett and Washburne (1931) obtained a correlation of .65 between mental age scores and sight word scores. A correlation of .65 indicates that 42% of the variation in group performance on the sight word test is accounted for by mental age. Yet, it should be understood that 58% of the variation in sight word scores *cannot* be accounted for by mental age and is instead related to other factors. These other factors would include such determiners as degree of child's motivational state, the quality of teaching, and the nature of the curriculum materials.

Developmental and Visual Differences

Younger children are believed by some to be more susceptible to emotional problems, disorders, and restlessness. They also are described as withdrawn and lacking interest in school tasks (Hemphill, 1953). Another belief is that the younger child is less able to concentrate adequately, to follow directions, to share the teacher's attention, and to work neatly with pencils and crayons (Hedges, 1977; Weinstein, 1968). Analysis of such differences is discussed in Chapter 11.

Several educators and psychologists identify visual problems in young children as a rationale for delaying school entrance. One belief is that children who are young for age for school have a high incidence of visual difficulties (Hedges,

1977). Another belief is that many 5-year-olds are not ready to use their eyes for reading (Ames, 1967). The visual apparatus of 6-year-olds also is believed to be "unstable" (Carter & McGinnis, 1970).

The belief about "eye readiness" is described in detail by Turley (1979, p. 91). According to her, because the tissues of young children's eyes are soft and pliable, concentrated doses of close work such as reading and writing are believed to cause muscle strain that can result in myopia. Moore and Moore (1979) also warn that nearsightedness (myopia) frequently is caused by "prolonged looking at near objects at an early age" (p. 151). Similarly, Hefferman (1964, p. 28) quotes a pediatrician as saying that the neurological system in 75% of the children has not attained the maturity for making connections between what is seen and what is understood and only time can provide this maturity.

Turley (1979) suggests the evidence is such that the delay of first-grade entrance tends to preserve the child's vision by delaying concentrated periods of close work for which the child is developmentally unready. However, collaborative data from medical sources are difficult to find.

An investigation of the visual status of 7,000 seven-year-olds in Great Britain revealed that 86.2% of the children were judged by physicians to have normal vision (Pringle et al., 1966). Although 13.5% were categorized as having a visual defect, the problems were not judged to be a handicap to normal schooling. Of importance is the fact that these children had entered school at an age younger than that of American children. That is, they had begun formal schooling between the ages of 5 years 0 months and 5 years 4 months.

In the United States a comprehensive visual examination was undertaken in the Denver public schools for children who had begun reading instruction in kindergarten (McKee & Brzeinski, 1966). The children's vision was checked during the first, third, and fifth grades. Vision was considered deficient if the students had a Snellen score greater than 20/40 or if they wore glasses. Vision of the children who had begun reading in kindergarten was compared with those who were taught reading in the first grade. Both groups included approximately the same percentage of children exhibiting visual difficulties.

The study showed that 6.2% of the children who began reading instruction in first grade were considered to have visual deficits; the corresponding percentage for children who began reading instruction in kindergarten was 6.9%. In grade 3, 13.3% of students who began reading instruction in grade 1 were found to have visual deficits. Only 12.5% of third-grade students who began reading in kindergarten demonstrated visual defects (McKee & Brzeinski, 1966).

Physiological Indicators of Readiness: Teething

Some educators (Ames, 1967; Hedges, 1977; Ogletree, 1975) have emphasized that certain physiological characteristics are dependable indicators of children's developmental readiness for school. Specifically, dental development of the child is viewed as a factor that reflects the child's maturational level and thus influences the proper time to begin instruction.

The position taken by Ames (1967, p. 53) is that a child's teething is one clue to body age. It is viewed as important because "slow teething tends to go along with slow development of behavior." Hedges (1977) concurs, maintaining that a close correlation exists between physiological maturity as found by the level of teething and behavioral maturity of the child.

Ogletree (1975) maintains that second teething is a definite indicator that the head has attained its full physical growth. Therefore, since the "growth forces" have completed the task of physical development, they are then "released (gradually) from physical growth for the processes of thinking; this accounts for the transition from preoperational (noncontrollable) to concrete operational (controllable) thinking in the child. The child now has greater voluntary control over his thinking processes" (p. 26).

In a study of Weston, Connecticut, schoolchildren, Ilg and Ames (1972) state that 96% who were ahead of schedule in teething were doing acceptable academic work. However, 80% of the children who were advanced in teething development were girls. It is therefore possible that sex of the child, not teething development per se, may have been the important underlying variable in regard to achievement (Harrison, 1979; Kaufman, 1970).

However, little empirical data have been collected in support of the various theories on teething. Except for the study of 80 children in Weston, Connecticut, conducted by Ilg and Ames in 1960, it is difficult to find any research studies in defense of teething development as a valid indicator of school readiness in the child.

In a study with a sample of over 300 children that was controlled for sex, Chase (1970) noted that dental development was *not* an important variable when differentiating characteristics of first-grade children who failed from those who succeeded. Specifically, Chase studied 309 first-grade children in a midwestern school system, 65 of whom were retained. She classified the child's dentition growth on a continuum of seven levels (level one—no deciduous teeth shed to level seven—deciduous teeth shed and/or eruption of upper lateral incisors).

Further analysis of Chase's data indicates that teething development was not closely related to the child's pass-fail status. Twenty-three percent of those who failed first grade also demonstrated a low level of dental maturity. However, 27% of the children with irregular development were retained, and 18% of those at a mature level of teething failed. (See Table 7-2.)

There is a difference of only 5% (i.e., 23%–18%) in the percentage of children retained who demonstrated mature dentition status and those with immature teething. In addition, the great majority of all first-grade children at each dentition level were promoted at the end of the year. (See Table 7-3.) A difference of only

Table 7–2.
Percentage of First-Grade Failures in Relationship to Maturity of Teething

Teething levels	Percentage of children retained
Immature (Levels 1–3)	23.00%
Irregularity in teething (Level 4)	27.30%
Mature stages (Levels 5–7)	18.00%

Note. Data from *Differential Behavioral Characteristics of Non-Promoted Children* by J. A. Chase, 1970. Unpublished doctoral dissertation. Request for use approved by Graduate School, University of Maine.

1.3% is found between the promotion status of Level 1 children and Level 4 children. One of the highest promotion rates is found in Level 2 children (immature teething) and is only 2% less than the promotion rate of those children with the most mature teething level.

Another important investigation of the relationship between dental maturity and school achievement was completed by Kaufman (1971). He measured a child's teething level on a 10-point scale ranging from 0 = no loose teeth and none missing to 9 = five to $5\frac{1}{2}$ teeth in place. In this scoring system 6-year molars, incisors, cuspids, and bicuspids were all allocated the same weight in counting the number of permanent teeth that were in place (Kaufman, 1971a, p. 62).

The subjects of this study were from an upper-middle-class population living on Long Island. Kaufman determined that two thirds of his sample obtained a dental rating of 0 (either the children had no new teeth, no missing teeth, or no loose teeth) (p. 96). These results, from children whose ages ranged from 5-0 to 6 years 2 months, were startlingly different from Ilg and Ames' study where three fourths of their $5\frac{1}{2}$- to 6-year-old children showed either some teeth partially in or eruption of new teeth. Kaufman correctly interprets his low, nonsignificant correlation (.14) between Gesell readiness scores and teething status as indicating "that advanced teething [is] not associated with a high score on the readiness test" (p. 97). Kaufman adds that "GSRT test-users ought to be aware that teething level may be a very misleading indicator of a child's behavioral maturity . . . " (p. 97).

More recently Harrison (1979) studied the teething level of first-grade children living in a rural northeast Georgia county. Dental development was assessed by determining the number of loose primary teeth and the number of erupted permanent teeth. An 11-point scale was used to measure teething level where 0 = no teeth loose or displaced to 10 = six or more teeth had erupted.

Harrison's results indicated a nonsignificant relationship between dental development and first-grade achievement. The correlation between the measure of dental development and achievement test results was −.09. Harrison also found a significant negative correlation between a measure of cognitive ability (the McCarthy) and dental development (−.28). In other words, children with a higher level of cognitive ability in the sample tended to have a lower level of dental development. This finding is completely opposite to the theoretical assumptions made about the importance of dental development.

A more recent investigation by Bird (1987) also demonstrated a lack of a relationship between physical maturity, as measured by maturation of tooth development, and academic achievement. Bird attempted to ascertain if such physiological maturation did account for a significant portion of the variation (variance) in the academic achievement scores of third-grade boys. Tooth development was determined by comparing the children's x-ray charts with the normative tables established to measure maturation of permanent teeth. According to Bird (1987, p. 32), the x-rays of the teeth were rated on a growth continuum and scored on a scale from 0 to 10 based on level of calcification, crown formation, and root development of the tooth. These ratings were assigned to the x-rays by dental hygienists. Each rating was then translated into a maturity score. Bird found a nonsignificant correlation of .04 between maturation as measured by tooth development and reading achievement. These results are similar to Harrison's findings. That is, maturation, as measured by tooth development, is *not* an important factor in children's reading achievement.

Table 7–3.
Percentage of Children Promoted from First Grade in Relation to Their Teething Status

Teething status		Percentage promoted at end of first grade
Immature	Level 1	71.4%
	2	83.4%
	3	76.1%
Irregular	Level 4	72.7%
Mature	Level 5	82.9%
	6	78.2%
	7	85.4%

Note. Data from *Differential Behavioral Characteristics of Non-Promoted Children,* by J. A. Chase, 1970. Unpublished doctoral dissertation. Request for use approved by Graduate School, University of Maine.

The studies by Chase, Harrison, Kaufman, and Bird should end the arguments over the importance of tooth development as an indicator of readiness. Bird's study should not be replicated as it will needlessly expose children to increased radiation. In addition, statements about the negative effects of slow teething should not be accepted as fact. Included are comments such as that slow teething is related to the slow development of behavior (Ames, 1967); if the 6-year-old has not lost his two lower middle teeth, the chances are his behavior will be behind the average (Hedges, 1977); the proper teething stage "signifies that the child is ready for academic training" (Olgetree, 1973, p. 12). The results of the research described in this section should end the controversial practice of considering tooth development as an important part of school readiness.

Physiological Indicators of Readiness: The Birth Process

A recent data sheet prepared for the Society for Developmental Education (Uphoff, 1988) includes a number of controversial statements about the birth process and school readiness. The document states that the child is more likely to experience problems in school when (a) labor continues for a "long time," (b) labor is less than 4 hours, (c) labor is unusually difficult, or (d) the child is delivered by Caesarean section. "Short labor and/or C-section is associated with reduced social skill development. Some studies have found birth trauma to be associated with later emotional problems including, in the extreme, suicidal tendencies" (Uphoff, 1988, p. 1).

The relationship between various obstetrical and birth factors is complicated, however, and does not lend itself to facile interpretation. The four most common methods of child delivery are spontaneous vertex (i.e., "normal"), breech, forceps, and Caesarean section (Neligan, Prudham, & Steiner, 1974). Any abnormal method of delivery can increase the risk of asphyxia (Neligan et al., 1974). However, it is quite a different matter to state that *all* such children are at risk and that all will have educational difficulties after they enter school.

Whereas 98.2% of children born of "normal" deliveries establish a regular respiration rate within 4 minutes, 81.4% of Caesarean babies do so (Neligan et al., 1974). The important fact to remember here is that the great majority of Caesarean babies do not have difficulty establishing a regular respiration rate.

Low birth weight is also cited as a factor in later school problems. However, it has been determined that the social class of the child is also an important variable. Seventeen percent of low birth weight children from fathers with manual occupations were found to have severe educational difficulties at age 7 compared to 1.5% of low birth weight children from fathers with nonmanual jobs (Davie, Butler, & Goldstein, 1972). As these authors state, "this is another example of the modifying effect which social factors can have on perinatal circumstances . . . " (p. 173). It is ironic indeed that such interview questions are used most often by maturational school psychologists and educators in schools that enroll children from middle-class families. It is these children who thus come from favored environmental circumstances.

Davie et al. (1972) also investigated the influence of different obstetrical factors individually on the educational achievement of children. They checked prolonged labor, abnormal method of delivery, and early or late bleeding in pregnancy and found no association with later school performance of the child. In a most important study, Bale (1981) also investigated prenatal factors and poor reading performance in 9-year-old boys. In a sample of 134 boys with severe reading problems he found 52 who were either moderately or severely impaired in perceptual functions as well as in reading performance. This group demonstrated a considerably higher incidence of abnormal pregnancy and delivery, a shorter gestation period, low birth weight, and premature birth. Of Bale's control group of regular class children, 14.8% of their mothers had an abnormal delivery, whereas 36.2% of the children with severe perceptual difficulties were in that category; this is a rate almost 2.5 times greater than that found in the normal group of children. However, the majority of the mothers (i.e., 64%) whose children demonstrated severe perceptual difficulties and poor reading performance did *not* have an abnormal birth experience.

It is a combination of factors of prenatal and perinatal difficulties rather than one individual factor that may cause neurological impairment and contribute to the child's poor academic performance (Bale, 1981, p. 142). The particular factors regarding the birth experience should not be marshalled against the child so as either to delay admission to school or to mandate automatic placement in an alternative class to kindergarten.

A recent study not only indicates our limited ability to predict later learning problems adequately but also suggests that early hazardous medical events may not necessarily be associated with later learning problems (Cohen, Parmelee, Sigman, & Beckwith, 1988). The 89 children studied by Cohen et al. had been born preterm (i.e., birth weight below 2,500 grams and gestational age less than 37 weeks). The criteria used to designate a learning problem were that children either had been recommended for retention, had been retained, or were achieving at or lower than the 25th percentile on a standardized achievement test. The children's development was monitored from birth to 8 years of age using a variety of neurobehavioral, medical, social, and developmental measures.

The rate of learning problems found in this population of children of average intelligence was 25% at age 8. This compares to the 3% to 7% estimated for the general population of children. Thus, although there was a higher incidence of learning problems, the authors emphasized that most of the children were performing adequately.

Most important, the children with learning problems in the Cohen et al. study were not perceived by their teachers or parents as showing any higher degree of social and emotional maladjustment when rated at age 8. Although it was hypothesized that medical problems during the first year of life would be associated with later subtle learning deficits, the learning problem group did not differ as to their overall medical status from the no learning problem control group during the perinatal period and the first year of life. However, some differences were demonstrated at the end of the second year (i.e., receptive language). The researchers conclude that although early deficits were apparent for some children in the learning problem group (i.e., receptive language), most of the preterm infants did not in fact show learning problems at 8 years of age.

Behavioral antecedents predictive of learning problems at a later age also were not found when comparing the child's medical status at birth or during the first year of life with learning status at age 8. As stated previously, some language and symbolic deficits did appear in the second year of life. But, as the authors conclude: "it is not the prematurity itself that is the salient feature but instead special factors within the premature child that are associated with learning problems. The study points to the need to be sensitive to the infant's own behavior rather than to the medical status itself" (p. 505).

Sex Differences in Reading

A frequent statement by education personnel is that girls are better readers than boys. A common argument is that learning differences between the sexes occur because boys "mature" later than girls. The difficulties of boys with the reading process are supposedly so persuasive that several educators and maturational psychologists have called for a delay in the entry of males to school or for raising the legal limit for entrance from 6 months to 1 year (Ames, 1967; Baer, 1957, 1958). However, such a policy does not eliminate the problem. This issue is discussed in the section on policy implications of higher entrance age.

One study, conducted by McGuinness (1985), indicates that females have a distinct advantage in comprehension skills and in producing language. Also, although boys were superior in gross motor skills, girls appear to have an advantage in fine motor skills. This advantage facilitates learning to write for girls. However, McGuinness adds that the major differences between the two sexes are found mainly in the lower range of the verbal skills distribution which includes more boys than girls. The largest percentage of children in remedial classes also is from this group.

One belief, expressed by Moore and Moore (1975, 1979), is that verbal ability differences between the sexes are related to physical maturity. They argue that girls mature faster than boys and are ready for school 6 to 9 months earlier. Specifically, girls are approximately 1 year ahead of boys in skeletal maturity and also "stabilize their verbal skills earlier; they seem to possess an advantage in learning" (p. 185).

Thompson (1975) notes that boys do lag behind girls in skeletal maturity from birth to adulthood. However, skeletal maturity does not provide information about the "maturation of the cerebral structures which mediate learning of the reading skill" (p. 20).

Dyer (1973) and Berk (1989) both discount a biological explanation for the differences in verbal abilities between girls and boys. First, no relationship has been demonstrated between physical differences and reading achievement. Second, girls do not demonstrate uniformly higher achievement across all subjects (Dyer, 1973). Specifically, boys are ahead of girls in spatial and math abilities (Berk, 1989).

Research conducted in other countries also indicates that sex differences are not consistent across cultures. Vernon, O'Gorman, and McLellan (1955) reported no significant differences between English boys and girls on tests or oral word reading in the 6- to 9-year age range. Teacher assessment of the reading ability of 7-year-old children in Great Britain indicated that 69.2% of the boys and 82.8% of the girls were average or above average (Pringle et al., 1966).

A study of schoolchildren near Glasgow found that girls scored slightly higher in reading at age 7 than did boys (Clark, 1970). However, the difference was neither statistically nor educationally significant. At age 9, the boys scored higher on reading tests. However, the differences again were not educationally significant. Neale (1958) also found no consistent sex differences in reading in her sample of 6- to 9-year-old English children. Her results included measures of reading accuracy as well as oral reading comprehension (Thompson, 1975).

One of the most important studies that provides evidence of boys' competence in reading was reported by Preston (1962). Investigating the reading achievement of German and American children in the fourth and sixth grades, he found that German boys were superior to girls on tests of reading achievement but that the reverse was true for American children. In addition, more cases of reading retardation were found among German girls. Preston accounted for these differences by differences in the culture. That is, most elementary school teachers in Germany were male, and the German culture placed more emphasis on reading as an appropriate activity for males.

Dyer (1973) emphasizes the importance of cross-cultural research when she states: "This complete reversal of sex differences in reading [as found in the Preston study] as we know them in America argues most strongly against acceptance of an explanation of sex differences based on innate human physical or maturational characteristics" (p. 465).

Other important research evidence that refutes a simple biological explanation to account for the superiority of American girls in reading achievement is that certain educational interventions have proven successful in reducing the gender gap in verbal skills (Berk, 1989). One such intervention was the use of computer-assisted instruction for boys in the Palo Alto public schools (Atkinson, 1974). Such instruction resulted in improving first-grade boys' reading performance to the level of the female students. This study is reported on in more detail in Chapter 11, on remediation.

Another example is the use of the initial learning alphabet (ITA) by Thackray (1971). The ITA method of teaching reading is an attempt to simplify the traditional orthography of the English language and to make easier the deciphering of the print code by providing an alphabet based on the 40 sounds of English speech. Thackray compared children taught with the ITA method vs. those taught by conventional methods (i.e., a traditional orthography approach). He was able to demonstrate that the reading achievement scores of boys were *not* significantly different from girls when the children were taught by ITA methods. However, in the group taught by traditional methods, significant differences in achievement in favor of girls were found (Thackray, 1971).

Thackray (1971) comments on the results by stating that these differences clearly indicate "that boys can learn to read with ITA as easily as girls, and make similar progress in reading achievement. However, boys learning to read with traditional orthography (t.o.) do not learn to read as easily as the girls, and their progress in reading is slower" (p. 274).

Policy Implications of Raising the Entrance Age

As indicated earlier, one proposal for addressing entering differences between girls and boys is to delay school entrance for boys from 6 months to 1 year. Such a delay, however, would not eliminate the differences. This phenomenon has been illustrated in the research conducted by Clark (1959). He constructed distributions of mental age for various chronological ages and then compared them. The tables were based on a mean IQ of 100 and a standard deviation of 16.

For an entrance age of 5 years 6 months, Clark (1959) determined that 28.8% of the boys had a mental age of 6 years. If the entrance age was changed to 6 years, 50% of the boys would have a mental age of 6 years or more. Raising the entrance age, therefore, "helps" 21.2% of the boys. However, raising the entrance age *also penalizes the 28.8% who had attained a mental age of 6 years at the earlier chronological age of 5 years 6 months.*

Clark is one of the few educators who recognized the extensive variability in mental age present in any age group within a chronological range of 11 months. The conclusions he reached are equally true today. Specifically, "changing chronological entrance ages for boys and girls is an inefficient way of meeting the problem (of ability to learn) and will create as many problems as it will solve" (p. 74).

In addition, Jones (1968) described the range of expected mental ages in a first grade in which the entrance age is 6 years by September 1 and the majority of children are in the 80–120 IQ range. She estimated that the children's mental ages would range from 4 years 9 months to 6 years 2 months, a spread of 29 months.

Raising the entrance age to 6 years 6 months increases the range of mental ages to 31 months. Moreover, an entrance age of 7 years increases the range to 34 months (Jones, 1968). In other words, higher entrance ages do not lead to a reduction in the range of individual differences in the classroom. The educator may react by stating that the use of a higher entrance age results in a greater number of children who succeed. Other evidence, however, indicates that grades will be assigned on the basis of a normal curve distribution. (Chapter 3, on entrance age studies, illustrates this point.)

Raising the entrance age also introduces other questions about the education of young children. In a review of research and policy options, Gray (1985) made the following important observations about entrance age:

(1) Chronological age is a useful criterion for school entry because it clearly states the obligations of the government for the provision of educational services for its citizens and it is administratively convenient.

(2) Although much of the research literature denotes higher mean achievement for older children than for younger children in the primary grades, satisfactory achievement was found for the majority of younger children.

(3) Many handicapped children who are in need of specialized educational services are not served until they enter school. Raising the entry age would increase the delay of provision of such services.

(4) Disadvantaged children, who are in special need of early educational services, would be hampered in skill development by delay in entrance age (p. 14).

(5) Overall the research literature does not support raising the entrance age. Parents in Illinois currently do not have to enter their children if they believe they are not ready. However, arbitrarily raising the entry age would discriminate against the children who are ready for school (p. 15).

Despite these cogent reasons, the maturational lobby was able to influence the Illinois legislature to change the entrance age to September 1.

Several proposals also were made to raise the entrance age in Maryland schools. Entrance age cutoff for that state is December 31. The State Board of Education (Shilling, 1989) did not change the policy for the following reasons:

(1) Research does not provide "compelling evidence" linking chronological age at school entry to success in school.

(2) The number of children who would be handicapped by a change in the entry age far exceeds the number who may benefit. Besides excluding disadvantaged children who may benefit from early schooling, also excluded would be "the large percentage of younger children who are able to satisfactorily meet the

expectations of kindergarten and first grade" (Maryland State Department of Education, 1987, p. 1).

(3) Parents still have the option of keeping younger children out of school if they feel they are not ready (Maryland State Department of Education, 1987).

(4) Absolute entry age is not the important variable; rather it is the relative age of entry. No matter what the cutoff date there will always be a group younger than the others because allowable age at entry spans a year of time (Maryland State Department of Education, 1987).

(5) Preoccupation with the child's readiness for school neglects the many problems of the school's readiness for children (Maryland State Department of Education, 1987).

The Relative Age Concept: The Heart of the Problem

As indicated in the prior sections, the entrance age issue is more complicated than it first appears. Many assume that increasing the age of entrance to school will automatically benefit children. The belief is that children will perform more adequately in the future and failures will be reduced because younger children are being delayed from entering until they are the appropriate age to begin school.

In American education the entrance age for first grade has risen steadily in the past 30 years. A legitimate expectation, therefore, is that a higher entrance age should reduce the problems of the young child. However, educators continue to refer to the young group as "at risk." Uphoff and Gilmore (1985), for example, refer to the "summer child" as being at risk. As indicated in the prior section, the problems cited for the young child in the 1950s (poor vision, immaturity, and poor development) are also attributed to the young child in today's schools. Thus, it appears that raising the entrance age has not reduced the problems of the young child.

Equally important is that the young and, therefore, at-risk child is a relative concept. In today's classroom September 1 is the accepted cutoff date for attaining the age of 6 years and entry to first grade. Thus, the at-risk child is the one born in the summer months of June through August. However, according to the cutoff date in use 30 years ago, December 1, the summer child is not at risk. Instead, the child is in the midrange age group. (See Table 7-4.) Stated another way, the child described as at risk in the 1990s classroom would not have been considered in jeopardy in the 1950s classroom.

In other words, the basic problem is that, *regardless of the cutoff date selected for attaining the required entry age,* children's ages in any one classroom will vary by 12 months. Therefore, changing the cutoff date as a mechanism for raising the entrance age does not change the variability of age within the classroom. The age groups illustrated in Table 7-4 will continue to be present.

The different perspective of chronological age that defines who is older and younger also differs across cultures. For example, British children enter school a full year earlier than their American counterparts. Children in the British system considered to be mature and ready to undertake academic work are the older children, whereas the younger children are described as immature and unready (Gredler, 1978). However, the mature child in the British system, if classified according to American criteria, would be labeled as at risk because *the older child in the British system would be included in the youngest age group in the United States.*

A similar observation about many Swedish children being too young is made by Malmquist (1958). In a study of reading disabilities in first grade, he states that he found only one good reader whose mental age was less than 7 years 6 months! Because Swedish children begin school a year older than American children, the oldest first-graders are approaching their 8th birthday and the youngest children are barely 7. Uphoff and Gilmore (1985) laud the Scandinavian schools for setting the entrance age for first grade at 7. However, Malmquist found 21% of the first-grade sample in his study with significant problems in reading at the end of first grade.

Academic Progress of Relative Age Groups

A legitimate question to be answered is: How young does a child have to be to qualify as "too young"? One way to investigate whether summer children are at risk because they lack readiness, as Uphoff and Gilmore (1985) state, is to study the academic progress and adjustment status of these children when they are *not* the youngest in their age group. Such an investigation was undertaken by Barnsley (1986), who investigated the achievement of children in the Lethbridge, Alberta, Canada, school system. There, children may enter school in September if they

Table 7–4.
Age Groupings of First-Graders Under December and September Cutoff Dates

Cutoff dates	
December 1	September 1
1) Youngest children are born in September–November	1) Youngest children are born in June–August
2) Midrange group are born in March–August	2) Midrange children born in December–May
3) Oldest children born in December–February	3) Oldest children born in September–November

become 6 years of age by December 31 of that year. Barnsley found that the children in his young group demonstrated lower achievement and a higher failure rate than the other children within the 1-year time span. However, if the Uphoff and Gilmore (1985) thesis has any validity we would expect the summer-born students to be developmentally unready and consequently to show poor achievement and an increased rate of failure. But Barnsley found this not to be the case. The summer children in his Canadian sample did quite well, and the autumn group (the youngest children in his sample) *alone* were the high-risk group.

As Barnsley states, " . . . it would seem that it is the younger children in any group who are at risk—not children of any particular age. It is the *relative age* hypothesis that predicts that the young children in a group will be at risk, and it is the *relative age* hypothesis that appears to handle both the Uphoff and Gilmore data and the data from our local school system" (pp. 91–92).

As would be expected, Uphoff and Gilmore (1985) reject the implications of Barnsley's thesis and counter by stating, "we found when *all* children in a grade are chronologically older, thus developmentally more ready for today's curriculum, nearly all children (especially the younger ones) will find more success" (pp. 92–93). However, Uphoff and Gilmore offer no evidence that this is so.

This writer has been unable to find any American research that investigated achievement and failure rates *after* a school system raised its entrance age. However, Viewger (cited in Mandl, 1976) demonstrated that when West Berlin, Germany, schools raised the entrance age, subsequent analysis of school failures showed that the percentage of failures *remained the same or increased in some instances.*

The importance of relative age also was underscored by Weinstein (1968). Gredler (1975) also commented on this concept over 17 years previously, but the serious implications for teaching children have been little considered by educators and psychologists until recently.

Weinstein investigated the relationship between the child's academic progress and adjustment status in first grade and membership in the youngest groups in the class. She theorized that young children were likely to be at risk in first grade due to being less mature mentally as well as less mature physically, socially, and emotionally. But Weinstein also speculated that the children's adjustment and academic problems would be associated with the children's entrance age *relative* to their classmates' age rather than with the *absolute* age of the children at school entry time.

To test her hypothesis of the importance of relative age versus absolute age, Weinstein first recorded the ages of children who had been referred for behavioral and learning problems to two residential schools in Tennessee and North Carolina. The entry age for school differed in these two states at the time. The cutoff for first-grade entry was reaching the age of 6 by October 16 in North Carolina and by December 31 in Tennessee.

If the relative-age theory had any merit one would expect to find that the same percentage of young children would be referred for lack of academic performance and emotional maladjustment. However, the children's absolute age would differ because the entry age to school in the two states differed. This was precisely what Weinstein found. Forty-seven percent of the children in the North Carolina residential school formed the youngest group, whereas 46% of the children in the Tennessee school comprised the youngest group. However, because of the difference in entrance age of the two states, *the young children in the North Carolina sample were actually older than the younger children in the Tennessee sample.* The youngest children in North Carolina were born in the time period from June 17–October 16 and comprised 47% of the sample of children referred. The percentage of children referred in the Tennessee school in that same age group was only 33%, which does not differ from the expected incidence for that group.

For Weinstein these results clearly demonstrated the importance of the relative age concept in referring children for emotional and academic problems. Such results heighten the importance of understanding the relative age concept and raise questions as to the best way to address the implications. The frightening implication of this research is that children who form the youngest of *any* group will be subject to lower grades and more academic problems. Thus, increasing the entrance age to school instead of eliminating the problem of the young group establishes a new group of children who are now the youngest and who will be at risk for learning problems unless the condition of relative age is clearly recognized.

Criteria for Successful First-Grade Performance

An important educational issue is concerned with the establishment of the criteria for successful school achievement in first grade. Research studies typically mention that a statistically significant difference is found between the average achievement of older and younger children. However, when statistically significant differences are found between older and younger children as to achievement, can the conclusion be drawn that the *younger* pupils have performed inadequately? The reliance on statistically significant differences between older and younger children as an indicator of lack of progress by the younger children means that success is being defined in terms of what the older child does.

However, a more legitimate question is, Given a certain level of readiness, what can we reasonably expect in the way of academic performance by the end of first grade? And is the level that is finally attained an indication of sufficient mastery of reading and arithmetic skills? The question that should be asked is, What is an acceptable level of performance at the end of 1 year for children who differ up to 1 year in chronological age? For example, in one study older children within the IQ range of 117 to 142 obtained a grade placement score of 3.82 at the end of second grade while younger grade-2 children obtained a grade placement score of 3.32. This difference is statistically significant. However, it must be noted that the performance of both groups of children is quite acceptable and both groups were well above the end-of-year norms of 2.9 (Gott, 1963).

Green and Simmons (1962) make an important point when they state that older pupils can be said to have learned more in school only if the assumption is made that the older pupils did not know more than the younger group when they began school. They go on to say that this assumption is false, because scores on readiness tests show a positive relationship to the child's age.

Green and Simmons also emphasize that, in comparing older groups with younger groups, we are comparing two groups that are unequal on many measures. Therefore, it is foolhardy to expect that the younger group should be *equal* to the older group on achievement measures at the end of the school year. Instead of always comparing absolute performance at the end of the year, we should also consider measuring gains from year to year and use such an index as a criterion of performance.

Analysis of many entrance-age studies indicates that the younger child often scores at a lower level of performance on classroom achievement tests and in grades received. However, a number of studies also indicate that while the younger children receive lower grades they do *not* score lower in performance on standardized achievement tests. In her study of children in the Camden, New Jersey, school system, Koch (1968) demonstrated that there was no difference in reading test scores for older and younger boys. However, a significantly greater number of younger boys were retained in comparison to older boys. Garrett (1956) also found no difference in the achievement test results of older and younger children in the Warren, Ohio, school system. And while there was no difference in the number of Fs given to older and younger children in the Warren schools, a larger number of younger children received Ds in reading.

Prince (1966) also states that early entrants to first grade cannot be expected to compete with the older group of children in school. What needs to be emphasized is that in its evaluations the school should not use practices that automatically put the younger group at a disadvantage. Bloom (1968) indicates that teachers are often using some variant of the normal distribution curve in assigning marks. With older children coming into school with up to an additional year of experience accruing from their extra year of chronological age and scoring higher on achievement tests, the younger-aged children are thus relegated to a lower position in a total ranking of students.

Bloom (1968) speaks to the point when he states that the failure of students is often "determined by the rank order of the students in the group rather than by their failure to grasp the essential ideas of the course. Thus, we have become accustomed to classify students in about five categories of level of performance and to assign grades in some relative fashion" (p. 1).

Dickson (1923) provides us with some data that illustrate Bloom's point quite well. He obtained grade distribution data given by two first-grade teachers whose children differed by 14 months in average mental age. Teacher A's children had a median IQ of 85 and were awarded grades which followed a normal curve distribution. Teacher B's children had a median IQ of 108 and also were awarded grades which followed the normal curve. For example, Teacher A awarded 13% Bs and 47% Cs while Teacher B awarded similar percentages of Bs (14%) and Cs (46%) despite the large difference in the median IQs. It is my contention that this type of grade distribution is repeated year after year in schools, regardless of the established entrance age. As stated previously, an analysis of grade distributions of schools with differing entrance ages should be conducted to provide information from a wide sampling of school systems.

Baer (1957), in his study of early and late entrants in the Kansas City system, alluded to this question when he commented that before concluding that younger children should be delayed entry to school, it should be remembered that most of the young children who entered school made acceptable school progress.

Once again we come back to the question of what is *satisfactory* performance. It is obvious that most investigators who urge that the entrance age be raised are implying that the characteristics of the older group should *set* the performance standards for achievement. When such an argument is used, the scores obtained by the older group are being considered standards to be reached instead of normative data.

Summary

An extraordinary amount has been written about entrance age issues in the United States. With regard to differences in the performance of boys and girls, the perception that boys perform more poorly is overemphasized while the overlap in performance of the two sexes is downplayed. Developmental factors in vision and teething have been overly stressed; in some schools the level of the child's tooth development is actually considered a primary indicator of the child's readiness for school, and placement decisions are made on the basis of such data! Although the entry age has risen steadily over the past 30 years, an even higher entrance age is advocated by some as a solution to the problem of individual differences found in the classroom. Overlooked in the call for increased entrance age is the fact that as the entry age is increased, a new younger group is formed and this group is now found to be at risk. There is no absolute entry age cutoff which is the "best"; evaluation of the performance of the young children is often found to be relative to the older children's performance. Thus the problem is really one of how to set curriculum objectives properly and to evaluate the children fairly.

8

THE INFLUENCE OF
ENTRANCE AGE ON ACHIEVEMENT:
AN ANALYSIS OF STUDIES
AND TRENDS

Extensive discussion and study of the relationship between entry age and school achievement have been conducted over the last 50 to 60 years. During this period, the trend has been to raise the entrance age. Moreover, many school systems have included additional requirements for entry into first grade.

One important concern influencing such policies, however, is the nature of the evidence claiming that school entry at a young age will result in poor achievement. The major purpose of this chapter is to review a number of the studies on entrance age. Typically, these studies compare the average achievement of children in the elementary grades who were younger and older in school entrance age. Much of this research may be described as causal comparative. That is, age is considered to be the important independent variable that "causes" significant differences in school achievement.

Social and educational situations, however, are complex settings in which a variety of factors are operating. Thus, a second purpose of this chapter is to discuss other variables that also can account for differences in the performance of younger and older children when they do appear. These variables include differences in ability level at school entry, rate of gain, and overall school success.

Included in the discussion are studies conducted prior to 1970. Some individuals indicate that such studies are not relevant for contemporary education which now includes educational television, preschool programs, compensatory schooling such as Operation Headstart, and competency testing (Carrington, 1982). However, many of the earlier studies continue to be cited by educators. Therefore, they are included in the discussion in this chapter.

Research Prior to 1970

Studies of entrance age typically report achievement differences between older and younger children in the same grade. Often these differences are statistically significant, with the older children earning higher scores. Equally important, however, are factors such as ability at entry, performance of the younger children in comparison to grade-level norms, and the rate of gain for older and younger children.

Entering Ability and Achievement

The relationship between entering ability and later achievement is illustrated in an early study conducted by Bigelow (1934) in the Summit, New Jersey, school system. Differences in reading achievement in grade 1 for two groups of children were analyzed. The older children were between 6 years and 6 years 4 months and the younger children were under 6 years. Although a greater number of older children were above average in reading performance, all of the successful children were in the IQ range of 110 or higher, and 85% of the successful younger children also had IQs of 110 or higher.

A more recent study, conducted by Gott (1963) in Chula Vista, California, also indicates the importance of considering entering abilities. The study investigated the effect of 9 to 11 months' age differences on achievement and adjustment in later grades. The ages of the younger group in kindergarten were between 4 years 9 months and 4 years 10 months. The older group varied from 5 years 7 months to 5 years 8 months. The majority of the children at all grade levels were from middle-class White families.

Standardized achievement tests were administered at the end of grades 2 through 6. (Social and emotional adjustment data also were collected and are discussed in Chapter 6.) In 25 comparisons of reading achievement, 14 of the comparisons indicated that older children obtained significantly higher grade placement scores. In arithmetic, 16 of 25 comparisons were significantly higher, with the same results in 18 of the 25 comparisons in spelling. Gott concluded that entrance age was a significant factor in achievement.

From this brief discussion it would appear that Gott indeed has made a definitive case in favor of increased entrance age. Her conclusions often are cited (e.g., Uphoff & Gilmore, 1985) as evidence of the need for a higher entrance age.

However, further analysis of the data raises questions as to the accuracy of that conclusion. Gott had divided her sample into five ability groups (IQs of 85–100, 101–108, 109–116, 117–124, 125–132). A comparison of the performance of the younger children in these five ability groups with grade norms indicates a different pattern.

In three ability groups (IQs of 125–132, 117–124, and 109–116), the mean reading scores of the younger children exceeded the expected grade placement score. Therefore, although the older children obtained higher average reading scores that were statistically significant, the performance of the younger children indicated that they were successful according to grade norms.

For third-grade children in the 117–124 IQ range, Gott reports statistically significant differences in favor of the older children. The average grade-placement score of the older children was 5.28. However, the average grade-placement score for the younger group was 4.49, well *above* the expected norm. Therefore, it is somewhat foolish to report that older children perform "better" than younger children, when in fact both groups perform considerably beyond the end-of-year norms of 3.9 and demonstrate a very high level of achievement. Further, a comparison of the achievement of the older and younger children in the lowest ability group (i.e., IQ 85–100) indicates that none of the older or younger children in grades 2 through 6 reached the end-of-year grade placement norm. Of real importance in the Gott study are the detailed data that are given on the performance of children throughout a wide range of ability. Such information is missing from many other studies of entrance age differences.

However when an analysis of the Gott data is undertaken of different IQ groups, both age groups (i.e., younger and older children) are found to make essentially the same average rate of gain from grades 2 through 6 despite the 9 to 10 months' difference in chronological age. For example, older children in the 85–100 IQ range gained 1.01 years each year from grades 2 through 6 on a standardized reading test. Younger-aged children with the same IQ bracket gained .995 years during the same time period. Older children within the IQ range of 125–132 gained 1.21 years on reading tests each year from grades 2 through 6 while younger children within the same IQ group averaged a gain of 1.25 years on the reading test. Such data raise questions about the supposed inability of younger children to progress academically at a satisfactory rate.

Gott's statement that "young children achieve less than older children of equal ability at all grade levels in reading" (p. 102) is technically true. However, as indicated in the above analysis, the performance of the younger children in many instances is quite adequate, and the rate of gain in reading scores over the course of an academic year for both groups is essentially the same.

Studies with IQ Held Constant

As stated above, the study conducted by Gott included five different ability ranges of IQ. In some studies, however, only one level of IQ is used. King (1955) studied the sixth-grade achievement of older and younger children in the Oak Ridge, Tennessee, schools. The average age of the younger children when they entered school was 5 years 10 months, while the average age of the older group was 6 years 7 months.

At the end of the sixth grade, the older group obtained an average grade equivalent score of 7.68 which was significantly higher than the young group's mean grade score of 6.20. That the curriculum might have been a difficult one is seen in the fact that one third (32%) of the older children failed to meet the grade norm when the achievement test was administered. King's study is widely quoted today despite the fact that her sample was restricted to children within the 90–110 IQ range. Moreover, 10 of her 54 younger children had been retained and were also included in the sample. Eight of these retained children were still among the lowest achievers in her sample. In order to delineate clearly the possible differences in achievement between younger and older children, retained children should have been deleted from the sample.

Baer (1957, 1958) investigated the achievement and adjustment status of younger and older children as they progressed through 11 years of the Kansas City schools. Older children obtained significantly higher average achievement scores than did the younger children. However, Baer noted that the underage children made acceptable school progress. Underage children in his sample had birthdates in November and December.

Baer's study also is restricted in its generalization, because his sample was composed of children whose average IQ was 111. A more complete understanding of the relative achievement of younger and older children would have been obtained if Baer had sampled a broader range of ability levels in his school district. It was impossible to ascertain the educational significance of the differences between achievement levels of the younger and older children in Baer's study because the variability in range of student performance was not reported.

In 1964 Halliwell and Stein reported on the comparative achievement of fourth- and fifth-grade students classified into younger and older groups according to their age at school entry. Mean IQ of the children ranged from 110 to 114. Younger students ranged in age from 5 years 10 months to 6 years 3 months, while older students entered first grade at an age of 6 years 4 months to 6 years 9 months. Halliwell and Stein stated that their findings were similar to those of Bigelow (1934), Baer (1957, 1958), and King (1955).

However, Halliwell and Stein (1964) mentioned one important aspect of their investigation that has been ignored by many of those who constantly emphasize the importance of a higher entry age. They noted that despite the fact that the younger students were "inferior" in performance to older students in most academic areas, when raw scores were changed to grade equivalent scores, all the scores were found to be above the group's actual grade level. Such results raise the question (discussed in the prior chapter) about the criteria for successful performance.

The Relationship Between Entrance Age and Achievement and Retention

One important investigation completed in the 1960s was undertaken by Koch (1968). She studied kindergarten entrance age as a factor in school progress in selected school districts in Camden County, New Jersey. She attempted to determine the relationship between entrance age and school achievement of older and younger children who had been continuously enrolled in school for a time period of from 5 to 7 years. At the time of her study, children were required to be 6 years old by October 1 to enter school. This entrance age was higher than most New Jersey school districts mandated at the time. Koch analyzed differences in reading and math performance for both older and younger children overall and for different IQ levels. The children were predominantly from middle-class families, with average and above-average IQs. The two disparate age groups were also compared as to teachers' grades received and retention rates.

An important finding was that for the total group of children, school entrance age was not significantly related to academic achievement as measured by standardized test scores of reading and arithmetic, nor were there significant differences between the older and younger children in reading grades. However, when the performance of specific subgroups was analyzed, a number of differences between older and young students were found. When comparing older and younger children with IQs of 110 or higher at the end of first grade there were no significant differences on achievement tests, grades in reading, and rate of retention. However, the older children within the IQ group 90–109 scored significantly higher on achievement tests at the end of first grade, obtained higher grades in reading, and had a lower retention rate.

Koch's data thus illustrate that the younger children in her lower IQ range (i.e., 90–109) were most at risk in assignment of lower grades, lower test scores, and higher retention rates. Further analysis also indicates the complicated relationship among grades, test scores, and retention rates.

Whereas only 5% more of the young boys than the older boys obtained a test score more than 1 year below grade norm (i.e., 20.9% vs. 15.9%), almost four times as many young boys received a reading grade below C (26.1% vs. 6.8%). And although 26% of young boys were given a reading grade below C, 39.1% of this group were retained in comparison with 9.1% of older boys. It should also be noted that whereas 15.9% of the older boys performed poorly on the standardized reading test, less than half (6.8%) of them obtained a grade below C.

Koch states:

> The picture of more successful older pupils and less success for younger pupils which persists (even with a relatively high minimum entrance age) suggests that there is not yet real

acceptance of a range of developmental levels among children
entering school together. (p. 127)

Koch was concerned especially about the very high level of failure experienced
by the younger children in the elementary schools of her study. The large difference
between the percentage of younger boys retained and the actual percentage of
younger boys who received low grades or low reading test scores indicates that a
number of teachers were making retention decisions based on factors other than
academic performance. Such data indicate that retention decisions should be made
cautiously, and the various factors that enter into the decision must be clarified.
Further study of the ways that retention decisions are made should be undertaken.
(See the discussion in Chapter 10, on retention, for a fuller account of important
attributes of the problem.)

The Miller and Norris Study

Miller and Norris (1967) studied entrance age and school success in the
Murfreesboro, Tennessee, school system. Fourth- and fifth-grade children were
separated into groups categorized as to school entrance age: early entrants (5-8 to
5-11), normal (6-0 to 6-7), and late (6-8 to 6-11). Mean scores from readiness tests
administered in kindergarten and achievement tests from grades 1 through 4 were
then compared. Statistical tests were computed to test the significance of differences in means for these three groups on 30 readiness, achievement, and
intelligence measures.

Significant differences were found between early, normal, and late entrants in
average scores on three of the six readiness scores. However, these differences in
tested readiness did not continue as significant achievement differences beyond
grade 1. At the end of 4 years the mean achievement of the early entrants in all areas
measured by the Metropolitan (word knowledge and discrimination; reading,
spelling, and arithmetic computation and problem solving) was not significantly
different from the performance of the normal-aged groups or the older-aged groups.
At the end of the fourth year of school, the mean difference between the normal-
aged group and the young group was less than 3 months on the Metropolitan
Achievement Tests. Miller and Norris attribute the lack of significant educational
differences to the effectiveness of the flexible instructional grouping in force.

The Importance of Determining Rate of Gain

Few investigators prior to 1969 studied the rate of growth as an index of the
performance of early entrants compared to the performance of the late entrants.

This would appear to be an appropriate measure of the degree to which children are progressing in school. This index has the advantage of not relying on absolute growth at the end of a school year as the criterion of performance. Absolute growth is often biased in favor of the older child (Ilika, 1969).

Rate of scholastic achievement for older and younger children was compared by Ilika. He believed that the developmental status of the child was more important than the extra length of time a young child was in school. However, it was his presentation of gain rates in his study of entrance age that is of the most significance. Analysis of Ilika's data indicates that the rate of scholastic achievement was essentially the same for early entrants and late entrants in many of the comparisons of the two groups of children. For example, early entrant boys increased 0.97 months in mean reading age for each 1.00 month in chronological age. Late entrant boys increased 1.00 month in mean reading age for each 1.00 month in chronological age. This is important evidence that both groups of children were making adequate progress in school because the rate of achievement gain was essentially the same for both groups.

The results of this study would indicate that it might be appropriate to construct tables of gains in achievement for younger and older children. Variability within classrooms of the same level of socioeconomic status as well as classrooms representing different socioeconomic levels could then be compared. Based on the findings from the Ilika study, it is our hypothesis that, other factors being equal, the rate of gain in achievement for the early entrants should be approximately the same as for late entrants. Gain status could be used as one marker for possible referral for instructional intervention. Such an approach would be somewhat more sophisticated than automatically condemning a whole group of children as unable to profit from instruction because they were considered too young.

Such a finding would also tend to show that both age groups could profit from schooling at the age period at which they enrolled. Therefore, school personnel perhaps might be more relaxed about age differences in the classroom.

Twenty years after Ilika's study, two other studies have demonstrated the importance of ascertaining rate of progress of children as opposed to focusing only on the measurement of the current level of student skills. Subjects in one study were kindergarten children categorized as a delayed-language group. It was found that estimating the slope of pupil progress over a period of 6 weeks contributed substantially to an accurate evaluation of the child's risk status (Good, Kaminski, Schwarz, & Doyle, 1990). Morrison (1989) investigated the progress of younger-aged grade-1 children with children who just missed the cutoff date and went instead to kindergarten: "If younger grade one children are, in some absolute sense, not developmentally ready to benefit from formal instruction, they should as a group make no more progress in basic academic skills like reading and math, than a matched group of kindergarten children, almost identical in age" (Morrison, 1989, p. 4).

Morrison investigated this problem using three groups of children. It is of particular importance to note the ages of each of the three groups of children that he studied in the Edmonton, Canada, school system. This is a school system that has the latest cutoff for school entrance of any school system in North America (March 1). Morrison studied young first-grade children whose birthdates fell in January or February of the year following entry into grade 1; kindergarten children with birthdates in March or April of the same year and therefore who just missed the March 1 cutoff date; and older children whose birthdates fell in March or April of the year preceding their entrance to first grade.

Morrison traced the academic progress and emotional maturity of these three groups of children through the first and second grades. He discovered that the *rate of progress* of the young children on a reading test was the same as that of older children. The younger children ended first grade 2 months behind the older group because they had begun first grade 2 months behind. The young group in first grade also made significantly more progress than the young group who had remained in kindergarten. The importance of the comparison of the two groups of young children who were only 2 months apart in age is that such results also question the doctrine of developmental maturity as espoused by the maturationalists. If these young children who were in first grade were not developmentally ready for formal schooling, then, as Morrison points out, we would have expected little or no academic progress when compared to an almost same-age group of children who had not been exposed to a formal reading program.

Although teachers and parents rated younger grade-1 students as adapting less well than older first-grade students, the low social adaptation scores did *not* predict poor academic achievement. Low-adaptation young children made as much progress in reading and math as did older children with low adaptation scores.

When reading performance was examined at the end of grade 2, the differences between older and younger children had completely disappeared.

In another study of the same age groups of children, Morrison and Smith (1990) were also able to determine that formal instruction in grade 1 had enhanced the memory development of the young children: " . . . being a year older when receiving formal grade one schooling did not enhance memory development beyond that shown by the children receiving the same schooling experience a full year younger" (p. 20).

Studies from Ohio School Districts

In the 1950s several Ohio school districts investigated the problem of entry age and subsequent school failure. The results of these studies are quite important but they did not receive wide distribution because much of the research was never submitted to professional journals for publication.

Described in this section are the results of important studies completed in the 1950s concerning entrance age and success in first grade. These studies reflect the complicated nature of the entrance age issue. They also demonstrate that local school studies can provide data useful in shedding light on important educational issues.

Warren, Ohio

Garrett (1956) investigated the achievement of first-grade pupils of different ages in the Warren, Ohio, school system. Entrance age cutoff for first grade at the time was December 1. Garrett investigated the number of first-grade children who would be eliminated if the entrance age was changed from December 1 to September 1 and catalogued statistics for this group of young children.

He found that the great majority of young children (107 of 145) received acceptable grades in reading (i.e., 73% obtained an A, B, or C). All these children would have been denied entry to school had the entrance age been changed to September 1.

Germane to this analysis of the below age 6 population is the issue of the performance of the young group in comparison with older children. This comparison can be found in Table 8-1.

The data indicate that, although grades are significantly higher for the older (6-0+) group, almost three of four children in the 5-6 to 5-11 group made satisfactory progress as determined by grades received. A higher percentage of the younger children (69%) obtained a grade placement score of 2.0 or higher at the end of first grade compared to the older children (67%).

The Warren, Ohio, study is a good example of a research study undertaken by school system personnel in order to answer some of the questions raised about entrance age. It is apparent from the results of the study that the younger-aged children were able to perform quite adequately at the time in the Warren, Ohio, first grades. Note also should be made of the fact that, although a greater percentage of younger children than older children attained a grade placement score of 2.0 or higher, a larger percentage of young children received lower grades from their teachers.

Canton, Ohio

In 1956 the entrance requirement in the Canton schools was 6 years of age by December 1. This study documented the first-grade failure rates for children for each of four age groups. The groups were determined by the quarter of the year in which the child was born. The older group had January–March birthdates, and the youngest children were born in the October–December quarter (Gredler, 1956).

Table 8–1.

Reading Test Scores and Reading Grades of Older- and Younger-Aged Children in Warren Schools

Criterion measures	Grade placement scores	Chronological age	
		6 years 0 months and older	5 years 6 months– 5 years 11 months
Reading test scores	Below 2.0	34%	31%
	2.0–2.9	44%	48%
	3.0–3.9	22%	21%
Final reading grades	C or above	82%	73%
	Ds	10%	19%
	Fs	8%	8%

Note. Data summarized from *Factors Relating to School Entrance Age* by W. Garrett, 1956, Warren, OH: Warren City Schools. Used by permission.

A significant difference was found in first-grade failure rate with the youngest group having the highest rate. However, further analysis revealed a tremendous variability in failure rate from school to school. In this analysis the following data came to light:

a. Four (14%) of the 28 schools in the system contributed one third of all the failures.
b. The four high-failure schools were all situated in low-socioeconomic sections of the city. Removing the first-grade failures of these four low-SES schools from the data resulted in a nonsignificant relationship between failures and being underage.
c. Six of the 28 elementary schools contributed 45% of all the first-grade failures. These six schools included the four schools already mentioned and two schools that served a lower middle socioeconomic group.

In view of the disproportionate influence of these few schools on the total failure rate, the superintendent recommended no change in the entrance age. The conclusion was that a large number of children in the school district would be penalized if a decision were based on the excessive failure rate in 4 schools. In other words, entrance age policy for 28 elementary schools should not be dictated by the failure rate found in only four schools. Therefore, instead of raising the entrance age for the whole school system, the Board mandated extra consultant help to the personnel in those four schools to try to lessen the failure rate. (See the section on

Table 8–2.
Distribution of Final Grades in Reading in Older- and Younger-Aged Children in Warren Schools

	Final grade in reading		
Age group	C or above	Ds	Fs
6-0+ (older) group	82%	10%	8%
5-6 to 5-11 (younger) group	73%	19%	8%

Note. Data summarized from *Factors Relating to School Entrance Age* by W. Garrett, 1956, Warren, OH: Warren City Schools. Used by permission.

social significance of data later in this chapter for further elaboration on the decision process.)

Lakewood, Ohio

Personnel in the Lakewood school system compared the achievement at the end of first grade of all children who were 6 years old before September 15 and those who were 6 after that date. Median grade placement scores were 2.2 for the older group and 1.9 for the younger group. No statistical tests were undertaken in the original study. However, the author (Gredler, 1975), using the median test, found a significant chi square at the .05 level in favor of the older group.

The Lakewood investigators also examined the relationship between underachievement in reading (i.e., below actual grade placement of 1.9) and chronological age. They concluded that if the entrance age were changed to September 15, 32% of the young group would be eliminated. However, the researchers also reviewed the percentages of those who then showed poor academic performance. They found that the number of children who were underachieving had now declined from 38% of the total group to 34% when the young age group was eliminated. Thus, an exclusion of almost one third of the class would have resulted in only a 4% reduction in the number of children who were making poor academic progress.

The importance of the Lakewood study is that school personnel became aware of the effects of eliminating a large number of young children, many of whom were adequate achievers. The final result would be only a minor reduction in the actual number of underachievers. Therefore, they decided that a change in entrance age would penalize too many children who were adequate learners.

Toledo, Ohio

School personnel in Toledo in the 1950s approached the entrance age problem by studying the success of normal-age pupils in grades 1–8. The criterion used was promotion or nonpromotion at the end of the year. At the time, entrance age regulations in Toledo stated that a child who reached age 6 by December 31 could enter first grade in September of that year. (See Gredler, 1975.)

In the first grade, 87.5% of the older-age group were promoted compared to 83.1% of the younger group. It was also noted that there was a high failure rate in first grade for both the older and younger groups (12.5% for older children and 16.9% for younger children).

Several generalizations can be made from the Lakewood and Toledo data:

a. Emphasizing only the failures of pupils born after September as a basis for changing the school entrance age from December 31 back to September would tend to penalize the very high percentage of younger pupils who demonstrated that they could succeed.

b. Within the limits of the established entrance age, the Toledo committee found that the chronological age was a far less significant factor than had been previously assumed. Because of this fact school personnel indicated that changing the school entry age was not warranted.

The importance of the Lakewood and Toledo studies is that school personnel considered a number of variables which are not discussed in much of today's research on entrance age. Such variables include determination of the actual number of poor learners (underachievers) as well as adequately performing "young" students who would be eliminated if the entrance age was indeed raised.

Recent Entrance Age Studies of Importance

A number of improvements can be found among many of the entrance age studies completed in the 1980s. In general, more careful attention is given to obtaining a sample of adequate size than was found in the older studies. Also, more attempts are made to control for a number of variables such as social class and ability levels. Many studies from the 1930s through the 1960s used very small samples and usually included only average or above-average ability levels.

A study by Carrington (1982) reflects the trend toward a more sophisticated approach in investigations of entrance age differences in achievement and adjustment. Carrington selected a predominantly White, middle-class school district in New Jersey for her study. She studied four groups of children. They were (1) young normal-age entrants (5-0 to 5-3), (2) intermediate normal-age entrants

(5-3 to 5-6), (3) older-age entrants (5-9 to 6-0), and (4) young entrants who were admitted early to kindergarten before they reached the entry age cutoff. These children were 4 years 9 months to 5 years 0 months. (The reader should note that these early entrance children comprised the *regular* younger group in the 1950s and 1960s before many schools raised the entrance age.)

The achievement and social adjustment of these groups were examined in the first, third, and sixth grades. Carrington found no overall effect of age upon achievement. Although the young groups scored below the achievement levels of the older group, the difference was not statistically significant. It was also determined that age affected school achievement differentially among the grade levels. Although older-age children performed better in language and math in first grade, age differences in these achievement areas were not noted at the third grade. Moreover, there was no significant age effect on reading achievement at any of the three grade levels.

Carrington also determined that children whose entry to school had been postponed did not perform any better than the younger-age children. This is an important observation because some middle-class parents tend to delay entry of their late birthday boys to the following year, hoping for superior academic performance. Also, it was shown that although girls consistently demonstrated higher achievement than boys, these differences were not related to entrance age. "[These] data clearly dispute the premise that age affects the achievement of boys to a greater extent than it affects the achievement of girls" (p. 139). This study is also important from the viewpoint of the demands placed on children by the current school curriculum. It would appear that quality teaching plus lack of "push down" curriculum resulted in adequate academic performance by both young and older children.

In another study, Campbell (1984) investigated the academic achievement of younger and older entrants in the Fairfax County, Virginia, schools. Her study provides some data that indicate how complicated the entry age issue can become. The differences in achievement were found to be statistically significant for children in grades 4 and 6, with older children performing at a higher level than younger children. However, an analysis of these differences by Gredler found them to be of no educational significance (i.e., of no practical significance). Differences in achievement between boys and girls also were not of practical significance. (See further discussion in Chapter 15 concerning the importance of practical significance.) Although Campbell found achievement test differences between younger and older children, teachers did *not* give a greater percentage of Ds and Fs to younger entrants. However, they did retain considerably more young entrants. It is also important to note that over a 2-year period, younger entrants made the same rate of gain on achievement tests as did the older entrants.

It is obvious that serious questions should be raised concerning the results of the Campbell study. That is, younger entrants made similar gains in achievement when compared to older entrants, did not receive remedial services in excess of older entrants, received no more Ds and Fs on their report cards, *yet* were retained three and one half times more often in number by the teachers than were older entrants. Unfortunately, nowhere in this study is there consideration of the adequacy of the achievement test scores earned by both older and younger entrants.

The Elizabethtown Studies

In 1962, Longnecker investigated the achievement of early and late entrants in the Elizabethtown, Pennsylvania, schools. She compared the achievement of children who entered school in the age range 6-0 to 6-6 (older group) with pupils in the age range of 5-7 to 5-11 (younger group). The achievement of children who were overage and underage also was compared at different ability levels. All achievement results were then converted to stanine levels, and comparisons between groups were made.

Longnecker first demonstrated that the mean performance of both the older and younger children was above the national norm levels. Similar results also were obtained in a comparison of the achievement of boys and girls. Close relationships between the mean intelligence score and the mean achievement score were found for both age groups. Such a relationship was correctly interpreted as indicating that ability level was more important as a measure of success than was either sex or age.

In analyzing the results obtained from grades 1 through 5, Longnecker found that the achievement discrepancy between overage and underage children in the early grades decreased as they moved through the grade structure. Comparisons of children who were the youngest (i.e., birthday in December and January) were made with the oldest (i.e., birthday in the previous February and March) and resulted in the finding of no significant differences in achievement.

The importance of Longnecker's study is that in at least one school district in a state where the entrance age was relatively low in comparison to other American communities at the time, early entrant children performed quite adequately. Although there was a trend for the older group to achieve at a higher level and for girls to do likewise, these differences were neither statistically nor educationally significant.

In 1985 another study of the performance of younger and older children in the Elizabethtown schools was undertaken by Dockery. In the intervening 23 years the entry age had been changed. A comparison can thus be made as to how younger and older children fared when the entrance age was changed. Table 8-3 illustrates the different birthdates between those labeled younger and older in two research studies.

It is readily seen that the majority of children originally labeled as older in 1962 in the Longnecker study now comprise the majority of the children in Dockery's

Table 8–3.
Ages of Children Labeled Young and Old in Elizabethtown Schools in a 23-Year Time Period

	Longnecker (1962) Birthdates	Dockery (1985) Birthdates
A. Older	Feb., March, April, May	Sept., Oct., Nov., Dec.
B. Midrange	June, July, Aug., Sept.	Jan., Feb., March, April
C. Younger	Oct., Nov., Dec., Jan.	May, June, July, Aug.

Note. Data summarized from *A Comparison of the Academic Achievement of Children Entering First Grade at Different Chronological Ages,* by R. Longnecker, 1962; and *The Effects of I.Q., Sex, and School Entrange Age on the Achievement and Self-Esteem of Ten- to Eleven-Year-Old Students,* by K. A. Dockery, 1985, unpublished doctoral dissertation, Temple University, Philadelphia.

midrange group. This shift results from changes in Pennsylvania educational entrance age regulations in the intervening quarter century. Schools were allowed to change the minimum entrance age from 6-0 by February 1 to 6-0 by September 1. Thus, the younger children in Dockery's study are the children who would form the midrange group in Longnecker's study.

Seldom is it possible to find in-depth studies of the achievement of first-grade children in the same school system before and after the entrance age has been changed by almost 6 months. Therefore, the Elizabethtown studies are important in understanding the myriad problems associated with this issue. It should be remembered that Longnecker in 1962 found no significant differences in achievement between younger and older children. Twenty-three years later, Dockery arrived at the same conclusion—no differences in achievement between older and younger children in the same school existed.

Dockery (1985) also investigated the influence of IQ, sex, and school entrance on the achievement and self-esteem of 10- to 11-year-old children. The population consisted of a predominantly White (97.5%; 2.5% Asian), middle-class group of children. Her subjects were divided into three IQ groups (mean scores of 95, 108, and 122), as well as groups according to sex and age.

Dockery found that achievement scores increased as IQ increased, a result that would be expected and which has been documented in many previous studies. Boys performed less well than girls on reading, but Dockery found no significant difference between younger, midage, and older students on achievement measures of either reading or math. In addition, young girls performed less well than did young boys on the composite achievement measure which was composed of 11 subtests from the Stanford Achievement Battery. This is a factor of some importance because so many American studies indicate that girls are superior in academic achievement.

Dockery (1985, p. 76) also noted that the perspective of the Gesell Institute is that girls do best if they are 6 years old prior to school entry and boys do best if they are $6\frac{1}{2}$ before entering school. In the sample studied, approximately half of the boys would be considered overplaced by Gesellian standards. The average composite achievement and math scores, as well as many of the self-esteem scores of younger boys, also were found to be adequate. Therefore, Dockery recommended that efforts be made to meet the boys' needs in reading and in self-esteem within the classroom, rather than to delay or retain a large percentage of younger boys.

Dockery comments that one possible explanation for the lack of age differences is that the February 1 cutoff date was changed to September 1 for that school system. This date ensured that all students were at least 6 years of age at the beginning of school. As already indicated, however, when, 23 years earlier, children were allowed into the Elizabethtown schools up to 5 months younger, *no differences in achievement between the younger and older children were found.* Such a finding indicates the necessity of investigating entry age cutoffs over a period of years and ascertaining whether actual changes in reading performance have occurred.

One can only speculate as to the reasons for the lack of differences in average achievement between the two age groups when entrance age cutoffs were drastically different. It is quite possible that the majority of teachers in the Elizabethtown schools were able to provide instructional strategies that were attuned to the individual differences of the children. The fact that this one school system was able to reduce the differences between disparate age groups *regardless* of the changes in entrance age should lead to closer inspection of the instructional climate of all schools.

One negative fact noted from Dockery's 1985 study is that 17.5% of the boys and 10.5% of the girls were in a lower grade than that expected from their chronological age. This fact implies that despite the increase in entrance age and despite the addition of learning disability classes, retention continued to be practiced as a primary means of addressing children's learning problems. These percentages demonstrate that an increase in entrance age does not eliminate individual differences in learning or the propensity of teaching staff to retain children.

Social Significance of the Data

Understanding the social significance of the entrance age studies is just as important if not more so than reporting that a particular score is statistically significant or educationally significant. However, the phrase *social significance* must be carefully defined. Used within the context of the entrance age issue, the social significance factor means that a thorough review of all the variables involved in an entrance age decision must be undertaken.

For example, one aspect of entrance age studies often ignored is the *actual* level of achievement demonstrated by younger-aged children. DeWitt (1961) found statistically significant differences between younger and older children in North Kansas City schools at the end of second grade. The older children obtained a grade placement score of 3.59 and the younger children an average score of 3.28. Note should be made that whereas the older children outperformed the younger children, and though the differences were statistically significant, *both* groups of children were achieving at more than an adequate level for second grade. Attempting to change the entrance age policy for the North Kansas City school system because the older children scored significantly higher than younger children on the achievement test battery would have been foolish because both groups of children were achieving considerably above the educational level of the average second-grade child.

Another example of the importance of understanding the social significance of a study is found in the results of an investigation of the achievement of younger and older children in a Canadian school system. In this study Andreas (1972) analyzed the progress of children over the first three grades of school. A child was considered to demonstrate normal or satisfactory progress in reading if four reading units were completed by the end of the year.

Children who required 4 years to complete 12 curriculum "units" were considered to have been retained 1 year. Andreas linked the progress of young and older children to the number of reading units completed within the 3-year time span. The data are presented in Table 8-4. Andreas determined that older-aged children did complete a greater number of reading units at the end of 3 years and this result was statistically significant. Moreover, he recommended that if the school systems that participated in the study would change their entrance age to 74 months, they would dramatically lower the failure rate.

It is obvious from the data given in Table 8-4 that if the entrance age was changed to 74 months the failure rate would be lowered, *all* other conditions being equal. Changing the entrance age to 74 months would eliminate 27 of the 40 failures, thus reducing the number of failures by 67.5%. But, in so doing, the schools also would be eliminating 57 young children who had been successful, i.e., 35% of the successful reading group. A total of 84 young children would now be denied entrance to school, 68% of whom had successfully mastered the reading objectives of the first three grades. It should be noted that reporting the results of this study only in terms of statistical significance differences between younger and older children thus masks important data.

School personnel and parents must consider whether the change in entrance age is worth the related outcomes. That is, for each young child who failed in this school system and who would now be eliminated by raising the entrance age to

Table 8-4.
Relationship of Chronological Age of Students to Time Span for Completion of 12 Curriculum Units

Chronological age		Chronological age	Number of children who completed reading units within the time span shown[a]		Percent successful
Years	Months	Months	3 years	4 years	
5-8		68	3	5	38
5-9		69	11	5	69
5-10		70	9	5	64
5-11		71	16	5	76
6-0		72	10	3	77
6-1		73	8	4	67
[b]6-2		74	14	4	78
6-3		75	18	1	95
6-4		76	22	2	92
6-5		77	19	4	83
6-6		78	19	0	100
6-7		79	9	0	100
6-8		80	4	2	67
6-9		81	1	0	100
6-10		82	1	0	100
6-11		83	1	0	100
Totals ($N = 205$)			165[c]	40[d]	

Note. Data from *School Entrance Age and Subsequent Progress,* by V. J. Andreas, 1972. Unpublished master's thesis, University of Northern Colorado. Used by permission.

[a]Six children took 5 years to complete the 12 units. Three of the children were below a chronological age of 74 months and three above 75 months. These children were excluded from this chart.

[b]Recommended new entrance age.

[c]"Successful" students.

[d]"Failing" students.

74 months, two young children who would have been successful are denied the opportunity to enroll in school and successfully complete the first grade. The total failure rate in this school system over the 4-year period was 19.5% (40/205).

By eliminating all of the 84 young children (i.e., 5-8 through 6-1), the failure rate for the total group would theoretically become 11% (13/121) or a reduction of 8.5%. In order to achieve a reduction of 8.5% in failure, it should be noted that 68% (57/165) of the young children (CA 5-8 to 6-1) who had been successful are now denied entrance to school. It must be emphasized that whether school personnel decide to change the entrance age or not, the decision to be made is a *socially significant* one. Such a decision must take into account a variety of factors. *But,* the decision should not automatically be made based on one piece of data: the statistically significant difference in the achievement of older versus younger children.

Summary

Review of entrance age research has produced several important findings. A number of studies have demonstrated that younger-aged children, although obtaining a lower grade placement score than older children at the end of first and second grade, have still earned a score that has exceeded the expected grade placement score for that grade. Other studies have shown that the failure rate for younger-aged children is not that much different from the failure rate earned by older-aged children. In addition, some of the research indicates that although standardized achievement test performance of younger entrants is similar to older entrants, the retention rate of younger children is far in excess of older children, raising the possibility of subjective factors being involved in the decision to retain.

Most important, recent research (Carrington, 1982) on entrance age has produced findings showing that younger-aged children do as well academically as do older children. And in one of the few studies of the comparison of performance of older- and younger-aged children over a period of 23 years (Elizabethtown, Pa.), younger-aged children have performed as well as older-age children, despite changes in entrance age that have occurred in the ensuing years. Such results lead to the logical conclusion that entrance age differences do not constitute as important a variable affecting achievement in school as some educators and psychologists have insisted.

9

THE TRANSITION
ROOM EXPERIENCE

For several years American schools have used the transition room as a means of placing young children who are judged "unready" for the regular first-grade experience. Also referred to as a *readiness room* or *junior* or *pre-first grade,* the transition room separates young children from the regular class for a period of time. This chapter first describes the characteristics of transition rooms and then discusses the research studies conducted on the effects of the transition room experience.

Major Characteristics of Transition Programs

Transition programs are based on a particular philosophy about the development of children. They also are characterized by a particular curriculum focus.

Rationale for the Transition Program

Adherents to the transition room philosophy express their views with a simple phrase, i.e., the program provides "the gift of time." The central belief behind this view is that children have "inner time clocks" for growth (Bohl, 1984). Also, they state, many of the stresses of first grade are not academic; instead, they involve social, physical, and emotional factors as well. Proponents of a transition room maintain that not all children are ready for first grade because successful development can occur only with the passage of time; instead, some may be functioning behaviorally as 5-year-olds. School personnel who hold such a philosophy typically support a transition program that is a year in length in order to allow the child to "mature."

Within the past few years, as kindergartens have become more popular, some school systems have introduced a transition program known as a junior kindergarten. Children considered unready for regular kindergarten are first placed in the junior kindergarten, followed by regular kindergarten, and then first grade.

The typical belief is that the transition placement, whether a junior kindergarten or a pre-first class, will automatically be of value to the young child in that he or she will be able to mature emotionally, socially, and intellectually. The assumption is that the child will, after the experience, be better able to cope with academic tasks. Because the inner time clock is supposedly the major force at work in the development of these children, educational personnel who organize transition programs consider that providing any reading instruction is inappropriate in the pre-first grade curriculum.

School personnel often state that the main reason for introducing a transition program into the school is to reduce school failures. However, few studies, if any, have been conducted by school systems to test the effectiveness of the transitional year.

Major Characteristics of the Transition Room Program

The most prevalent transition program is one in which an extra year is added to the child's school program between kindergarten and first grade. However, in a few cases, the separation of the child from the regular class has varied from the typical 1-year transition experience. In one New Jersey school district, children were separated up to 5 years from the regular instructional program. In a suburban Detroit system, two of eight elementary schools established a Readiness I, II, and III classification system (Bell, 1972). Children were promoted each year from Level I through III prior to being returned to the regular class program.

In the late 1950s a variable-time version of the transition room program was developed for the Quincy, Illinois, schools. Liddle and Long (1958) devised a transition room for low-SES children who were having difficulty with the regular school program. Children were placed in the transition room for a variable time period based on their progress in the program. The purpose was to integrate the child into the regular school environment as soon as possible. Liddle and Long report that such a program was of value in improving the academic performance of many of the children.

Initial versions of the transition room took the form of a junior or pre-first grade. However, over the last 10 years, implementation of transition room programs in a number of school systems has changed. Currently emphasized is placement of the child in a junior kindergarten (at the same age that other children would enter regular kindergarten) followed by progression in the graded school structure. In some schools, the junior kindergarten is a 1-year alternative program for children who are not considered to be "developmentally ready" for kindergarten—socially, intellectually, emotionally, or physically.

Whether a prekindergarten, developmental kindergarten or pre-first grade, readiness room program, or transition class, the result is the same: A minimum of an extra year is added to the child's educational program. However, advocates of transition rooms do not consider the extra year(s) to be a form of retention. Instead, the year is described as "a grade between two grades, a line or a progression, not a pattern. Transition is proactive; retention is reactive" (Grant, 1989, p. 1).

In the average prekindergarten or transition program, the teacher is the major participant in the selection and identification of children to be placed in the program. In Broward County, Florida, elementary teachers and a primary specialist identify the children for placement, and school psychologists play little if any part in the process (Sincere, 1987). However, in many New Hampshire schools, the school psychologist also is the developmental examiner and plays a major role in the identification of children for such placement.

The Chippewa Valley, Michigan, school program guide expresses the philosophy of the readiness room program at the kindergarten level. Specifically, "developmental kindergarten is not a nursery school, nor is it a 'watered down' kindergarten; it is a program designed specifically to meet the needs of young five-year-olds" (Tisci, Lowe, Rice, & Rivard, 1984–85).

The curriculum for the readiness room in this school system includes a number of varied activities. The daily program planned by the teacher attempts to implement a curriculum that emphasizes various listening and speaking activities; "gross and fine motor skills [are included which] involve balancing, galloping, and creative movement, building with blocks, prescissor skills, and some paper-pencil tasks." The program guide also stresses the inclusion of science tasks, "to alert the children to observe, reason, infer, and draw conclusions" (p. 9). Math as well as music activities also are part of the curriculum.

Review of the developmental kindergarten program in the Eastern Lancaster County School district, Narvon, Pennsylvania, (ND), indicates that the emphasis is on social and emotional development, perceptual motor skills, work habits, and reading and math readiness. The transition room program (pre-first) in Alton, Illinois, schools emphasizes six areas of classroom instruction. They are language development, perceptual motor and visual perceptual development, reading and math readiness, and social-emotional development (Matthews, 1977). The curriculum is described in Table 9-1.

Raygor (1972) discussed some of the differences between a regular kindergarten program and a transition room (pre-first) program. While 10 to 15 minutes was spent twice a week teaching the letters of the alphabet in kindergarten, the same

Table 9–1

An Example of a Transition Room Curriculum

Curriculum area	Classroom activities incorporating curriculum objectives
Development of oral language skills as well as listening skills	Activities engaged in that stress speaking in complete sentences; using words adequately to describe objects and events. Development of listening skills so child will remember what is heard.
Perceptual-motor development	Activities stressed that will aid in development of large and small body muscles; learning to hop, skip, and jump. Increasing knowledge of body parts; understanding directional concepts (i.e., left and right). Development of balancing skills.
Visual perceptual development	Curriculum will include activities to aid in eye–hand coordination, learning different sizes and shapes; increasing attention on one activity without becoming distractible; understanding concepts such as front–back; up–down.
Reading readiness development	Activities provide instruction in recognizing letters, saying the sounds of different letters, stating the difference between letters and also sounds.
Social-emotional development	Provides instruction to help the children understand themselves and others; learning how to get along with peers and accepting responsibility.
Number readiness	Helps child to learn to count, learn number values and to understand concepts of more, less, how many, etc.

Note. Adapted from *The Effect of Transition Education, a Year of Readiness and Beginning Reading Instruction Between Kindergarten and First Grade,* by H. W. Matthews, 1977. Unpublished doctoral dissertation, St. Louis University.

amount of time was spent on letter sounds and names in the transition room (i.e., pre-first) program. No worksheets were used in kindergarten and printing was not taught, but worksheets were frequently used for practice and drill on academic skills in the transition room. An informal class structure was common in kindergarten, but in the transition room there was a definite program which reflected activities similar to those found in a first-grade classroom. However, Raygor emphasized that no formal reading instruction was provided. In general, transition rooms emphasize behavioral development and typically do not provide instruction in specific academic skills, such as printing and reading.

Example of a Reading Readiness Program

The Aumsville, Oregon, school system inaugurated a readiness room program in 1982 because school personnel believed many of the children entering first grade lacked "the developmental and academic skills needed to be successful in the first grade" (Pheasant, 1985, p. 2). The rationale for the program cited by school personnel is the Gesell Institute's estimate that 50% of school failures could be prevented if children were properly placed.

The cost to the Aumsville school system was $35,000 in 1982 for a full-time readiness teacher and an aide (one-third time) to staff the readiness room. The school also produced a parent handbook that contains "first-grade entry skills" which the child is expected to master. In essence the list is a parent version of a school readiness test that is ordinarily administered to the child in school.

Children are screened during the first week of school, attending only half days. The first-grade teachers rotate through the classrooms, leading the children in various activities and at the same time informally "assessing their skills and development." Each child is then evaluated individually by specialists in reading, speech and language, and learning disabilities, and by a first-grade teacher—all of whom engage in formal testing of the child. Tests used in the screening process included the Brigance, the Metropolitan Readiness Test, a teacher-developed screening instrument, a speech and language screening measure, and the Gesell School Readiness Test. In addition to these measures, the parent is required to complete the readiness skill rating scale referred to earlier. The decision on placement of the child in a regular first grade or the readiness room is made at the end of the first week of school.

The maturationalist philosophy of the program is reflected in the following statements. "Sometimes it is difficult for parents to accept that their child is not ready for regular first grade. [We explain] to the parents that the first grade team believes it would be better for the child to spend two years in the first grade." School personnel consider that the first year of the program allows the child to "grow," and in the second year a "strong academic program is presented" (Pheasant, 1985, p. 11).

Although extensive testing is used, Aumsville school personnel concede that they are uncertain about the placement of a few children. Their answer to that dilemma is to enter the child in a "readiness first grade" or regular first grade for a month in order to assess the child "in more depth." However, little attention is given to the reactions of children and parents if children are returned to the readiness room a month later.

School personnel emphasize that most parents understand the need for such a program. However, the school requires that the parents sign approval forms concerning readiness room placement. Also included on these forms is the statement that the child will be in a regular first grade, rather than a second grade, the following year and that to finish first grade the child invariably takes 2 years. Such a procedure reflects the lockstep nature of the program.

Aumsville school personnel evaluate the program through teacher testimonials. "[We have] received many good reports from second-grade teachers about these students. Informal monitoring of student progress shows that they have not encountered discipline or academic problems, and for the most part, they are achieving in either the average or upper groups" (Pheasant, 1985, p. 20).

The only data presented on the children's performance is a comparison of fall and spring testing scores from Level II of the Metropolitan Readiness Test. Analysis of scores for 2 consecutive years indicates that the mean percentile score was 13.21 in September and had risen to 66.47 in April.

Note must be made of four children whose percentile score was either at the 1% or 2% percentile mark in September but had risen to an average 64th percentile in April. Such an extraordinary increase raises the question as to whether the original test score was an accurate one.

A large block of time in the Aumsville program is assigned to assessment activities. However, using a teacher-devised screening test of skills without providing for any standardization of the test and without collecting any normative data does not follow proper test procedures.

No results are provided about the at-risk children who proceeded directly to first grade, their Metropolitan scores, or their current learning status in second grade. Note should be made of the fact that in the Aumsville schools, the parents of children recommended for placement in the readiness room are told during the *first week* of school that their child will spend 2 years in the first grade. It is doubtful that school personnel should make such a statement about a child's future placement at such an early time in the school year when the child has yet to begin formal work in the first grade. Such an evaluation appears to be speculative screening at its worst.

Summary of Research Conducted on Transition Programs

Research on the effectiveness of transition programs typically compares the first-grade academic performance of transition room children with that of their at-risk peers who, instead of being retained, went directly on to first grade. Some studies include additional comparison groups, and others compare academic performance several years after the early school experience. In the initial comparisons, each group is tested at the end of the first-grade experience. Thus, the transition room children are tested a year later than the at-risk children who went directly on to first grade.

Two-Group Comparisons

Three studies by Bell (1972), Talmadge (1981), and Day (1986) compared standardized test performance of transition room children with that of at-risk children who went directly to first grade.

In discussing these studies, the group that received the transition room experience is referred to as the TR group. At-risk children who went on to regular first grade instead are referred to as the AR-RF group (At Risk-Regular First).

The performance of 64 TR children in six schools was compared to that of 12 AR-RF children in a seventh school by Bell (1972). The scores of the AR-RF children on the Stanford Early School Achievement Test at the end of first grade were higher than those of the transition room groups at the end of first grade. Also, the Stanford Achievement Test was administered to each group in second grade. The AR-RF group in second grade also achieved at a higher level than the TR group on each of the four subtests although the results were not statistically significant.

These results indicate that the at-risk children fared relatively well when allowed to progress through the regular class program and also performed at a higher level than the transition group at the end of both the first and second grades.

In another study, Talmadge (1981) investigated the value of a transition room program that had been in existence for 12 years in a Washington state school system. A number of relationships among family environmental factors, cognitive variables, behavioral ratings, transition room placement, and early reading achievement were studied. Of interest here are the findings with regard to the transition program.

In this study, children were identified at the end of the kindergarten year and recommended for transition room placement on the basis of the kindergarten teacher's opinion and a low score on the Metropolitan Readiness Test. Following their 1-year placement in the transition room, the children were promoted to first grade.

Controlling statistically for cognitive ability and reading-readiness status, Talmadge found that the reading achievement of the TR group who had 2 years of schooling was no higher than that of the first-grade performance of the AR-RF group. Reading achievement was measured by performance on the Gates-MacGinitie reading test. Talmadge states that his results challenge the value of transition room placement.

In a recent study, Day (1986) investigated the effectiveness of a transitional first-grade program in a suburban school district in northeast Texas. Twenty-one children in the TR group and 12 children in the AR-RF group were tested on the Iowa Test of Basic Skills at the end of 1 year for achievement in reading and mathematics. At the end of the first year, the mean for the AR-RF group was twice that of the mean of the TR group. However, comparisons of the two groups of children were, in one sense, biased against the TR children, because reading was not emphasized in their curriculum. Of importance is that children who were identified as at risk for first-grade problems, and who would have been in the transition program except for their parents' refusal to allow such placement, were able to achieve substantial progress in reading. Nevertheless, results of this study must be considered tentative because the numbers of children in each program were small.

Multiple-Group Comparisons

Some of the studies on transition rooms also have compared the performance of the TR and AR-RF groups to the performance of regular first-graders who were not labeled as at risk. Meeks (1982) compared three such groups in the Gwinnett County, Georgia, schools (N =577). Of interest is that the Metropolitan Readiness Test administered to the children in kindergarten indicated differences between the three groups at the end of the kindergarten experience.

Files of all children attending second-grade classes during 1980–81 and 1981–82 were reviewed. During the spring of the second-grade year for each group, the Georgia Criterion Referenced Tests were administered by the classroom teachers. The tests measure 25 reading objectives and 20 mathematics objectives. No significant differences were found among the three groups at that time.

Meeks notes that school personnel believe attendance in readiness classes and participation in a manipulative curriculum affect later academic performance in a positive way. However, the data indicate that the group recommended for the transition room experience and who did not attend readiness classes (the AR-RF group) "also made enough academic gains to be considered like the other two groups" (Meeks, 1982, p. 51).

Meeks states that it is possible that the parents of the AR-RF group may have been sufficiently energized to have made an extra commitment to help their children. It is also possible that extra supportive help was forthcoming from special personnel such as reading specialists and counselors, along with instructional provisions that provided a more adaptable curriculum for these children. However, these reasons are only speculative. It is important to note that the AR-RF group were able to perform at a similar academic level in math and reading when compared to the regular group of children who also were in first grade.

In this school system, 25% of the total group of kindergarten children (142 children) were placed in a transition room; thus, a large number of children were required to attend an extra year of school. This extra year did not pay off in an achievement performance superior to the at-risk children who skipped the readiness room placement and who did not spend an extra year in school.

Note should be made of the importance of using a control group of children in studies of readiness room programs. Without the existence of this third subgroup of children, teacher testimonials would have been the major evidence presented that transition room placement was an effective one for at-risk children.

An achievement and behavioral study. One three-group study (TR, AR-RF, and regular first-graders) compared both achievement and behavioral problems (Caggiano, 1984). Middle- and upper-class children in a New Jersey school district participated. Only 3 of the 431 children in the study were from a minority group.

Children in grades 2, 4, and 6 who belonged to one of the three groups (TR, RF, and regular first grade) were tested using the Iowa Test of Basic Skills. No significant differences were found among the groups on vocabulary, reading, spelling, and math problems and concepts. In other words, the at-risk children who went directly to first grade performed at the same level as the children who spent 1 year in a transition room.

Among the researcher's concerns, however, were the differences he found among the groups as to attention problems, conduct disorder, anxiety/withdrawal, and motor excess problems as measured by the Quay-Peterson behavior rating scale. Statistically significant differences were found between the three groups, with the at-risk children who went on to regular first grade having the highest scores. However, of major importance in the interpretation of the data is that the at-risk children who did not participate in the transition program were still well within the range of normal behavioral adjustment.

In Caggiano's study, transition room children earned a total behavioral score of 9.60, at-risk children who went directly to first grade obtained a score of 13.83, and regular class children earned a score of 7.49. The data represent the scores of children from grades 1 to 7 who belonged to the various groups described above. The reader should refer to Table 9-2 for a comparison of those scores with children in Quay's normal and clinical groups.

Caggiano noted that the mean score for the at-risk children on the total test was higher than that of the TR group and the regular first-graders in the sample. However, *all* three groups fall *below* the mean scores of children in the normal sample. Thus, while the at-risk children who went directly to first grade did have a higher behavioral problem score, this group still demonstrated better adjustment than the normal sample reported by Quay-Peterson. In addition, all of Caggiano's students had scores substantially below those earned by children referred to clinicians for behavioral problems. (See Table 9-2.) Also, Caggiano's at-risk children who went directly to first grade obtained an attention problem score of 6.75, while his regular class children earned a score of 3.39 and his transition room children had an attention problem score of 1.96. These children were all tested when they completed the first grade.

Table 9–2.
Behavior Rating Scores of Normal and Clinical Groups from Quay's Data

	Mean scores (grades 1–7)[a]	
Behaviors	Scores of normative group	Scores of clinical sample
Conduct disorders (CD)	6.06	20.40
Attention problems (AP)	5.56	12.27
Anxiety; withdrawal (AW)	2.31	6.94
Motor excess (ME)	1.52	4.63
Totals	15.45	44.24

Note. Data from *Interim Manual for the Revised Behavior Problem Checklist,* by H. C. Quay and D. E. Peterson, 1983, Coral Gables: University of Miami. Copyright 1983 by University of Miami. Used by permission.

When these scores are compared to the attention problem scores from Quay's data for first-grade children (see Table 9-3) it can be easily seen that *all* of Caggiano's first-grade groups were also well *below* the average score of Quay's normal first-grade male students for attention problems.

The total behavioral problem scores of all three groups were all below the mean total scores of Quay's normative data. (See Table 9-3.) Specifically, the total behavioral scores of transition room children (5.66), at-risk children who went directly to first grade (13.50), and regular class children (8.04) are all well *below* the mean behavioral score of Quay's normative sample (female mean score 16.42; male mean score 20.50).

Thus, although the at-risk students showed more problems than did the transition room and regular class children, their total score compared well to that of Quay's normative sample for both male and female first-grade children.

Differences were found in referrals for psychological services and special education placement between the TR group and AR-RF group. Twenty-two percent of the TR children were referred for special education evaluation compared to 12% of the AR-RF children. Also, 14% of the TR group were placed in special education classes, whereas only 8% of the AR-RF group were so placed.

In summary, it can be concluded that at-risk children who went directly to first grade and therefore bypassed the transition program did not differ in academic achievement from transition program children. In addition, they also demonstrated normal adjustment to the demands of school.

Reading, language, and math comparisons. The performance of TR children, AR-RF children, and regular first-graders was assessed by Simpson (1984) in three academic areas. The 56 children included in the study were administered the Gesell test at the end of the kindergarten year, and children were recommended for transition room placement (a pre-first class) on the basis of their test scores and teacher recommendation.

The developmental lag scores of the three groups also were compared. The lag score is defined as the mean difference between the chronological and developmental age score obtained from administration of the Gesell. Differences between the three groups were minimal. The TR group mean was −14.6 months, the AR-RF mean was −13.25 months, and the mean for regular first-graders was −13 months.

In the conclusion, Simpson emphasized the growth in academic skills of the TR group after 1 year in the program. He considered the program a success as a result of this growth. The mean for the TR group was the 91st percentile on prereading skills, whereas the mean at the end of kindergarten for the AR-RF group was at the 31st percentile. A comparison of the academic performance of the three groups at the end of first grade indicated that the children who attended the transition room program had a mean percentile score of 58 in reading, the AR-RF group were at the 49th percentile, and regular first-graders had a mean percentile score of 68. Math performance for the transition room group was at the 81st percentile, for the AR-RF group at the 75th percentile, and for regular first-graders was at the 91st percentile (Simpson, 1984). Thus the data indicate that all groups demonstrated satisfactory achievement at the end of first grade.

Table 9–3.

Behavior Rating Scores of First-Grade Male and Female Children from Quay's Normative Group

	Quay's normative data for first-grade children	
Behaviors	Male	Female
Conduct disorders (CD)	6.13	4.70
Attention problems (AP)	8.20	5.64
Anxiety; withdrawal (AW)	4.01	4.56
Motor excess (ME)	2.16	1.52
Totals	20.50	16.42

Note. Data from *Interim Manual for the Revised Behavior Problem Checklist,* by H. C. Quay and D. E. Peterson, 1983, Coral Gables: University of Miami. Copyright 1983 by University of Miami. Used by permission.

Several questions as to the value of the transition program can be legitimately raised. Does a difference of 9 percentile points in reading skills justify the extra year of school for the TR children? The at-risk children who went directly to first grade scored at the mean percentile of the norming group in language (i.e., the 50th percentile) and almost at the 50th percentile for reading (i.e., 49th percentile). Also, they were above the norming group in math, scoring at the 75th percentile. These scores were achieved *without* an additional year of schooling.

Note should be made of the scores of the regular first-grade children. In kindergarten, the mean for these children in prereading skills at the end of the year was the 97th percentile. This performance level indicates a high-achieving school population.

One problem with the Simpson study, however, was the small number of children involved. Only 10 children were in the TR group in 1980, and only 7 at-risk children went directly to first grade.

Longitudinal Studies

A few studies have investigated children's progress beyond the first or second grade. May and Welch (1984) conducted an investigation of kindergarten retention in a suburban New York school system. All the children who were currently in grades 2 through 6 and who had been administered the Gesell test in kindergarten were included. Three groups were identified in the study. Children who had obtained a developmental age of below 4 years 5 months were retained an extra year in kindergarten and were named the "Buy a Year" (BAY) group. The second group was composed of children also with developmental ages below 4 years 5 months, but whose parents requested that they advance to first grade. This group was named the overplaced (OP) group. A third group of "mature" students, referred to as traditional, was also identified.

In the sixth grade, the reading performance of the three subgroups was compared. Seventy-seven percent of the traditional group were reading in sixth-grade or seventh-grade readers. Also, 71% of the children considered developmentally immature, who had proceeded directly through the regular grades instead of going to the transition room, were at the same reading level as the transition room group. However, only 41% of the developmentally immature group who had stayed behind a year (BAY) read at the sixth-grade or the seventh-grade level.

Although the number of children in the study was small ($N = 39$), the findings are comparable to other studies already cited in this chapter. In other words, placing children in kindergarten the extra year did not lead to improved reading status.

A three-group study undertaken by Raygor (1972) in the Roseville, Minnesota, schools compared TR children ($N = 37$), kindergarten-retained children ($N = 25$),

AR-RF children ($N = 30$), and regular first-graders at the end of first grade and 2 years later.

Comparisons on the Stanford Achievement Test of all children when they were in first grade indicated that the AR-RF group performed significantly lower than the other groups. However, teacher ratings taken at the end of third and fourth grades indicated that the TR group was rated significantly higher in only two of the eight comparisons—reading achievement and gross motor skills. No significant differences in teacher ratings were found for overall academic achievement, arithmetic and language achievement, or emotional adjustment. Of importance in this study is that the third-grade children were compared by the teacher to other third-grade children whereas the AR-RF group (who were one grade ahead) were compared with fourth-grade children.

Also of importance is the comparison of the AR-RF group on a standardized achievement test with a random sample of regular-class children in the fourth grade. Only scores of 2 of 10 subtests from the Stanford Achievement Test were found to be significant in favor of the regular fourth-grade children. Also, while the TR group and kindergarten-retained children obtained mean grade placement scores of 3.80 and 3.70 on the Stanford word meaning subtest at the end of third grade, the AR-RF group obtained a mean grade placement score of 4.30 at the end of fourth grade. Unfortunately, Raygor did not obtain achievement test data on the TR and kindergarten-retained children when they reached fourth grade. Therefore, it is not known whether these children would have reached or surpassed the mean grade placement score of the AR-RF group. Raygor's data indicate the importance of following the progress of children variously classified as retained, transition room, at-risk first-graders, and so on through at least 3 to 4 years of schooling.

A study by Kilby (1982) provides us with another view of a junior first-grade or transition room program. This program should be discussed because of the contradictory interpretation of the study by the author and by Shepard (1989). A junior first grade was established in Sioux Falls, South Dakota, as an early intervention program. Educators implemented a year-long transition room program following kindergarten "to provide a smooth transition into first grade" (Kilby, 1982, p. 5). It is important to note that the Sioux Falls program had enrolled 473 children over a period of 11 years with no review of the effects of the program until Kilby undertook an evaluation.

Kilby compared the readiness and achievement status of transition program children and a similar group of children who went directly to first grade. No significant differences were found between these two groups of children at the end of first grade, second grade, or in the fourth grade (Kilby, 1982; Shepard, 1989). Although Kilby states that her junior first-grade children had fewer grade retentions, Shepard (1989) comments quite correctly that the conclusion only holds if the extra year in the transition room is not counted. "If junior first-grade had been counted as retention, the junior first-graders would have had by far the greater number of retentions" (Shepard, 1989, p. 68).

A well-designed study that followed children through 4 years of schooling was conducted recently in a midwestern school system by Mossburg (1987). Two groups of children identified in the large sample ($N = 298$) were compared. One was a TR group composed of children who were placed in an extra year of schooling between kindergarten and first grade. They were compared to a group of children considered at risk who went directly on to first grade. Subjects were matched on the variables of sex, socioeconomic level, readiness test results, and entrance age to kindergarten.

Issues that were considered included differences between TR and the AR-RF groups on academic performance at the end of first, second, third, and fourth grades and whether the students were developmentally mature for middle school. The study is an important one for the school system, Mossburg noted, because the system had placed over one third of the students in transition rooms. The extra transition year cost the system $2,000,000 in 1986 alone.

The results indicated that the AR-RF group had significantly higher mean scores in reading and math in the second, third, and fourth grades. The TR group obtained higher mean scores in reading and math in the first grade, although the differences between the two groups were not statistically significant. However, this advantage was not maintained in subsequent years.

Teacher judgment was used as the measure of the children's social, emotional, and academic readiness for fifth grade. The teachers judged the AR-RF group to be more socially and emotionally mature and also to be more adequately prepared academically than the children in the TR group.

Results of this study indicate that older students (the TR group) did not demonstrate a significantly higher level of academic achievement or social and emotional maturity than younger students. Mossburg concludes by stating: "Why do we continue to promote the idea of having so many children 'buy a year' between kindergarten and first grade when the positive effects are so undramatic in first grade and nonexistent for most after first grade?" (p. 82).

Mossburg's study is considered to be a well-controlled study (Shepard & Smith, 1989b). The value of the research is enhanced because transition room children and at-risk children who went through the regular grades were followed for a period of 4 years and because the study involved a large sample of children. Thus the study provides important information about the longitudinal effects of the transition room experience.

A multiple-group study conducted by Matthews (1977) used four comparison groups in addition to 163 children in the TR group. The groups were 60 at-risk children who went directly to first grade (AR-RF), 30 regular first-graders, 45 children who had been retained in first grade, and 30 children who had started kindergarten 1 year later than the children in the other groups.

Test data indicated that transition room placement did not result in achievement in second or third grade similar to that of regular class children. Also, the AR-RF group achieved at a relatively higher rate in the second or third grades than did children who had been retained in first grade. Consistent differences between these two groups were found on 7 of 10 of the achievement test comparisons at the third-grade level in favor of the "potential first-grade failure" children who were mainstreamed. The obvious implication is that the retention of students was not an effective method in improving school achievement.

When the transition room children reached second grade, they did not perform significantly higher than the retained children or at-risk students who remained in the regular class. Also, in the third grade, the transition room children did not perform significantly higher on the total achievement battery than at-risk children who were mainstreamed.

Furthermore, in the third grade, the transition room children attained a significantly higher mean achievement score than those children who had earlier been retained in first grade. However, transition room placement did not help those children who had been identified as academically deficient to catch up and perform at the same level in the third grade as the average student.

The Matthews study (1977) is one of the most important projects conducted on the effects of transition room placement. The relatively large sample of children involved, the careful delineation of the experimental group, the inclusion of well-defined control groups, and the follow-up of the children over a period of 3 years all add to the significance of the educational findings.

The Effectiveness of a Prekindergarten Program

A recent study in a Minnesota school system investigated the effectiveness of a prekindergarten program (Burkhart, 1988). The purpose of this study was to ascertain the effects of a developmental kindergarten program on the academic performance and behavioral adjustment of children in kindergarten and first and second grades.

One hundred fourteen children enrolled in a suburban school system adjacent to Minneapolis were designated as "developmentally delayed" based on their low scores from the Gesell School Readiness Test (GSRT). Of these 114 students, 26 kindergarten children were randomly chosen for participation in the alternative kindergarten program (i.e., prekindergarten). The other 88 eligible children were placed in the regular kindergarten program because of space and staff limitations.

These groups were then compared at the end of the first year on several indices of student performance. The indices included a test of conceptual development

(Boehm, 1971) and teacher report cards. Although the developmental kindergarten children earned significantly higher scores on their report cards, there were no differences noted on the test of conceptual development.

All of the prekindergarten children were then promoted to the regular kindergarten. Of the prekindergarten-eligible children who attended regular kindergarten instead, 41% were promoted to regular first grade without the "benefit" of having attended a prekindergarten. Of 40 developmental kindergarten–eligible children who were placed in regular kindergarten and who had *the same Gesell scores* as the children who had been placed in the developmental kindergarten, 50% were promoted to first grade.

Burkhart also followed these developmental kindergarten–eligible children through the second grade. Of all the developmental kindergarten–eligible children who attended regular kindergarten, 52% were now in second grade; 46% were in third grade, while 1 child was in first grade.

Thus it needs to be emphasized that 46% of all the children designated to be placed in a prekindergarten program because of low Gesell scores, but who were instead placed in regular kindergarten because of space and staff limitations, had progressed normally from regular kindergarten to third grade.

Furthermore, when Burkhart compared the group of prekindergarten-eligible children who progressed normally from kindergarten to first grade to second grade, he found no significant differences in academic achievement or in behavioral adjustment from a random sample of second-graders.

This study has profound educational implications. A suburban school system was committed to a program of adding an extra year of schooling by requiring prekindergarten placement for many of their children. Yet analysis of the program indicated that a substantial percentage of children with low Gesell scores, when allowed to attend "regular" grades, were able to complete the kindergarten program successfully, were able to progress satisfactorily in first grade, and in fact demonstrated adequate achievement in second grade.

No test should be used for placement decisions when 50% of low-scoring children, when given an opportunity to attend regular kindergarten, are considered by their teachers to be a good risk for first grade. Furthermore, 46% of all prekindergarten-eligible children progressed normally from the regular kindergarten and first and second grades and were promoted to third grade.

This school system compounded its placement errors by maintaining a pre-first transition room for children who were considered developmentally immature. At the end of the kindergarten year, if almost half of the developmentally immature children at the kindergarten level made satisfactory progress in school without being placed in an alternate program, common sense alone dictates consideration of a new policy that would include provision of educational interventions with children while they are in the regular kindergarten and first-grade program.

The Importance of Curriculum

The overall impression obtained from these studies is that the transition room, as currently operated in the American school system, does not result in adequate progress in reading skills for the children so placed. This conclusion is reinforced by the results of a recent study of the effectiveness of transition room placement. Leinhardt (1980) undertook a study of transition room progress in the Pittsburgh public school system that is one of the few studies to utilize a predominantly Black population. Transition room−eligible children who were integrated into a regular first-grade class were divided into two groups. One group was taught with a carefully designed individualized reading program within the regular classroom, and the other group was taught using regular basal instructional material. The progress of these two groups of children also was compared with that of children placed in a self-contained transition room who were taught using the individualized reading program.

Results of the year-long program indicated that the children eligible for transition room placement but placed instead in a first-grade class and given the individualized reading program outperformed transition room−eligible children in the same regular class who were given only conventional classroom instruction. The integrated children taught with specialized materials also outperformed students who were given the special instructional program but were placed in the transition room. Leinhardt attributes these results to a combination of (a) the specialized instructional curriculum that was used and (b) the fact that the children were integrated into a regular classroom setting.

The most valuable contribution of the Leinhardt study is the description of the ways in which the instructional climate differed in the two settings. Transition-room children received an average of $2\frac{1}{2}$ hours a week less reading instruction than the transition room−eligible children placed in the regular class, and, of course, less reading material was covered in the transition room (50.4 lessons vs. 26.8 lessons). In addition, the teachers in the regular classes tested their children 15 times whereas the transition children were not tested at all. All this was accomplished despite the fact that the adult/student ratio was three times higher in the transition room.

The Leinhardt study highlights a number of facets of transition room programs that have been surmised by some investigators. The curriculum of such programs may be watered down too much; negative expectations of school personnel may contribute to the poor educational outcomes (i.e., "We know they haven't matured; therefore, we can't really do too much with them in class this year"). However, because of the very small number of transition room−eligible children placed in a regular class and involved in a specialized curriculum ($N = 9$), replication of the study is recommended.

Simply to group children based on some arbitrary factor such as maturational age will not be helpful. As has been previously mentioned, the validity of such arbitrary practices will be increasingly challenged. Immaturity and maturity are defined so differently by teachers that the terms have become instructionally useless. Some teachers state that an "immature" child is one who has social adjustment problems. Others insist that what is primary is the maturity of the child's visual perceptual performance (Dennler, 1987).

An example of the inappropriateness of the "immaturity" label for children's learning problems is demonstrated in a recent study of school placement (Rapala, 1990). One hundred thirty-nine children in the West Boylston, Massachusetts, school district were screened with the Gesell School Readiness Test in the spring prior to entry to school. Twenty-five were identified as "immature" (i.e., behavior age scores 4.5/5 or below). These children were subsequently placed in a prekindergarten program followed by placement in regular kindergarten. One hundred fourteen children were considered to be ready for kindergarten (i.e., behavior age scores 5 or above) and subsequently attended regular kindergarten in the fall following the spring screening process. The records of these 139 children were reviewed when they were in first and/or second grade. Thirteen of the 25 immature children (or 52%) were now in special education programs, whereas 16 (or 14%) of the "ready" group were enrolled in special education.

Rapala emphasizes that a large percentage of those labeled immature were identified as having learning difficulties which necessitated some form of specialized instruction. She suggests that the "gift of time" was not sufficient for this group of children and the prekindergarten program could be considered inappropriate because so many of the children performed poorly in the classroom subsequent to their prekindergarten placement. Rapala believes that the poorer performance of these so-called immature children probably reflects specific cognitive deficiencies rather than developmental immaturity. She points out that placement on the basis of behavior age scores from the Gesell is inadequate in that such a placement typically results in nonspecific, nonacademic-type activities. Instead she recommends that more active remedial intervention programs be substituted (p. 3).

The gift of time, which meant an extra year in prekindergarten, was not sufficient for the children in this Massachusetts school. "Fortification against school failure was not afforded to the children who participated in the prekindergarten program" (p. 3). Rapala continues: "Assignment to a program that is simply less academic has no empirical basis" (p. 4). Her conclusion is similar to that reached by Shepard and Smith (1985) in their study of kindergarten retention in the Boulder, Colorado, schools and by Gredler (1984), who also raised serious questions as to the effectiveness of transition rooms. School districts that continue to offer only programming based on labeling a child as immature will find that such placement will be increasingly challenged. School districts will also find ever-increasing amounts of time taken up in individual and legal confrontations.

A study by Dennebaum (1991) also raises questions as to the efficacy and value of a transition classroom program. Ninety-five children who were currently in the fourth and fifth grades of a Rhode Island school comprised the population that was tested. Children were chosen on the basis of their fit into one of four groups as well as test scores available in their file folders. One group consisted of children retained in kindergarten; one group was made up of children placed in a transition room before first grade; another group was composed of children recommended for retention or transition room placement but who went on to first grade anyway. The fourth group was a control group who were promoted from kindergarten to first grade without teacher reservation. Ability scores among the groups were not significantly different.

Comparisons of achievement scores in grades 2 and 3 indicated that the children who were recommended for retention and/or transition room but who went directly to first grade performed as well as the regular class children in first, second, and third grades. Although children who were retained in kindergarten performed at a lower level than transition room–placed children, the transition room children, now a year older, did not perform any better than children who were recommended for the extra year program but went on anyway to first grade.

A study of the use of a transition room program in a suburban school district near Rochester, New York, underscores the need to examine carefully the assumptions and organization of any intervention program for young children and the value of an approach different from that reported by Rapala. The particular school district in question provided "transition" classes after kindergarten for children considered to be "not ready" for grade 1.

The decision to place children in such a program was based on teacher identification of children as they were observed and interacted with during the kindergarten year. A school counselor then administered to the children designated as at risk a "battery of screening instruments predictive of first grade success" (Dolan, 1982, p. 102).

Dolan states that a flexible curriculum program was followed to accommodate children with varying levels of perceptual, language, and social deficiencies. That this curriculum was more than the watered-down version usually found in a transition room program is indicated by the number of children who went *directly* to second grade at the end of the transition year. Of the 123 children placed in this district's transition program over a 6-year-period, 53 (43%) were subsequently placed in second grade at the end of the year, thus bypassing first-grade placement.

Such data illustrate two important facets of this program. First, school personnel were in effect offering a true remediation/intervention program rather than a "time to grow" program. Second, the large percentage of children who made rapid progress and were placed in second grade challenge the maturationalist view that additional time is the critical variable in school progress.

Dolan emphasizes that the transition to first grade children performed at a higher level on reading and math tests than did the at-risk children whose parents refused transition placement and had them go directly to first grade. However, these differences should be questioned for several reasons. First, the parent refusal group was very small, numbering only 16 in three different grades. Second, Dolan did not adjust for the initial differences between the three groups (Shepard, 1989, p. 70). Thus the significance of the differences that were found is not clear.

In addition, more attention frankly should have been given to the children whose parents refused placement in a transition class. The comparisons made by Dolan were with at-risk children who went on to first grade, but were then *not* provided any extra help once there. Only the children whose parents placed them in the optional first-grade class received extra help. This assistance consisted of small classes of 12 to 15 children with a teacher and full-time aide. That such help can make a positive difference is seen in Leinhardt's study (1980) where promoted at-risk children, given special help, performed better than retained children (Gredler, 1984). The emphasis on individualized assessment, continuous evaluation of the children, and placement in a regular grade throughout the year transformed this so-called "transition" program into a truly intervention/remedial program. Because of the large percentage of children who were placed in the second grade by the end of the year (43%), it would appear that with even further refinement of the program, such as including elements of intervention approaches similar to the Reading Recovery and Writing to Read programs, fewer children in fact would need to be retained and spend the following year in the first grade.

Summary

The use of transition rooms as a placement option for at-risk children has increased dramatically within the last 30 years. In the state of New Hampshire, 80% of the public schools use a transition room placement for children considered to be "unready" for first grade. (See Chapter 10 for further information on New Hampshire transition programs.) Analysis of a broad sample of research studies on transition rooms raises definite questions about the degree of educational "payoff" obtained with such programs. The research clearly indicates that transition room children either do not perform as well or at most are equal in achievement levels to transition room–eligible children placed in regular classrooms.

Ostensibly the transition room program provides an opportunity for the child to mature within an appropriately structured environment; yet, as the careful investigations of Carrington, Talmadge, and Matthews demonstrate, this type of program does not produce the positive results that the maturationalists insist will occur.

Although attitudes of school personnel toward the transition room generally are quite favorable, few, if any, schools collect any data to indicate the educational status of children so placed. Instead, statements of faith from school personnel abound. Few programs maintain effective monitoring systems to indicate the progress of the children. Although a small teacher/student ratio often exists in the transition room, research also indicates that less time is devoted to academic activities than is given to children who are eligible for the transition room but who are placed in the regular class.

The importance of evaluating such programs cannot be overestimated. Real-life consequences that are negative for the children involved are frequently a result of such placement. Twenty-five percent of a group of kindergarten children in Gwinnett County (Ga.) were placed in a transition room instead of first grade. But as has been reported in this chapter, the at-risk children whose parents refused to let them attend such a program and instead placed them in first grade were found to have made satisfactory progress when evaluated at the end of second grade and in 1 year less time than the at-risk children who were sent to the transition room program. Fifty percent of Minnesota children with Gesell scores as low as those placed in a prekindergarten but who were instead placed in regular kindergarten were promoted to first grade and also demonstrated academic achievement similar to regular class children when in the second grade.

Implementation of an educational program based on a maturationalist philosophy does not appear to be adequate. Approaches other than placement in a transition room program need to be considered by school personnel.

Arguments for transition rooms usually emphasize the benefits of a class size smaller than would be found in the regular first grade and an instructional program that is more geared to children who have been labeled as immature and who thus need additional time before they will be ready for first grade. Dolan's (1982) study of a transition room program, one that instead offered an intervention program based on the specific needs of the children, is one example of a remediation program that helped a large percentage of students (43%) to join the regular classroom at the end of the year. Thus many children profited from the intervention program without having to remain in school an additional year.

10

RETENTION IN KINDERGARTEN AND FIRST GRADE

Retention has been an established policy in American schools since the turn of the century. In recent years, concern over educational excellence and the imposition of higher promotion standards in some school systems have generated increased interest in the use of retention as a school policy. However, few topics bring forth more concern from parents than that of possible retention for their child in kindergarten or first grade.

Several issues are important in the discussion of retention as a school policy. One is that using retention in kindergarten as a method to alleviate learning problems differs from the retention of children in the fourth or fifth grade. When a child is placed in a prekindergarten instead of kindergarten—one form of retention—the retention is occurring *before* the introduction of formal learning and *before* the child has an opportunity to respond to instruction (Gredler, 1978). A similar situation exists when a child is recommended to repeat kindergarten.

Related to the issue of retention is the issue of educational standards. In recent years, discussions of educational standards have escalated. The loss of American preeminence in world affairs and its emergence as a debtor nation in the last 11 years has contributed to increased anxiety among the American people. This anxiety is reflected in part in the increased concern about the educational system. As a result, there has been a call for higher educational standards.

The concern about possible lax educational standards has led to an increase in student retention. In New York City, for example, the school system introduced a "gate" policy in the fourth and seventh grades. Students who did not perform adequately were placed in a remedial class. They were not allowed to progress beyond these grades until they attained a minimum competency level as defined by standardized test scores and teacher evaluations.

However, over the years, the policy broke down; the quality of some of the remedial classes also became an issue. It was found that 40% of students formerly in the Gates program dropped out of school before graduation compared to 25% of the students with comparable reading levels who had obtained a waiver from being retained (Berger, 1990). Obviously the New York City retention policy is due for a much needed review.

Currently, public schools in the United States retain 2.4 million children a year, or 6% of the total school population. The cost of this extensive use of retention as a means of improving academic performance is estimated to be $10 billion a year (Berger, 1990). An educational policy that involves so many children and at such a high cost certainly should be examined in more detail, particularly because a large percentage of the retained students are found in kindergarten and first grade.

It is therefore important to discuss at length the relevant facets of retention as a school policy. In this chapter, issues related to retention are discussed, including retention rates, teacher beliefs and practices, and research studies on retention.

Incidence of Retention

Retention as a school practice became commonplace when grade schools were introduced into American education in the 1840s (Moran, 1988). During the early years of the public grade school, up to one half of the students were retained at least once (Bucko, 1986). Even at the turn of the century it was determined that half of all elementary school students had been retained in grade.

During the years from 1930 to 1950 it was estimated that 20% of the students had been retained once (Ypsilantis & Bernart, 1957). However, with the increased demand for minimum competency testing, retention rates have increased significantly (Wolf & Kessler, 1987).

Retention rates continued to vary in the 1980s. The state of California reported a retention rate of 4.4% for the primary grades in 1985–86. In other states, kindergarten retention for 1985–86 ranged from 1.4% in Mississippi to 10.5% in Florida. For first grade, the retention rate varied from 1.6% in Hawaii to 20% in Arizona (Shepard & Smith, 1989b).

Nationwide, the annual failure rate changed little overall from 1979 to 1985. However, some states showed dramatic increases in their overall retention rate during those years. For instance, Arizona's annual rate increased from 3.5% to 7.2% in this 6-year period (Shepard & Smith, 1989b).

Retention rates also vary for subgroups in the school population. In a recent examination of retention rates for 13- to 15-year-old children, Moran (1988) compared the rates for males, females, Whites, and Blacks. In the period from 1978 to 1983, retention rates for all groups had increased. However, females were retained less frequently than males, with White females showing the lowest rates, i.e., from 13.9% to 19.4%. In contrast, retention rates for White males ranged from 21.7% to 32.7%. The rates for Black males were the highest, varying from 31.6% to 52.5%. These data indicate that the retention problem cannot be discussed without specific reference to the composition of the student body.

Also of interest are the retention rates of schools in other countries. Analysis of retention in the first three grades in elementary schools of Latin America indicates that average retention rates in the 1960s ranged from 29% to 74% (Schiefelbein, 1975). Recent data from Japan and the United Kingdom indicate that the annual rate of children repeating primary grades is 0% in the school systems of those two countries (Shepard & Smith, 1989b).

Annual Retention Rate Versus Cumulative Rate

The annual retention rate is reported as a percentage of a total number for a grade, school, district, or state. For example, retention of 35 first-grade children out of 150 for school X in 1990 results in a 23.33% rate for that year.

Reporting an average rate for a district, school, or state, however, can mask wide variations in specific units. For example, the state of California reported the average retention rate for the primary grades for 1985–86 as 4.4%. However, the retention rate in California school districts ranged from 0% to 50% (School Readiness Task Force, 1988). Similarly, the annual retention rate for Arizona in 1985–86 was 7.2%, but this figure masks the high rate of retention in kindergarten (8%) and first grade (20%) in that state (Shepard & Smith, 1989b).

Also of importance is the fact that the retention rate for any one year for a grade, school, or district does not reflect the full impact of retention policies. The cumulative retention rate (CRR) over several grades is a major consideration. Specifically, the cumulative retention rate for a particular school year is the sum of the retention rates for each grade for that year. For example, a school with a 1985–86 retention rate for first, second, and third grades of 7.8%, 6.2%, and 4.0% has a cumulative rate of 18%. That is, the 18% is an additive rate, not a percentage of a total number. It is used as a total rate index across years per school system. Any meaningful discussion of retention rate should include the calculation of the CRR in addition to the annual rate (Rodgers, 1970). The CRR is useful in comparisons between schools as well as in determining the extent of nonpromotion in a particular school system.

Educational researchers in 1920 recommended that the annual rate of retention should on the average be less than 2% per year and that at the most the cumulative rate should not exceed 8% by the beginning of grade 7 (Rodgers, 1970). The consensus among educators at that time was that a CRR of 20% was excessive. In an investigation of the extent of retention in Ohio schools for the 1965–66 school year, Rodgers (1970) classified schools with a CRR of 14% or more through sixth grade as having a high retention rate. In his analysis he found that 37% of all schools in Ohio had cumulative retention rates greater than 14% for the school year 1965–66.

To illustrate the utility of the CRR in the analysis of retention practices in a particular school district, data from school districts "A," "B," and "C" are used. (See Table 10-1.) All of these school districts are located in Delaware County, Pennsylvania. School district A had a CRR of 20.3% for kindergarten and first and second grades. The mean CRR of all schools in Delaware County for that school year was 10.36% for those three grades. It should be remembered that a 7% CRR for three grades indicates a high retention rate according to criteria established by Rodgers. That is, by the end of grade 6, the cumulative retention rate should not exceed 8% (Gredler, 1980; Rodgers, 1970). However, the computations did not include kindergarten, but represented grades 1 through 6. If Rodgers' criteria are followed, the CRR from kindergarten through second grade should be no larger than 3.4%.

It is important to note that both school districts A and C are located in upper-middle-class communities with students whose IQs are above average. School district B had a CRR of 21%, practically the same rate as middle-class school district A. Yet school district B is an inner-city school district where the children's IQs range from the high 80s to low 90s. The community encompasses a large number of families at the poverty level. A predominant reason for the high CRR in school district A at the time was probably due to the educational philosophy subscribed to by the staff. School personnel believed in the maturational point of

Table 10–1.
Comparison of Cumulative Retention Rate of Specific Delaware County Schools from Kindergarten Through Second Grade

School (Kindergarten, 1st-, and 2nd-graders)	Cumulative retention rate (CRR)
School District A	20.3%
School District B	21.0%
School District C	2.01%
Mean of Delaware County schools	10.36%
Ideal cumulative retention rate	3.4%

Note. Data from Pennsylvania State Department of Education, *Retention Rates in Pennsylvania Schools, 1970–71*, 1971. Unpublished report, Harrisburg, PA.

view concerning school readiness. They believed that children were being allowed to enter school at too early an age. The result of this philosophy is reflected in the very high CRR for the first three grades. On the other hand, the educational staff in district C, another middle-class school, were not committed to a maturational philosophy and their CRR of 2.01% reflects this different point of view.

Data from 22 school districts in Delaware County as found in Table 10-2 illustrate the average CRR for these school systems for 1 school year.

It would be enlightening to ascertain how instructional remediation programs were organized in the five schools with the lowest CRR (i.e., 0–4) and compare these with two schools with the highest CRR (20–22).

Cumulative retention rates in selected school districts surrounding Atlanta are illustrated in Table 10-3. As indicated in Table 10-3, all the districts (excluding Gwinnett County, which uses transition rooms) have exceptionally high retention rates. The cumulative rates at the end of second grade exceed the percentage (8%) recommended for *all* six grades (Rodgers, 1970).

Table 10-4 compares the CRR for grades 1–6 for four states for 1979–80 and 1985–86. The data indicate that the use of nonpromotion as a school policy has escalated over the 6-year period. For Arizona, the retention rate for 1985 has increased almost two and one-half times over the 1979–80 rate. For Mississippi, the retention rate was very high in both 1979 and 1985. In contrast, the rate of increase for New Hampshire was only one and one-third over the 6-year period. However, the CRR does not reflect extensive use of retentions in the form of transition room programs in that state. Also of importance is that the CRR for three

Table 10–2.
Cumulative Retention Rates for the School Year 1970–71 in Kindergarten Through Second Grades in 22 School Districts in Delaware County

No. of schools	Cumulative retention rate (%)								
	0–1	2–4	5–7	8–10	11–13	14–16	17–19	20–22	Total *N*
	1	4	5	1	2	5	2	2	22

Middle-class school district C is located here

Middle-class school district A and inner-city school district B

Note. Data from Pennsylvania State Department of Education, *Retention Rates in Pennsylvania Schools, 1970–71,* 1971. Unpublished report, Harrisburg, PA.

Table 10–3.

Cumulative Retention Rate (CRR) for K–2nd Grade for Selected Georgia School Districts in 1990[a]

	K	1	2	CRR
[b]City of Atlanta	10.9	10.6	6.8	28.3%
Clayton County	8.3	4.7	1.6	14.6%
Cobb County	6.4	4.3	2.0	12.7%
[b]City of Decatur	15.9	13.6	10.6	40.1%
DeKalb County	7.2	5.1	2.4	14.7%
Fulton County	7.5	4.4	2.9	14.8%
[c]Gwinnett County	0.0	0.1	0.4	0.5%
City of Marietta	6.6	8.6	2.5	17.7%
State of Georgia	8.7	7.4	3.8	19.9%

[a]Data from "Schools Flunk When Kids Fail a Grade, Experts Say," by B. White, May 6, 1990, *Atlanta Journal and Constitution,* pp. 1 & A-13. Copyright 1990, *Atlanta Journal and Constitution.* Used by permission.

[b]School districts that are predominantly Black.

[c]Gwinnett County schools use transition rooms.

states in 1985–86 (Arizona, Georgia, and Mississippi) ranged from 41% to 46% for the first six grades.

Table 10-5 illustrates the very high retention rates for the first 3 years of schooling for these states for 1985–86. For all states, the CRR at the end of grade 2 greatly exceeds the recommended rate (8%) for the first six grades. It should also be noted that at the end of grade 2 the cumulative retention rate is more than half of the total CRR accrued through grade 6. Such data indicate the liberal use of retention practices in kindergarten through the second grade.

In Table 10-5 the reader will also note that New Hampshire supposedly has the lowest CRR of the four states listed. However, as noted previously, the New Hampshire CRR of 17.2% for kindergarten through grade 2 is much lower than is the actual case because of educational practices that are not reported in these statistics.

First, the kindergarten retention rate of 4.4% in New Hampshire schools is based on a restricted number of schools because only 54% of New Hampshire schools had a public kindergarten in 1986. More important, the data also do not reflect readiness room placement of children. Eighty percent of New Hampshire public schools used a readiness room/transition room program in the school year 1986–87. Placement of children in such a program constitutes a retention and should be so noted as it is in California and Florida schools. Therefore it would

Table 10–4.
Cumulative Retention Rate (CRR) for the First Six Grades (Excluding kindergarten)

	1979–80 school year	1985–86 school year
Arizona	18.7%	45%
Georgia	27.4%	41.3%
Mississippi	42.5%	45.7%
New Hampshire	17.2%	23.4%

Note. Data from *Flunking Grades: Research and Policies on Retention,* L. A. Shepard and M. E. Smith (Eds.), 1989a, Philadelphia: The Falmer Press. Copyright 1989 by The Falmer Press. Used by permission.

be important to ascertain the CRR for New Hampshire children with the inclusion of the transition room placement.

Table 10-6 illustrates the average cumulative retention rates for three types of New Hampshire schools for the school year 1986–87. Group A includes schools with both public kindergarten and transition rooms; Group B includes schools with transition rooms only; and Group C includes schools with public kindergartens only.

As indicated, from 23% to 28% of the children eligible for first grade are retained through placement in transition rooms. Also of interest is that such placement does not lead to a greatly reduced retention in first grade, i.e., 7.22 and 7.51 as opposed

Table 10–5.
Cumulative Retention Rate (CRR) 1985–86 for Selected States for Kindergarten and First and Second Grades

	Average retention rate			CRR at end of grade 2	CRR K through 6
	Kindergarten	First	Second		
Arizona	8.0%	20.0%	8.0%	36.0%	53%
Georgia	8.0%	12.4%	6.7%	27.7%	49.3%
Mississippi	1.4%	16.1%	7.0%	24.5%	47.1%
New Hampshire	4.4%	9.1%	3.7%	17.2%	27.8%

Note. Data from *Flunking Grades: Research and Policies on Retention,* L. A. Shepard and M. E. Smith (Eds.), 1989a, Philadelphia: The Falmer Press. Copyright 1989 by The Falmer Press. Used by permission.

to 8.80 for schools with no transition rooms. However, all the retention rates exceed the criterion of an average cumulative rate of no greater than 8% established by Rodgers (1970) for grades 1 through 6.

Only with the inclusion of transition room data is it possible to learn the true retention rate for a school system. Although the reported cumulative retention rate for the state at the end of grade 2 is 17% (Table 10-5), the actual CRR for New Hampshire schools with transition rooms included ranged from 31% to 35% *at the end of first grade.* (See Table 10-6.)

Teacher Beliefs and Perceptions About Retention

Discussed in this section are teacher beliefs about the nature of development, rationales for retention, some effects of retention, and a decision-making process to examine all recommendations for retention.

Table 10–6.
Average Annual Retention Rate and Average Cumulative Retention Rate for Schools with and Without Kindergarten and Transition Rooms (NH State Department of Education, 1988)

	Average kindergarten retention rate (%)	Average transition room placement rate of first grade–eligible children (%)	Average annual first-grade retention rate (%)	Average cumulative retention rate at end of first grade
Group A: Schools with both kindergarten and transition rooms (N = 73 towns)	1.29%	22.76%	7.22%	31.27%
Group B: Schools with transition rooms only (N = 99 towns)	—	27.73%	7.51%	35.24%
Group C: Schools with kindergarten only (N = 44 towns)	5.23%	—	8.80%	14.03%

Note. Data from State Department of Education (1988). *Analysis of Schools with Kindergartens and Transition Rooms.* Unpublished data, Concord, NH.

Teacher Beliefs About Development

Basic beliefs about the nature of learning and development form the foundation for much of educational practice. Theoretical foundations of readiness described in Chapter 2 range from that of an internally controlled process to a process that is strongly influenced by social and educational events.

Similarly, teacher beliefs about the nature of development influence both their beliefs and practices related to retention. In a series of semistructured interviews of 40 teachers, Smith and Shepard (1988) found four beliefs about child development and the role of the environment. These beliefs are summarized in Table 10-7.

The belief referred to as nativist also may be referred to as Gesellian because it is consistent with the view of child development outlined by Ilg and Ames (1965). The other three belief systems are described by Smith and Shepard (1988) as nonnativist because each one advocates some environmental intervention. The major difference between the remediationist and the diagnostic-prescriptive is that remediation is a general instructional approach whereas the diagnostic-prescriptive approach targets a particular deficit.

Table 10–7.
Teacher Beliefs About Development

Belief system	Description
Nativist	The child's growth is primarily a psychological unfolding of abilities. Children who are having difficulty in kindergarten or first grade need time to mature.
Remediationist	Children of legal age for kindergarten are ready for school and should be taught. The curriculum is subdivided into smaller segments, and remediation is provided in the form of tutors, pull-out programs, and other adjustments.
Diagnostic-prescriptive	Inadequacies in school readiness result from a defect in one or more of the traits essential for learning, e.g., auditory memory. The belief is that the defect can be corrected by specific, concentrated training.
Interactionist	Learning is a complex interaction between the psychological characteristics of the child and the environments arranged by the teachers. Materials selected by the teacher should be based on an ongoing analysis of each child.

Note. Adapted from "Kindergarten Readiness and Retention: A Qualitative Study of Teachers' Beliefs and Practices," by M. L. Smith and L. A. Shepard, 1988, *American Educational Research Journal, 25,* pp. 317–319. Used by permission.

Smith and Shepard hypothesized that teacher belief systems would be related to their retention practices. They found that of those who held a nativist (i.e., Gesellian) belief system, 84% were classified as high retainers. That is, they retained more than 10% of their kindergarten children. Of those considered to be nonnativists, only 5% were high retainers.

Rationales for Retention

Several researchers (Byrnes, 1989; Gredler, 1978; House, 1989; Larrabee, 1984) note that retention is a frequently used approach for identified problems. Byrnes (1989) and Larrabee (1984) indicate that retention is used because it can be implemented without disrupting the organizational set of either the school district or the classroom. Teachers sometimes state that they would rather retain a child who possibly might not need it than to promote a child who should have been retained. Such a belief indicates the prevalence of use of retention practices and the lack of alternative programs available as viable options for the child.

However, the rationale for retention of first-grade children may be quite nebulous, as indicated by an analysis of responses given by teachers in a small southeastern school system. Comments included "immaturity" (28%); academic failure (32%); no reason given (24%); and miscellaneous reasons, such as poor attendance and late entry (15%) (Abidin, Galloway, & Howerton, 1971).

The widespread acceptance of retention is indicated by the fact that such decisions often are made early in the school year. Byrnes (1989) discovered that teachers pinpointed children who might possibly be retained in first grade as early as January. Gredler (1984) found one teacher who had "given up" on certain children in December of the school year, and labeled them as possible retainees. The teacher wanted an IQ test administered to bolster her case that these children had below-average intelligence and therefore should be retained. Also reported by Gredler (1984) was an interview with an elementary school principal who directed all his first-grade teachers to report possible first-grade retentions to him by February 1. The purpose was to forestall the problem of the previous year when teachers handed first-grade children their final report card of the year with the statement that the child was retained. No previous comment about possible retention had been made either to student or parent.

The value of retention as a school practice often is cited as a rationale for its use (Gredler, 1978; House, 1989). Moreover, the belief in the value of retention is so extreme that it has taken on the characteristics of a "tightly held ideology" (House, 1989, p. 209).

The beliefs about the positive effects of retention are indicated in one study conducted by Faerber and Van Dusseldorp (1984). Teachers in Alaskan school districts enrolled in graduate classes at the University of Alaska responded to several statements about retention.

Ninety percent of the teachers agreed that retention could be a positive step in a child's education. Ninety-seven percent believed that a child's lack of achievement could be the result of immaturity because the child's birth date fell in the last half of the year. Eighty-four percent of the respondents thought that retaining students would help them catch up academically. Only 40% thought that retention had a detrimental effect on a student's self-concept, and only 36% believed that retention had a detrimental effect on a child's attitude. Furthermore, only 3% of the teachers thought that retention had a detrimental effect on a child's academic growth. Finally, 94% were in agreement that retention provided a child with time to grow and mature and thus increased success in learning. Such beliefs indicate the importance of retention as a central tenet for these public school teachers.

Interviews conducted by Smith (1989) provide further support for the belief that retention is not a negative experience for the child. Most teachers, for example, rejected the possibility that children would be bored by repeating the classroom work they had had previously. Teachers also stated the following beliefs:

(1) There is no doubt in the teacher's mind that the child's achievement and adjustment will be improved by a second year in first grade.
(2) The teachers' own personal experience from the classroom has "proved" to them that retention was helpful. (However, this view is related to the fact that the child is already familiar with the work and the class routine.)
(3) No mention was made of the possible value of keeping a child with peers to enhance social adjustment.
(4) The teacher can't believe the child could have succeeded if promoted (Smith, 1989, pp. 129–150)

It is important to note that one Gesellian (Raygor, 1972) conceded that under certain conditions transition room children could probably have been successful if they had been directly placed in regular first grade. Raygor felt that a small amount of extra help given to these children could have provided the necessary aid that they needed.

Also supporting the practice of retention is the belief that no evidence exists to support alternative solutions. As Smith (1989) states, the use of a control group would provide the necessary information about the effectiveness of retention to the teachers. She says: "Two groups start out alike, one gets the treatment—in this case retention—and the other group gets an alternative treatment or control condition" (p. 148). Use of a control group demonstrates the outcome if the retained child had been promoted instead. "Since teachers lack this abstract information, they rely on their direct, but inadequate experience" (p. 148). In addition Smith (1989) mentions that teachers seldom obtain any information on what ultimately happens to retained children during their school tenure.

A psychologist who writes a newspaper column on parenting and who believes firmly in retention states there is "no reliable body of evidence [that] clearly supports or doesn't support retention" (Rosemond, 1989, p. 3-E). The usual practice of individuals who support retention is to cite testimonials from teachers as to the value of the practice. Typical is the kindergarten teacher in Long Beach, California, describing the seven "early birthday" children in her class. Quoted by Rosemond (1989), she stated:

> They were of at least average intelligence. Their only handicap was they were so young. The parents were all supportive of their retention. This year, they had a wonderful kindergarten experience and are ready and eager for first grade. (1989, p. 3E)

This attitude is similar to that noted by McDaid (1950) in his study of transition rooms in Detroit and discussed at length in Chapter 9, on transition rooms. In McDaid's study, transition room children performed no better than at-risk children sent directly to first grade. Nevertheless, the Detroit teachers *knew* that many children "blossomed" by being placed in the transition room for 1 year and that the experience was a helpful one for most of the children. These beliefs are expressed by many teachers despite the fact that the data collected by McDaid indicated no difference in the academic performance of transition room children and those at-risk children who went directly to first grade.

Beliefs and opinions also hold sway with much more tenacity in regard to the retention of young children because those being retained, i.e., the kindergarten or first-grade child, do not have the power to influence, argue about, or block the decision. Up to the present the power to retain has been one of the few decisions the teacher has been able to make without extensive review by other school personnel and parents. In contrast, placement of a child in a special education class cannot be made solely on the teacher's recommendation. Once the child has been referred, the recommendations of the school psychologist and other ancillary personnel also enter into the placement decision.

Also important is that the feelings of children often are perceived as being relatively unimportant in the process of retention. As Rosemond (1989) states: "Retention can, indeed, be initially traumatic for certain children, but I find with adequate adult support the trauma is usually short-lived" (p. 3E). Rosemond buttresses his opinion from his clinical experience but offers no other evidence. He also quotes Ames to the effect that it is "better to traumatize them once and get it over with than to have them face problems every day for the next twelve years" (p. 3E).

Effects of Retention

When asked about the negative effects of retention, few of the teachers interviewed by Smith (1989) named even one such effect. However, Byrnes (1989) states that children feel anxious about the reactions of their classmates to their retention, consider themselves as school failures, and view their retention as a punishment. (Chapter 13, on parental concerns, discusses this issue in more detail.) She also notes that the retained year provides little more than a repetition of the same curriculum for the child. In her analysis of retention policies, Byrnes found that the responsibility of dealing with the child's fears and concerns about retention is usually left to chance.

Another effect of retention is that learning problems may not receive needed attention. Byrnes comments in her study of children retained in primary grades (i.e., grades 1, 3, and 6) that a number of the children were found to have various visual and auditory perceptual disabilities. She states: "By implication it appears that children had typically been retained without any special intervention, either adaptation of instruction or in-depth assessment" (p. 127). Byrnes reports that only one teacher referred a retained child for a complete psychological assessment in order to determine whether the child needed special services. In Massachusetts, Chapter 766 regulations (1976) require that any child considered for retention be referred for a psychological examination *before* any such decision is made. It should be noted that the learning-disability movement received its impetus from the fact that many children who were not retarded or who were without major emotional problems were being failed (Gredler, 1978).

Response to the High Retention Rate

Moran (1988) accepts the fact that retention is a major part of the present-day school organization. He proposes that some form of structured decision process be established that would involve referrals of possible retainees to an advisory committee. This committee would then examine several sources of information. Included are demographic data, the school progress of retained students in subsequent years, the records of students promoted with or without summer school, and those placed in a junior first grade.

Moran understands that many retention decisions are made without adequate analysis of the student's progress. However, to attempt to have a committee be responsible for monitoring all the variables involved in a retention decision would be an overwhelming task.

Understandably, Moran is attempting to bring order out of what often is a chaotic school process. However, his proposal is not likely to succeed for two reasons. First, too few alternatives to retention are available in his proposed school program. Second, no attempt is made to establish a groundwork to change teacher perceptions and practices in the overuse of retention as a remedial program for children who demonstrate learning problems.

Moreover, Moran's attempt to set up a committee to pass on the worth of placement of children into junior first grade (transition room) also fails to recognize the value of the research studies already completed. These studies, some of which have been reviewed in prior chapters, demonstrate the failure of junior first-grade placement as a viable option for young children with learning problems (Gredler, 1978).

Lieberman (1980) also attempts to organize a coherent policy but states some qualifications. He says that retention offers a valuable programmatic option for kindergarten through second grade. However, Lieberman goes on to state that retention of a child always means that the student will have a need for service above and beyond those offered in regular class programming. "It is doubtful that retention in and of itself will work to the benefit of the child" (p. 272). Norton (1983) essentially makes the same point about retention as Lieberman. That is, such a practice provides students with more of the same program that the child already has experienced, and therefore it is unlikely to be helpful to students during their retained year.

Frick (1986) attempts to formulate a policy that is different from ordinary retention by dividing the kindergarten and first grade time period into four stages. Such a policy supposedly would help to erase traditional grade divisions; the plan is for the children to proceed at their own pace through these four stages. Although the policy does away with grade divisions, it is quite similar to a transition room program, where additional time and a watered down curriculum are the main variables. The question that logically can be asked is, Why can't educational help be organized and provided to the students during the year when they are in regular class? Such an effort is implemented in the Reading Recovery Program (Clay, 1979) which is discussed in Chapter 11, on intervention methods.

Related Research

Research on the effectiveness of retention policies must be carefully organized and implemented. Two studies of effectiveness with dramatically contradictory conclusions are described in the following sections. Each is reported in detail, as are other related studies.

The Turley Study

The progress of kindergarten children in the Lafayette school district of Contra Costa County, California, was investigated by Turley (1979).

This school district had implemented a policy of kindergarten retention for more than 10 years. Annually, 15.5% of the kindergarten children were recommended to repeat the kindergarten year. According to Turley, the school district at the time of the study also was proposing that a child be required to stay in kindergarten for

2 years before being able to qualify for special help from a resource specialist (Turley, 1979, p. 8). The school district had established specific procedures to find kindergarten children who lacked "developmental readiness" for grade 1.

Turley compared the achievement in reading and math of three groups of children:

a. children who had been retained in kindergarten and therefore had spent 2 years in that educational unit, labeled K2;
b. children who had been recommended to repeat kindergarten but instead went on to first grade, labeled K1; and
c. children who went on to the first grade after their kindergarten year and for whom no recommendation had been made to repeat kindergarten (Turley, p. 1). This latter group was composed of "normal" children; i.e., they had not been flagged by the teachers as being in need of kindergarten retention.

The two kindergarten (K2 and K1) groups were matched on a number of test and interview variables. The developmental test battery included material taken directly from the Gesell School Readiness Test, as well as subtests of visual perceptual performance, vocabulary, and auditory memory and comprehension from established tests such as the Detroit, Binet, and Wechsler. The Stanford Achievement Test was administered to the group at the end of grade 1.

The results indicated that the K2 group scored significantly higher in reading and math on the Stanford than did the K1 children. However, both groups scored lower on these tests than the children who went on to first grade and who had not been recommended for retention.

For example, the K2 group (2 years in kindergarten) obtained a grade placement score of 2.81 in reading on the Stanford at the end of first grade. The K1 group (1 year in kindergarten; then on to first grade) obtained a grade score of 1.94. Regular kindergarten children scored at the 3.19 grade placement level at the end of grade 1. Similar results were noted in math for the three groups.

Turley interprets her results as clearly demonstrating that children who were considered developmentally young benefitted from the year of retention in kindergarten. In addition, 46% of the K1 group of children (i.e., those considered to be at risk but who went directly to first grade after 1 year of kindergarten) were retained in grades 1, 2, or 3.

Turley emphasizes the performance differences in reading and math between the K2 and K1 groups. Of importance, however, is that the at-risk kindergarten children who went on to first grade instead of being retained were right on target at the end of first grade with grade placement scores of 1.94 in reading and 2.09 in math.

Turley's study was undertaken in a school district deeply committed to the use of kindergarten retention as a major strategy in attempting to improve a child's school achievement. As stated previously Turley emphasizes that 46% of the children labeled as at risk but who went on to first grade were retained in grades 1, 2, or 3. She cites this fact as evidence of the "effectiveness" of the 2-year kindergarten experience. However, it should also be noted that those children who attended the 2-year kindergarten already had been retained once! In view of the popularity of the retention policy among the teachers in the Lafayette school district, it would not be unusual to expect a large number of at-risk children, who did not "take advantage" of the kindergarten retention, to be retained later. This indicates the need for a careful standardized test assessment of the 1-year kindergarten children as well as the 2-year kindergarten children. The number of children who score at the 26th percentile, 50th percentile, and 75th percentile also should be documented. Evaluation data that report only the mean score mask the variability found in the achievement level of both groups of children. Such a policy would help clarify the adequacy of the academic performance of both groups.

The Boulder Study

A study by Shepard and Smith (1985) as to the effectiveness of kindergarten retention resulted in diametrically opposite conclusions to those of Turley. Four elementary schools with very high retention rates in kindergarten in the Boulder, Colorado, school system were identified, and all of the first-grade children who had been in the 2-year kindergarten formed the retained sample. Children in the control group were selected from Boulder schools with a low retention rate. The two groups were matched on a number of variables including age, sex, readiness test score, and use of a second language (Shepard & Smith, 1985, p. 5). The readiness test sampled a number of developmental factors such as conceptual and language development, auditory and visual memory, visual perception, and motor coordination.

It is important to note that this school system was composed of kindergarten and first-grade teachers who held markedly different beliefs concerning the promotion and retention of kindergarten children. Shepard and Smith chose 40 retained children from a group of schools where the retention rate ranged from 16% to 20%. The 40 control children were obtained from schools with low retention rates which ranged from 9% to 4%. The subjects were matched on a number of factors present when they *entered* school: sex, birthdate, free-lunch participant, first language status, and scores on a school readiness inventory. The advantage of the matched study conducted by Shepard and Smith is that several schools within the district (unlike the Lafayette schools in Turley's study) had disparate retention philosophies. A child who had been flagged for kindergarten retention from a high-retaining school was matched with a child with similar psychological and educational characteristics from a low-retaining school who had been promoted to first grade.

Therefore, the comparison of the academic performance of the children is between a group of children who had been retained in kindergarten and with a group of children who had been promoted to first grade. It should be remembered that these promoted children would have been retained if they had attended a high-retaining school in Boulder.

Children were matched as to level of conceptual and language development, auditory and visual memory, visual perceptual development, and motor coordination. The children were compared on a number of outcome measures that included several teacher rating scales as well as standardized tests. Thus, the children were evaluated on such variables as math and reading achievement, social maturity, and self-concept. Standardized test scores were obtained from the reading and math subtests of the Comprehensive Tests of Basic Skills (CTBS). The results of the teacher ratings and test scores can be found in Table 10-8.

Table 10–8.
First-Grade Outcome Measures for Previously Retained[a] Children and Matched Controls (Smith & Shepard)

Teacher ratings	Retained in kindergarten			vs.	Matched controls		
	M	*SD*	*N*		*M*	*SD*	*N*
Reading	2.65	1.31	40		2.50	1.32	40
Math	2.80	1.29	40		2.68	1.33	40
Social maturity	2.83	1.15	40		2.65	1.29	40
Learner self-concept	2.90	1.30	40		2.55	1.20	40
Attention	2.73	1.20	40		2.63	1.35	40
	Mean score				Mean score		
Standardized tests	63%ile				56%ile		
CTBS Reading	[b]GE 1.9				[b]GE 1.8		
CTBS Math	78%ile				81%ile		
	[b]GE 2.2				[b]GE 2.3		

[a]The retained group included children who spent 2 years before first grade either because they repeated kindergarten, or entered a two-level kindergarten program, or were placed in pre-first.

[b]GE = Grade equivalent.

Note. Adapted from the *Boulder Valley Kindergarten Study: Retention Practices and Retention Effects* by L. A. Shepard and M. E. Smith, 1985, Laboratory of Educational Research, University of Colorado, Boulder. Copyright 1985, Boulder Valley Public Schools, Boulder, Colorado. Used by permission.

The data indicate that both groups were rated in a similar fashion by their teachers on different educational dimensions, i.e., maturity, achievement, and self-esteem. Standardized test results also indicated a very similar performance. The retained group scored 1 month higher on the reading test, whereas the promoted group scored 1 month higher on the math test.

A 1-month gain in reading as found in the kindergarten retention group in a time period of 1 year would appear to be an inadequate payoff for such a time investment. Similarly, the retained children were not rated as being any more mature or as possessing a more healthy self-concept than were the children who were promoted. This finding is particularly important because advocates of retention emphasize the need for time for the child to gain maturity. However, in this study the at-risk children who were promoted were perceived as just as mature as their retained counterparts and they reached this maturity level in 1 year less time.

Another aspect of this study that makes it an important one is that Shepard and Smith also reviewed the achievement test data of the children found to be below grade level in reading. Approximately the same number of children were judged by their teachers to be below grade level in reading in both the retained and promoted groups (12 vs. 13). It is important to note this fact because retention/transition room literature often emphasizes that children who go on to first grade against the wishes of school personnel must then be retained in that grade because of inadequate achievement. Yet the Shepard and Smith data indicate that *a similar number of children, as noted by their teachers, were performing at a low reading level* although one group of children had already had the "benefit" of an extra year in kindergarten.

Review of the standardized test data (Table 10-9) indicates that 6 of the promoted children scored at or below the 40th percentile on the reading subtest, whereas only 1 of the kindergarten-retained children did so. Conversely, 34 of the promoted children either scored at or above the 41st percentile level, compared to 39 of the retained group.

If it is granted that the 40th percentile reflects inadequate performance for children in this school district, then 6 children from the promoted group needed additional help as opposed to 1 in the retained group. However, the results of this study indicate quite clearly that 85% of the promoted children were able to perform at an acceptable educational level by the end of the first grade *without having to repeat kindergarten.* Furthermore, 14 of the retained children, or 35%, scored in the top one-fourth of the group on the standardized test, while 11 of the promoted children, or 28%, scored at the same level.

The results of the Boulder study demonstrate the similar educational performance of two groups of at-risk children—one group with 2 years of kindergarten experience and one group with 1 year. In summary, careful analysis of teacher ratings and the achievement test results of individual children indicates that a high

Table 10–9.
Distribution of Reading Scores of Retained and Control Group Children

First-grade performance of
at-risk children retained in
kindergarten and those
promoted directly to first grade   At-risk children

National percentile score breakdown on CTBS reading	Second year of kindergarten	Promoted directly to first grade
92nd percentile	8	6
77–91 percentile	6	5
66–76 percentile	7	7
59–65 percentile	8	3
53–58 percentile	6	2
47–52 percentile	1	7
41–46 percentile	3	4
33–40 percentile	1	3
26–32 percentile	0	3
N	40	40

Note. Adapted from the *Boulder Valley Kindergarten Study: Retention Practices and Retention Effects* by L. A. Shepard and M. E. Smith, 1985, Laboratory of Educational Research, University of Colorado, Boulder. Copyright 1985, Boulder Valley Public Schools, Boulder, Colorado. Used by permission.

percentage of the at-risk children who went directly to first grade without repeating kindergarten performed at an acceptable level in both math and reading on standardized achievement tests.

Discussion

In the Boulder, Colorado, schools, as stated previously, Shepard and Smith were able to choose the retention group from a number of high-retaining schools that were spread out through the school system reflecting diverse socioeconomic neighborhoods. In some retention studies the choice of control subjects ("promoted") is made from the same school as the retained subjects. The element of teacher bias may be present and thus threaten the validity of the findings.

A control subject in such a retention study is often one because the promoted child has been sent on to first grade due to parental insistence. The child will be attending first grade in a school that has adopted retention as a preferred approach for children. Therefore school personnel typically consider that these children will have a difficult time in first grade. As a result, school personnel may have negative attitudes toward these promoted children, give only minimal assistance to the children if they have learning problems, and thus help insure that they perform below par. In effect, then, a self-fulfilling prophecy may operate.

In Turley's study in the Lafayette schools, kindergarten retention was a district-wide policy for all schools. In the Boulder, Colorado, system, a diversity of opinions among the schools as to the efficacy of retention in kindergarten was found. As has been stated previously, the retention rates varied widely in the Boulder system. Children who were marked for kindergarten retention in high-retaining schools could therefore be easily matched with children who had the same psychological and educational characteristics but were being promoted because they attended a low-retaining school. As Shepard and Smith point out, choosing the experimental and control subjects in this manner makes for a more rigorous controlled study.

It would appear that the at-risk children who were attending these low-retaining schools were part of an educational environment that provided an atmosphere in which a more positive attitude in helping the child succeed was emphasized, and it is probable that a more individualized instructional program was provided.

Other Studies of Kindergarten Retention

Troidl (1984) attempted to determine whether promotion or retention was a better educational approach for low-achieving children in the Mesa, Arizona, school district. Kindergarten children were identified for retention by kindergarten teachers in the district. Sixty-nine of the 174 children who were identified as potential retainees were actually retained; the remaining 105 were promoted to first grade. Troidl compared the mean scores on math and reading tests of these two groups of children as they progressed through school. He found a statistically significant difference between the retained and promoted groups in reading and math favoring the retained group. Troidl then states that retention "is to be preferred to promotion for low achieving kindergarten children" (p. ii).

However, Troidl's conclusions are suspect because no attempt was made to match the retained and promoted groups of children on significant variables. Because so many factors enter into retaining or promoting children at the end of kindergarten, a determined attempt must be made to ensure that the two groups being studied are comparable on basic aspects such as readiness scores, sex ratio, socioeconomic status, and emotional adjustment.

Stapleford (1982) attempted to determine whether a second year of kindergarten would improve the academic performance of the children. Four groups of children attending Department of Defense schools in West Germany were studied. One group consisted of children who went into first grade with no recommendation for retention. Two groups consisted of children who were retained in kindergarten in 2 successive years; and one group was composed of children whose parents did not follow the recommendation but enrolled them instead directly in first grade.

Stapleford found that children spending a second year in kindergarten scored higher on a listening comprehension test. However, these findings probably should be considered suspect for two reasons: first, the lack of evidence of comparability of the groups at the beginning of the study (Shepard, 1989); and second, the variability of scores found in two groups within a short time period in the second year of the project. A group of children recommended for kindergarten retention but who went on to first grade scored significantly higher on achievement measures in the fall of the school year than did a group retained in kindergarten. However, 8 months later the situation was reversed with the retained group scoring higher. Before one can state that kindergarten retention should be implemented as a policy, the kindergarten-retained group should be monitored after attending first grade and both groups should be followed at least through the second grade. As mentioned previously, Mossburg's (1987) study demonstrated a washing out of effects of special placement by the end of second grade.

Delayed Entry to School

If a child is considered to exhibit immature behavior by school personnel, the parents often are counseled to delay the child's entry to kindergarten or first grade. In the 1960s and 1970s the percentage of mothers who remained home was higher; therefore this policy was more popular. Currently this option has declined in use mainly because more mothers have entered the workforce and therefore fewer adults are at home to care for the child. It is also difficult to find any formal evaluation of the usefulness of delayed entry as a worthwhile intervention tool. However, one such study was undertaken by Haag (1980), who investigated the delayed-entry program in a Missouri school system.

The Brookfield, Missouri, school district had initiated a prekindergarten screening clinic in 1972. The rationale for such a clinic was that school personnel believed that a number of children did not demonstrate "sufficient maturity" to make adequate school progress or that they lacked basic developmental skills. First-grade teachers complained that some of their students were having difficulty making normal progress. They stated that they believed these children would be more successful if given the opportunity of another year to "mature and develop readiness skills before experiencing the pace of the regular first-grade program" (Haag, 1980, p. 21).

The screening process in this particular school district consisted of having the prekindergarten children actually attend a week of classes in the regular kindergarten facilities. In addition to observing the children's behavior during that time period, the children were tested with measures constructed by the local school staff. Included were various personal-social and developmental dimensions.

Haag evaluated the screening program after it had been in existence for 5 years. Prior to his study no formal evaluation of the efficacy of this type of screening program in the Brookfield schools had been conducted. When analyzing the operation of the clinic over the previous 5-year period, Haag found that 75 prekindergarten children had been recommended for delayed entry into kindergarten. Of the 75 children's parents, 40 accepted the recommendation for delay of entry and 35 rejected the recommendation.

The purpose of the study was to ascertain if there were important differences in first-grade achievement of children withheld from kindergarten entrance for 1 year compared to those children who were recommended to delay entry but who were not withheld. Complete data were available on 26 children whose parents agreed to delay their children's entrance to kindergarten and on 20 children recommended for delay whose parents disagreed with the school assessment and enrolled their children in kindergarten. The achievement scores on a standardized test (Iowa) were compared for both groups when the children finished first grade.

The results of the achievement test analysis indicated no significant differences between the delayed and nondelayed groups on four of the five subtests of the Iowa Test of Basic Skills: vocabulary, word analysis, reading and spelling. Only on the math subtest did the delayed group score significantly higher. This in turn led to a significantly higher composite score when all five subtest scores were totaled.

However, Haag mentions that there is no real significance to the difference in the composite test scores of the two groups. "The composite scores are an average of the grade-equivalent scores of the other five subtests, and the large difference between the two groups on the mathematics subtest probably inflated the difference between the two groups on the composite scores" (p. 41). Therefore, the difference on the composite score really is not a valid finding in this study. In summary, the results of Haag's research indicate that a 1-year delay in entry to kindergarten resulted in no real improvement in the child's academic performance.

Haag states that the delayed entry policy was initiated in the Brookfield school district because the "practical classroom experience of teachers . . . supported the belief that in order to be more successful in school some children should probably be given another year to mature before entering school" (p. 57). The preschool clinic set up in the district was modeled on the ideas of the Gesell Institute. According to Haag, teacher observation of the children who delayed their entrance to school indicated that many of the children "did exhibit greater competency in dealing with the formal school situation after having had the extra year" (p. 38).

However, as stated previously, the belief that the children did benefit from the extra year was based on the teachers' subjective evaluation. As Haag points out, this evaluation was not corroborated by the objective data that were obtained from the academic performance of the delayed and nondelayed children. Note should be made of the fact that the two groups of children were not matched prior to the implementation of a delayed entrance program on any variable. Instead, all of the 75 children were considered by the teachers to be at risk for first-grade problems.

Another study of delayed entry was undertaken in the Omaha parochial school system (Reichmuth, 1983; Wilson & Reichmuth, 1985). One hundred thirteen children were evaluated as to their risk status for kindergarten. Twenty-one children were considered to be high risk and the parents were advised to delay their entry into kindergarten. However, 8 parents decided to enroll their children directly into kindergarten while the other 13 parents kept their children out of kindergarten another year.

In a subsequent follow-up of these 21 children, Reichmuth (1983) determined that of the 8 nondelayed students, 5 (or 62.5%) were reading above the 50th percentile on a reading test in the second grade. Of the 13 delayed children, 8 of the 13 (or 61.5%) were reading above the 50th percentile when tested for reading in the first grade.

This study is an example of the type of follow-up evaluation that is needed when alternative methods of educational intervention are implemented. Reichmuth was able to demonstrate that the same percentage of children were reading above the 50th percentile regardless of whether their entry to school was delayed or not. As Wilson and Reichmuth (1985) conclude, "the decision to delay entry into kindergarten may not have been the best strategy or intervention method. In summary, predictive accuracy is sufficient only when students are provided better educational opportunity" (p. 188).

Summary

Retention as a school practice in American education became commonplace in the mid-1800s. Analysis of retention rates indicates a wide variation among different states and different school systems. Annual retention rates for particular grades, such as first grade, typically are reported. However, of primary importance is the cumulative retention rate, which is the sum of the annual rates for several grades. Although it is recommended that the cumulative retention rate for the first six grades be no higher than 8%, the cumulative retention for kindergarten through second grade often exceeds that rate. In addition, some states do not include kindergarten retention or transition room placement in the reported retention rates; thus, the actual number of children retained is underreported.

Contributing to the high incidence of retention are teacher beliefs about the nature of development and the effects of retention. Teachers who believe that the child needs a year to mature support retention as a policy. Also, teachers often indicate that retention does not negatively influence the child's attitude or self-concept.

Research conducted on retained and nonretained at-risk kindergarten children, however, indicates that a high percentage of the nonretained children make satisfactory progress in first grade. Similarly, the retained children were not rated as any more mature than the promoted children. Furthermore, two studies of delayed entry to school found no significant differences between delayed and nondelayed children as to achievement.

Frymier (1989) summarizes the retention issue bluntly and succinctly: "Research on retention in grade is like research regarding smoking: almost nothing about either practice is positive in human terms. ... [If] student learning is the basic purpose of schools, retaining students in grade appears to be unprofessional, unethical behavior" (p. 43).

11

INTERVENTION/REMEDIATION PROGRAMS FOR YOUNG CHILDREN

When a child is having difficulty in learning, efforts must be made by educational personnel to assess the difficulty and to implement some type of educational intervention to ameliorate the problem. Over the years, countless intervention methods have been suggested to improve the achievement of children with learning problems. Specific approaches advocated at one time or another represent a range of perspectives. Examples include color-cued words, changes in the English alphabet, directive teaching, task analysis, computer-assisted instruction, remediation of deficient processing abilities, and dozens of behavioral and motivational approaches.

Therefore, in this chapter, a variety of intervention approaches for children demonstrating possible difficulties in learning will be reviewed and evaluated. Major issues in the interpretation of intervention/remediation studies are discussed. Several research studies of different remediation intervention approaches that offer promising results for children in the primary grades are described.

Major Issues in the Interpretation of Intervention/Remediation Methods

The concept of implementing an intervention for learning problems is consistent with the adaptive growth/environment view of learning described in Chapter 2. That is, readiness to learn is a combination of the child's physical growth and social experiences. Therefore, when the child experiences difficulty in learning, a particular method, i.e., a different educational experience, may alleviate the problem.

Of particular importance, however, in developing an intervention is an adequate conceptualization of the problem. In other words, the success of a particular intervention may well depend upon the initial diagnosis of the nature and extent of the difficulty. For example, in diagnosing reading problems, both standardized tests as well as informal reading measures should be used. Further, administration of any assessment instrument should be accompanied by careful notation about the kinds of errors made by the child.

Several instructional models, each with their particular advocates, have been suggested at one time or another for use in the schools. An example is the process training model that calls for the differential assessment of specific perceptual abilities of the child with remediation based on such an assessment. This model has been popular ever since the learning disability movement gained favor in American education in the 1960s (Gredler, 1990).

In addition, the task analysis model, which emphasizes the characteristics of the task rather than the characteristics of the learner, continues to be popular with many school psychologists and educators (Gredler, 1990; Smead, 1977). Task analysts, however, have difficulty explaining the lack of successful learning for a child because they reject the importance of mediating variables such as motivation that may account for this lack of success (Smead, 1977). Process training advocates would attempt to pin the poor performance on a particular perceptual deficit (Gredler, 1990; Smead, 1977). However, neither model takes into account such important variables as the motivation and attitudes of the learner (Smead, 1977).

The current discussion of curriculum-based assessment (CBA) (Rosenfield & Kuralt, 1990) is in reality merely a restatement of the task-analysis approach. Included are assessing the child's performance, analyzing the results of the assessment, adjusting task level to the student's entry level, and measuring mastery of curriculum objectives over time (Rosenfield & Kuralt, 1990, p. 285). Once again, motivational variables are not identified as important.

Three main principles underlie the curriculum-based assessment approach. They are (1) "assessment should be taken from the curriculum in use"; (2) "the instructional activity itself should be the basis for most of the assessment activity"; and (3) "tests [must] be samples of the curriculum in use" (Hargis, 1990, pp. 79 & 81).

However, the CBA approach can be criticized as a substitution of another form of educational testing for the more traditional practice of using standardized tests. There is criticism of CBA for its emphasis on assessment activities based solely on materials taken from the local classroom curriculum. One very successful intervention program for young children, Reading Recovery, utilizes a different curriculum from that which is used in the regular classroom (Clay, 1987). The strategies that the child uses in learning to read are similar regardless of the differences in the specific curriculum materials being used.

Most important for successful intervention with children's learning is to understand that a number of instructional practices have proven to have been helpful.

Problems in Remediation Research

One major problem in some remediation studies is the identification of the children who are to receive a remediation program. Often the selected group is so heterogeneous that the remedial method may fail to improve achievement for the group. That is, possible positive effects for some students in the group are canceled out by little or no effect on other students. For example, suppose that a large discrepancy score between ability test performance and current reading achievement is used to select a group for remediation. The group will include both "true" learning-disabled children and those whose deficient reading performance may result from emotional difficulties or other variables. Such difficulties are likely not to be addressed by the particular remediation technique under study.

In other words, children whose current achievement level is 1 to 2 standard deviations below their ability level are likely to be identified accurately as having some type of learning problem. However, any study of such children that purports to identify appropriate remediation methods based solely on discrepancy analysis is automatically suspect because the use of such a formula alone is simply a screening method. That is, it should be followed by a careful, in-depth diagnostic assessment that indicates more precisely the nature of the problems to be addressed.

A second and related problem is that comparisons of the effects of different methods on the average performance of groups may obscure the effectiveness of an approach with particular students. One example is a modality study conducted by Cooper (1969). The premise is that a particular sensory channel may be more effective than others when learning to read. Cooper studied the differences in the learning modalities of good and poor first-grade readers of normal intelligence under four different learning methods: visual, auditory, kinesthetic, and a combination approach. The visual modality emphasized word length and configuration; the auditory modality focused on the sounding out and blending of syllables (basically a phonic approach). The kinesthetic approach emphasized tracing and copying the syllable; and the combination approach utilized parts of the three other approaches.

Cooper noted the number of trials required for a child to learn five syllables under each teaching condition (referred to as the acquisition score). Twenty-four hours later, the child's retention of the syllables was measured for each condition (referred to as the retention score). Cooper demonstrated that good readers were able to learn new syllables in fewer trials than poor readers regardless of the modality approach selected. The results also indicated that no modality approach was significantly more effective for good readers *as a group* or poor readers *as a group*.

However, significant differences were found in a number of *individual* cases as to the importance of modality preference. For example, one first-grade child was able to learn to read words to criterion in only two trials when using an auditory approach, whereas 10 trials were required for the kinesthetic approach. Another first-grade student was unable to learn any of the new words presented regardless of the modality method even after 10 trial attempts had been made with each approach.

The results of this study raise an important point. That is, although the mean (average) performance of the four groups did not differ, the data indicate that modality is important for some individual cases. Learning to read words in two trials with one approach and requiring 10 trials in another approach was important for at least two children. The implication of such a study is that school psychologists and other educational personnel must carefully tease out important variables during the assessment/intervention process.

A third major problem in intervention and/or remediation studies that is almost completely neglected is that of the Hawthorne effect (Roethlisberger & Dickson, 1939). It is so named from the demonstration carried out in the assembly room of the Hawthorne plant of the Western Electric Company in the 1930s. A number of different changes were made in work conditions at this plant, each of which was followed by an increase in worker output. Becoming suspicious, the researchers began removing the innovations. However, worker output remained high. Thus, the experimental changes were not responsible for the improved output. Instead, the increased interest in the plant workers shown by management positively influenced worker motivation, and output increased.

In the school environment, students often participate in a study that investigates a new method, procedure, or technique, and, therefore, one that is novel and different. Additional attention to students from teachers or other school personnel typically accompanies the installation of a new program. However, this variable, which is not a component of the particular treatment, may be responsible for posttest changes in student performance, i.e., the Hawthorne effect. The difficulty is that once the "new" method or approach becomes an accepted practice, the increased interest and the accompanying increased attention to students often are no longer present.

Educational or psychological personnel who become involved in research on new or different teaching methods are likely to be highly interested and involved in their work with the children. The students react positively to the new approaches, and an improvement in academic performance can be expected because a different approach and extra attention are provided.

Because the Hawthorne phenomenon should be seriously considered in research projects, the editor of one medical journal has stated that improvement in academic performance must be maintained over a 3-year period before the particular teaching technique can be considered to be an advance. The editor also states that research studies that do not meet this criterion will not be published in that particular journal (Lennox, 1983). However, few educational interventions with schoolchildren would qualify for either conference presentation or publication if such requirements were invoked for educational and psychological journals!

Problems in the Literature

Discussions of remediation methods in the literature are hampered by two problems. One is that the field is subject to "fads" in treatment methods. For example, the 1960s and 1970s were replete with studies purporting to demonstrate the primacy of visual-perceptual remediation. Curricula in kindergarten and first grade were revised to include structured visual-perceptual activities. Then, in the 1970s and 1980s, other approaches came to the fore. Included were behavioral methods and metacognitive strategies purported to produce significant improvement in children's academic performance. What is needed is an understanding that a number of different interventions can be utilized, many of which result in the improvement of the child's reading performance.

Another problem is that discussions of remediation are replete with unsupported testimonials, or doctrinaire statements. A recent review of American textbooks in special education indicates that a number of authors eloquently defend particular remediation techniques, yet fail to offer empirical evidence of superiority over other methods (Gredler, 1987).

One example of a doctrinaire approach is the exclusive emphasis on the use of criterion-referenced methodology for teaching and measurement of educational objectives (Duffey & Fedner, 1978; Shapiro, 1990). Advocates of this methodology maintain that "[special needs] children could literally work their way out of special attention by meeting identified criteria" (Duffey & Fedner, p. 249).

Close monitoring of children as they acquire skills is, of course, important in the classroom. However, substitution of this assessment/intervention process for one in which ability and perceptual variables are emphasized is merely a substitution of one set of limited variables for another. For the diagnostic/intervention process to be meaningful, superficial interventions for children in kindergarten and the primary grades should be discarded.

Process-Related Intervention/Remediation Approaches

Despite the various factors that may influence the validity of remediation research, a number of investigations have been carefully formulated and implemented. Discussed in this section are examples of research studies conducted on two important processes related to learning. They are psycholinguistic processes and perceptual processes.

Psycholinguistic Processes

Some educators and psychologists believe that important psycholinguistic processes are underlying correlates of learning disabilities. Therefore, strengthening these psychological processes leads to improvement in reading. The effectiveness of such an approach has long been a topic of discussion. Arter and Jenkins (1979) vehemently argue against the continued use of the process approach "until a more adequate research base" is established. In fact, they call for a moratorium on advocacy and the classification and placement of children utilizing the analysis of modality preferences or processing deficits.

However, evidence has been partially provided by the recent investigations of Naylor and Pumfrey (1983). Their work raises significant questions as to whether such a wholesale indictment against processing approaches should be accepted.

Naylor and Pumfrey worked with 60 poor readers aged 7 to 8 years. A deficit in psychoeducational functions as measured by the Illinois Test of Psycholinguistic Abilities (ITPA) was found in auditory closure and visual sequential memory. Three intervention programs were used. One group received a language program based on ITPA-type activities. Another group used materials from the Peabody language development kit. A third group, the control, worked with a number program. Intervention time totaled two 45-minute sessions of remedial teaching for 12 weeks. Children were tested for achievement level at the conclusion of the treatment program and again 10 months later.

The results indicated that both language subgroups improved in psycholinguistic development as measured by the ITPA. More important, the two language groups made significant gains in word comprehension and word recognition on standardized achievement tests as compared to the controls, both at the end of the treatment program and 10 months later.

Such research demonstrates the value of the use of a language program in improving psycholinguistic functioning achievement in reading with young children. Naylor and Pumfrey (1983) offer some thoughtful points as to the reasons for the improved reading performance. They comment that many of the ITPA activities suggested do not necessarily follow from the ITPA model. They mention that the ITPA program as outlined by Kirk and Kirk (1971) is multimodal (visual, auditory, kinesthetic), as well as multilevel and multiprocess. They view it as similar to other remedial programs but with a particular emphasis on conceptual and sequential activities.

Naylor and Pumfrey (1983) further postulate that the effectiveness of their remediation resulted from the use of some reading and writing activities in the treatment approach. They suggest that the ITPA treatment approach as recommended by the Kirks reflects more of a general language orientation in which a number of subskills are emphasized during the course of treatment. Thus the carefully conceptualized study of Naylor and Pumfrey has shown the efficacy of a process approach to the remediation of reading problems in one group of 7- to 8-year-olds who were in the second and third grades.

Further support for Naylor and Pumfrey's research is found in a previous study with poor readers (Pumfrey & Naylor, 1978) and from the research of Burkholder of over 20 years earlier. Burkholder (1968) worked with second- and third-grade children in the Tucson, Arizona, schools who were retarded in reading. She states that her instructional exercises were aimed mostly at the integrative language level. However, analysis of her program indicates that many more language skills than those at the automatic integrational level were taught. In addition, the program was designed to be an attractive option to regular school activities with a positive reinforcing environment (Gredler, 1980).

Psycholinguistic processing deficits as measured by the ITPA were first noted. A careful program based on the subtests of this battery was then used in the remediation program, which was conducted over a period of 3 months. Gains in such reading skills as oral reading, study skills, and word meaning were noted after the treatment program. And, most important, the gains were maintained in oral reading and study skills for several months.

According to Burkholder, five variables were important in the success of the remediation program. They were (1) the use of special materials, carefully prepared; (2) the programming of the presentation of such materials in small graduated steps; (3) the introduction of a different teaching personality, one from outside the school environment; (4) a positively reinforcing environment that was probably aided by the small-group structure (4–5 children); and (5) a relaxing atmosphere, where errors could be made without fear of punishment (Burkholder, 1968, p. 92). The reading gains most likely resulted from a complex interplay of these factors operating over the treatment period.

Burkholder's study is one of the best illustrations of the importance of considering a number of different variables when analyzing the improved performance of children who participated in a remedial program. It is refreshing to note that Burkholder freely acknowledged the influence of a "new teaching environment," the use of different materials, and a warm, supportive atmosphere for learning without threat of punishment. At the same time, it is important to recognize that significant gains were made in the children's reading performance utilizing an approach that stressed the underlying processes purported to affect reading development. And at no time was reading per se taught during the intervention process. The improvement in performance continued over a period of 6 months without further intervention.

Also of importance is that the interventions used by Naylor and Pumfrey and by Burkholder were implemented in second and third grades. Thus, these years are not too late, as Reynolds (1979) states, to implement a successful intervention program.

Perceptual Skills

An important research investigation using a perceptual remediation approach was undertaken by Arnold et al. (1977). Eighty-six first-grade children performing poorly on the Silver-Hagin SEARCH battery comprised the intervention group. The SEARCH battery is a school readiness measure that includes tests of perceptual areas such as visual matching, visual recall, auditory discrimination, sequencing, and verbal expression.

The design of the study was a parallel pretest-posttest type, with comparison of improvement among the intervention group children, a Hawthorne control group that received regular academic tutoring, and a no-contact group that would reflect possible changes from passage of time. Children were matched on such variables as sex, IQ, school, severity of perceptual deficit, and the presence or absence of neurological signs.

The intervention group received tutoring for half an hour twice a week from November through mid-May of the first grade. Tutoring was based on improving the child's perceptual performance in those areas deemed as deficits from the SEARCH battery. The academic remediation group was also tutored twice weekly and reflected the typical academic tutoring used in the public school classroom.

A number of important results were obtained by Arnold et al. Although nonsignificant differences among all three groups on the readiness posttest were found, some improvement was noted in behavioral ratings for the perceptual intervention group. On the Conners Behavior Rating Scale, the perceptual intervention group showed a trend in the direction of more acceptable classroom behavior, although the group differences were not significant. However, on a hyperkinetic rating scale, the intervention group demonstrated definite improvement while the ratings of both control groups significantly deteriorated.

Most important of all, the entire sample was assessed a year after the posttest. The results of the follow-up assessment showed dramatic changes in the performance of the intervention group. The intervention group had improved significantly on the reading measure and in spelling and on behavior rating scales. Lack of improvement occurred only on the arithmetic test.

Several important implications may be inferred from this study. First, the study demonstrated that the perceptual skills of the first-grade children spontaneously improved during the year in first grade with exposure to the regular classroom environment. However, while there was improvement in the perceptual area for all three groups (i.e., intervention, academic tutoring, and no-contact control), this improvement was not followed the next year by any spontaneous improvement in classroom behavior, reading, and spelling achievement for the academic tutoring and no-contact control groups. In fact, the two control groups showed a definite deterioration in all of the above-mentioned areas by the end of second grade.

The results of this study indicate that the processing approach can be an effective intervention method. It is significant that the perceptual remediation approach used did *not* involve specific instruction in reading activities. Nevertheless, the children demonstrated important gains in reading by the end of second grade.

A recent study of children retained in kindergarten in the Marin County, California, schools also indicated the presence of difficulties in perceptual, visual-motor, and visual integration areas (Mantzicopoulos, Morrison, Hinshar, & Carte, 1989). The same screening instrument (e.g., SEARCH) was used in the Marin County study as was used in the Ohio State medical school study (Arnold et al., 1977) of first-graders described earlier. In addition, the students were rated as more hyperactive and impulsive. The researchers emphasize that children with possible learning problems need more than just retention in grade. However, many school personnel consider that the review of the same material, when the child is retained, is sufficient to produce academic gains. As the authors state, "The multiplicity of the retained group's deficits . . . seems to be incompatible with the assumption that re-exposure to the same curriculum is enough to facilitate remediation" (p. 119).

The work of Burkholder with second-graders and Arnold et al.'s treatment program with kindergarten children indicate the efficacy of intervention with young children using sophisticated remediation approaches. Such investigations justify the importance of a specific assessment of the learning problems of children. These psychologists also emphasize the fact that developmental skills must be adequately assessed to be certain that the child will progress satisfactorily in academic subjects. The alternatives of retaining the children in kindergarten or placing them in a transition room offer *no* specific assessment and remediation for the children and thus are to be avoided.

Remediation Approaches in Reading: Some Promising Practices

Reading is a critical skill, both in school learning and later life. Thus, methods that improve the reading comprehension skills of poor readers are particularly important. Remediation approaches discussed in this chapter are a multisensory vocabulary approach, an educational therapy approach, computer-assisted instruction, the Writing to Read Program, and Reading Recovery.

A Multisensory Vocabulary Approach

An investigation of a multisensory whole-word method that uses a meaningful context for learning was conducted by Gredler (1979), replicating earlier studies conducted by Argyros and Rusch (1974) and Fricklas and Rusch (1974).

Subjects in the study were children between 7 and 9 years 8 months with a Hemmon-Nelson IQ average of 81. The 12 children in the study were selected from a group of 25 children identified by the teacher as poor readers. Selection was based on poor performance on the word recognition subtest of the Peabody Individual Achievement Test. Average performance of the 12 children was at the 6th percentile. The study was implemented for 2 months with an average of three lessons a week.

The program presents 59 words in 25 programmed units. Each lesson was contained in a cartridge that held a filmstrip loop and a continuous audiotape. The filmstrip pictures appeared on a video display unit (called a "teledesk") in front of the child, and the teacher's words were heard through a speaker or headphones. The child responded to the audio questions both by placing plastic word plaques on the video screen and by verbally responding to each question.

Two theoretical assumptions form the basis for the materials used in the study. One is that an emphasis on the microanalysis of phonemes and the use of routine sound exercises with deemphasis on meaning frequently contributes to some children's failure. The second is that a child will be able to read a word automatically, without iconic or pictorial clues, when the input-output frequency exceeds 100 (Higgins, 1971).

For example, in the program the child sees the word "same" 116 times, hears the word 137 times from the tapes; speaks the word 77 times (modeled from the tape or read in context), and then places a plaque on the interface 12 times. The total input-output for "same" is 342. It was anticipated that after a child used a word in a meaningful context, the child would then rely on the orthography of the word.

The pretest-posttest design of the study, with each student serving as his own control, indicated that substantial progress was made (Gourevitch, 1965; Hardyck & Petrinovich, 1969). The mean pretest score was 5.17 with scores from one to nine words correctly recognized. The posttest mean was 44.33; correctly identified words ranged from 26 to 54. Because the study was conducted with low achievers, some pre- to posttest gain was expected as a result of regression toward the mean. However, the gains, significant at the .001 level, cannot be explained away by this phenomenon.

Use of an instructional programmed system that provided an interesting format, along with a rich matrix of visual, verbal, and motor input-output, contributed to substantial gains in word recognition. Also, an important component of the method is that the children enjoyed and looked forward to the interaction with the assistant, who stayed with them while they completed the lesson. This gave the children an opportunity to interact with an adult in an essentially nonauthoritarian atmosphere.

Teachers had previously commented on the children's poor learning strategies. Nevertheless, the increase in number of words learned was indeed significant, both statistically and educationally. The children's progress suggests that such an instructional approach should be considered and incorporated in remedial strategies for children in the first three grades who are seriously retarded in reading.

A similar curriculum may be designed without the necessity of the equipment used in the program. The important factor is the immersion of the child in a rich instructional environment. The children enjoyed the new environment and their motivational level was enhanced. Also of importance is that curriculum planning within the regular classroom for the children in the study was minimal. In the absence of further attention from the regular classroom teacher and specialized instructional planning, the progress of these children in their classes would probably remain minimal.

Although these children had not been labeled as "learning disabled," their performance on oral recognition skills tests was similar to many children referred to as learning disabled. The importance of this study is that the results provide further evidence of the need for the school psychologist and educational specialist to be cognizant of a number of various instructional approaches that may be recommended for use with a minimum of time and expense.

An Educational Therapy Approach

The affective component of the instructional environment is seldom emphasized by educators in the intervention/remediation process. Often a child's emotional needs are either inadequately understood or neglected unless grossly disturbed behavior is shown. Much of the current remediation of children with learning problems takes the form of merely a direct attack on the mechanics of the reading process.

In an action research project undertaken by Gredler (1978), the establishment of a positive relationship with the child was of prime importance. School personnel referred children from the first, second, and third grades who had either failed in reading, were repeating with little current progress, or were in danger of being retained in grade. Emphasis was placed on two areas: (a) development of a positive relationship between a graduate student (who served as the tutor) and the child, and (b) use of sophisticated instructional methods. The Programmed Reading Kit (Stott, 1962; Stott, 1970b), System 80 Material (1977), and various behavioral reinforcement programs were introduced.

The Programmed Reading Kit was the mainstay of the instructional process. The kit materials consist of 33 games carefully constructed to reflect the basic tasks that make up the reading process. Stott considered that the process of encoding and decoding could be adequately presented within a game framework in which several procedures were emphasized. First, the games should be relied on to do the teaching; long explanations were "out." Second, phonic drills also were banned. Teaching the sound of letters in isolation from their context was to be avoided. Third, blending separately pronounced sounds into words was also to be avoided. Fourth, continual observation of how the child is coping with the learning process was to be followed up by further analysis if the child was continuing to have difficulties (Stott, 1970b, pp. 19–22).

Some referred children were so sensitive to their lack of progress in school tasks that they refused at first to become involved in the testing of their academic skills. Many children were fearful of responding and making mistakes and showed an initial distrust toward adults who were working with them in the remediation center.

Fear of the teaching adult, concern about possible failure, and anticipation of punitive reaction from the tutor were important behaviors that had to be dealt with during the remediation sessions. These reactions are common in children who are having continued difficulties in learning (Rie, 1974).

At the completion of the remediation sessions, 65% of the children were able to read material at the instructional level that when presented 12 weeks earlier had been classified at the frustration level. Instructional level was defined as being able to read the Houghton Mifflin reading passages accurately with no more than 10 errors for 100 words of material. Frustration level was defined as making a cumulative total of 11 or more errors when attempting to read a passage. Moreover, 65% of the children also were able to read at least one book level above their entering reading level. For example, they may originally have been at the primer level; at the end of the study, they were at the first-grade level. Further, 23% of this group of children were able to read material a minimum of two book levels above their original assessment.

Once again, improvement in performance was due to a combination of factors: emphasis on a therapeutic environment, motivated personnel, and use of a sophisticated remediation program. Also of importance is that this reading improvement resulted from a time increment of only 20 hours distributed over a period of 13 weeks. Further, the majority of children were first- and second-graders. Thus, this approach emphasizes the gains that can be accomplished with children in the early grades without necessarily implementing a screening program in kindergarten which attempts only to place the child either in a prekindergarten program or to delay entrance to school.

Lawrence (1971, 1972, 1973), in a series of pioneering studies, emphasized the value of counseling by volunteer adults in helping children to improve their reading performance. Reduction of the child's level of anxiety was the main objective in his studies, and *no* specific reading intervention was provided. The solid gain produced by these intervention studies also demonstrates the importance of a therapeutic environment when organizing any remedial intervention.

Computer-Assisted Instruction

The use of computer technology often is cited as a means of improving the child's reading performance. Some version of computer technology has been used in the American classroom for the last 20 years (McDermott & Watkins, 1983).

A CAI study completed several years ago has provided a detailed analysis of the utility of the computer with 6-year-old children. Fletcher and Atkinson (1972) compared the reading progress of children matched on appropriate variables. One child of each pair received CAI in reading in addition to regular class instruction while the other child received only regular classroom instruction.

The computer-assisted instruction was provided for 12 minutes a day for a 5-month period during the first grade. During the remainder of the school day, classroom activities were the same as those for the control group. Standardized test results administered at the end of the first year indicated an average increase of 5 months over that of the control group. Although the children received no CAI in the second grade, follow-up evaluation at the end of the second grade reflected a difference of 4.9 months in favor of the CAI group.

Also noteworthy is the fact that although the reading performance of both boys and girls improved when exposed to CAI, the relative rate of improvement was greater for the boys. This result is important because boys in many American schools typically lag behind girls at the end of the first and second grades. The results demonstrated that when appropriate curriculum modifications are provided for first-grade male students, they can perform at the same level as female students.

This study also indicated that supplementary instruction was definitely needed to reinforce the regular instructional program. Atkinson (1974) states that CAI should not necessarily be utilized in all phases of reading instruction. He considers that CAI provides individualized instruction that cannot be matched by the teacher even when working with a group of only four or five children. Atkinson attributes the typical higher performance of girls to the predominance of female teachers in the school. However, he also believed that girls were more adept at memorization. This skill in turn helped them to cope with a curriculum that emphasized sight word procedures.

The results of this CAI study by Atkinson is similar to the findings of several other investigations. Specifically, regular instruction, when supplemented by CAI, is found to be more effective than normal classroom instruction alone (Edwards, Norton, Taylor, Weiss, & Dusseldorf, 1975).

A number of different reasons have been set forth as to the effectiveness of CAI over conventional instructional approaches with children who are referred for remediation. These are as follows:

(a) CAI is better able to adapt to the pace of the student. Pupil control of the material makes it more manageable for the student (Clark, 1986; Martin, 1973).

(b) Information is provided the student as to correctness after he or she has made a response. Providing immediate knowledge of results or feedback is important (Annelli, 1977).

(c) Machine instructional programs appear to clarify the problem more easily and provide the "required frequency and subtlety of reinforcement" that is needed (Skinner, 1972); and a properly constructed program helps to narrow the gap between the abstract and concrete (Clark, 1986).

(d) CAI makes more effective provision for active and passive feedback during learning sequences than does conventional instruction (Annelli, 1977).

(e) The interactive dimension of the program helps to promote curiosity and increases personal involvement of the child with the educational material (Clark, 1986).

(f) The resultant higher level of interest increases the child's attention span (Clark, 1986).

Writing to Read Program

A recent approach to initial reading instruction is that of the Writing to Read Program (Martin & Friedberg, 1986). Designed to help young children learn to read more effectively, the program has been field-tested on 10,000 children in the United States. The program is composed of three parts: a computer program, in which the child is led through a sequenced, self-paced cycle of interactive learning; work journals that reinforce the learning activities and are similar to the computer program; and a language development program that provides the child with a number of different activities with which to apply the language arts skills.

In the program, children learn to write by combining the 42 phonemes into words. Students learn to spell the words phonemically. The computer provides a high degree of individual attention as well as multisensory experience in word construction. Words are typed into the computer; the children see the word constructed on the monitor; and then they repeat the phonemes along with the computer voice (Rotenberg, 1984).

In the Writing to Read Program kindergarten and first-grade children make use of a variety of equipment and language arts materials that are organized around six learning stations. As Martin mentions, the Writing to Read system is an important concept in that it not only teaches children to write before they begin to read but also teaches the children to use a typewriter and a computer. Most important, though, is the fact that Writing to Read teaches a child how to convert the sounds he or she already knows "into 'sounds' that can be written down" (Martin, 1986, p. xii).

Martin has emphasized that children can learn to write what they say—that they can write all the words they use in everyday conversation—*provided* that a program is used that offers structured activities.

Children go to a computer station, where they follow instructions that guide them through the words that are presented. They spend 12 to 15 minutes each day at each station listening to words and sounds; they then say these words and type letters to make words. At the writing/typing station, the students type words they have just learned at the computer station and begin to write and type their own words and stories. Additional stations include the work journal station, listening library station, multisensory materials station, and make words station (Martin, 1986, pp. 26–28). Properly used, this program is helpful in encouraging children to progress in reading performance at their own rate.

Preliminary results of this approach to initial reading are found in standardized test data from the Winston-Salem, North Carolina, school system. Mean reading scores of the CAI children at the end of the first grade were at the 89th percentile in comparison to the control group's mean score at the 69th percentile (Gredler, 1990).

Further evidence of the effectiveness of this programmed approach as a remedial intervention method is found in the results of a study of third- and fourth-grade retarded readers. Significant improvement in reading performance resulted after 12 weeks of using the Writing to Read Program for 55 minutes a day (Thompson, 1985).

In a recent study of over 2,100 first-grade students in Mississippi public schools, it was demonstrated that the Writing to Read Program significantly improved the students' reading and writing skills (West, 1991).

In another investigation of effectiveness of the Writing to Read Program, Chang (1989) demonstrated that first-grade children performed significantly higher on writing, reading, and language tasks at the end of the year than did a comparable group of children who remained in the regular first-grade program. Particularly important is that children of low and average readiness levels benefitted the most from the Writing to Read Program. The analysis by Chang is an excellent example of the high level of research that can be carried out by a school district.

Some educators have questioned the use of the Writing to Read Program. Freyd and Lytle (1990) are concerned that the program's use of a special spelling system is controversial, that the phonics instruction does not provide practice in blending sounds, and that the program does not focus on decoding. They are also concerned that talking with a computer is a poor substitute for interacting with a teacher.

Freyd and Lytle further state that their review of 17 studies indicates that whereas 7 of 8 studies reported positive gains in reading with kindergarten students, only 2 of 8 demonstrated gains with first-grade students as opposed to regular first-grade instruction. However, Nelms (1990) challenges the interpretations by Freyd and Lytle. Perhaps her most telling criticism is that little or no information on the methodological details of the 17 studies cited is provided.

Also of great concern to Freyd and Lytle is the cost of the Writing to Read Program. However, Abramson (1990) questions the cost figures mentioned by Freyd and Lytle. What is left unspoken by most educators is the cost of retaining students. Such costs far outweigh the expense of providing an intervention method such as Writing to Read or Reading Recovery.

Reading Recovery

Targeted for at-risk first-grade students, Reading Recovery originated in New Zealand. Developed by Marie Clay and field-tested in the late 1970s, the program was adopted in several Australian school systems in the early 1980s and the Columbus, Ohio, schools in 1984 (Clay, 1987). Approximately 228 Ohio school districts had been introduced to the program by 1987 (Pinnell, DeFord, & Lyons, 1988).

Children who demonstrate poor performance in reading and writing are selected for the program. Although the target group consists of the lowest achievers in these two skill areas, selection does not depend on screening by the school psychologist or elementary school counselor. No child is excluded on the basis of IQ, language background, learning disability status, or ethnic background (Clay, 1987).

The program provides individual tutoring for the children 30 minutes per day for 12 to 20 weeks. The children are removed from the classroom for the tutoring and work with a specially trained teacher. A critical feature of the program is that the first 2 weeks are spent in establishing a close relationship with the child and in assessing the child's learning strategies and knowledge in a thorough manner. Thus the program makes use of important features of therapeutic tutoring, as outlined by Rie (1974) and Gredler (1978) and discussed earlier in this chapter. Included are reducing the child's fear of the teaching adult; providing an atmosphere where concern about possible failure is reduced; and providing an emotionally supportive atmosphere wherein children will feel comfortable in using reading strategies they already know and learning new ones. As Clay (1987) points out: "an attractive feature of the program is the way in which it feeds back information on success to all participants from the beginning. Children who are turned off by reading take only a few weeks to show that they feel in control of their work tasks . . . " (p. 37). Of major importance is the preventive nature of the program. The program focuses on children when they are being introduced to the strategies of learning to read.

Sufficient data have been obtained from various research studies of the Reading Recovery Program to indicate that a large percentage of children who perform poorly in first grade can be helped to a sufficient degree that they are no longer candidates for possible retention in first grade. In Clay's work in New Zealand, over 90% of the children selected for the program attained the average level of their classmates within a time frame of 14 to 16 weeks (Pinnell et al., 1988). Clay (1987) also emphasized that the program is cost effective because two thirds of those who entered the program in three countries (Australia, New Zealand, and the United States) were able to improve their performance to the average levels shown by their classmates without further interventions.

In Ohio, analysis of the test performance of children in the Reading Recovery Program on specific subskills (i.e., text reading, writing vocabulary, dictation, letter identification, word test, and concepts about print) indicated that in May, 1987, the number of Reading Recovery children who achieved scores equal to or exceeding the average band of performance of regular students ranged from 68.5% (text reading) to 94.6% (letter identification) (Pinnell et al., 1988). Also, researchers found that a high proportion of Ohio children who exited from the Reading Recovery Program continued to make satisfactory progress for a period of at least 2 years after their treatment period had ended. Comparison children who were also from the bottom 20% in reading and were assigned to regular remedial instruction for the school year never reached the average score band attained by a random group of children (i.e., random sample mean ± .5 standard deviation) (Pinnell et al., 1988).

The program, if implemented appropriately, can also reduce first-grade retentions. A report from the school superintendent in a suburban Ohio school district stated that 95% of the children selected for the Reading Recovery Program in his school district were candidates for grade retention. However, at the end of the school year in June, only 10% of this group were actually retained in first grade (Pinnell et al., 1988).

The number of children who would have probably been either retained in grade or referred to a school psychologist for assessment of learning problems has therefore been considerably reduced. The small percentage of students who are still demonstrating learning difficulties can now be referred to the school psychologist for in-depth psychoeducational assessment and recommendation for additional intervention strategies.

The preceding discussion demonstrates that there are a considerable number of instructional interventions that have been successfully utilized with young children as they begin their primary school experience.

Restructuring Instructional Time

Sociologists have noted that individuals attempt to reduce the uncertainty of events that occur in their lives. One method of reducing uncertainty is to establish "timetables" or reference points that readily can be observed as indicators of progress toward a particular objective (Roth, 1963). Such timetables are constructed by hospital patients, for students within the school system, and by business executives within a corporation.

The American school is an example of an institution with a highly organized and standardized timetable. After children begin kindergarten, they are expected to march forward one grade a year in a "lockstep" until they graduate together from high school (Roth, 1963).

However, each entering group of students reflects a variety of individual differences. Addressing these differences during the academic year is a formidable task. One of the important side effects of well-organized intervention/remediation programs is that they often bring about a suspension of excessive "time-table" pressures to which the failing child has been subjected.

Also of importance is restructuring instructional time in the classroom to better provide for individual differences and thereby reducing lockstep instruction. For example, in Swedish schools, teachers in grades 1 to 3 offer a weekly 2-hour block of time for tutoring any child who needs help (Clay, 1979).

Another approach to individualization of instruction involves staggering first-grade attendance. One half of the first-grade class meets with the teacher for the first 2 hours of the day. The other half comes to school 2 hours later and stays 2 hours beyond the normal closing time. Such an arrangement offers a concrete way of reducing the number of students in the class and provides more individual instruction for specific children who have learning problems (Clay, 1979).

Three particular approaches to restructuring instructional time are discussed in this section. They are mastery learning, utilizing "time-to-learn" tests, and various forms of regrouping children within the classroom.

Mastery Learning

Developed by Benjamin Bloom (1968), an educational psychologist and researcher at the University of Chicago, mastery learning is based on an observation by John Carroll. Specifically, Carroll (1963) maintained that aptitude for learning, in large measure, could be defined as "time to learn." Bloom (1968) noted that, in the traditional classroom, a normal distribution of students (in terms of aptitude for the subject to be taught) also will be normally distributed on postcourse achievement. Such a process, in which approximately one third of the students adequately learn the concepts and principles being taught, is wasteful and destructive.

However, Bloom (1968) maintains that most students can master the subject matter if appropriate methods are found. He recommended that instruction be subdivided into units, and objectives and mastery standards be established for important concepts and principles. Then two or more mastery tests are developed for each unit, and alternative sources of information for each unit are identified (books, articles, films).

At the end of instruction for unit one, all students take the formative test. Those who do not attain mastery (typically set at 80% or 90%) are recycled through the alternate instructional materials. Those who achieve mastery may either serve as peer tutors for other students or pursue other projects for a few class periods until the recycled group retakes another formative test on unit one. At this point, most of the students should have attained mastery. Then instruction begins on unit two and the same procedure is followed.

Recent analysis of the effects of mastery learning on children's learning suggests that immediate improvement in academic performance may be accounted for by frequent testing and feedback provided to children. However, advocates of mastery learning emphasize that the entire teaching-feedback-corrective process used in the diagnostic-prescriptive cycle is needed (Slavin, 1987b).

Nevertheless, any "new" remediation approach may increase achievement by providing frequent opportunities for testing and feedback. Close monitoring of a child's learning process in a positive way is an action to be applauded. However, motivation and attitudes are important mediating variables. Thus, unless children are motivated to learn, they may continue to perform below grade level after several weeks of school and may require a more involved assessment/intervention.

"Time-to-Learn" Tests

In a study of important instructional variables, Gettinger (1978) developed measures of time-to-learn for academic tasks that included vocabulary, math concepts, reading comprehension, reading for facts, math computation, and dictation for spelling. She then compared these learning-rate measures with measures of intelligence and school achievement. Learning rate was defined as the number of trials necessary to master a specific task.

Results demonstrated that some students learned the academic material to the same achievement criterion level from six to nine times as fast as the slowest students in the class. Correlations of time-to-learn measures with achievement were higher than with IQ/achievement measures (e.g., .84 to .89 in comparison to .58 to .74 for IQ/achievement).

Gettinger suggests that describing that a child needs three times as many trials to learn 12 spelling words or two times as long to learn 12 vocabulary words will be more helpful information about the child's learning performance than the identification of the student's IQ score.

This suggestion has obvious implications in working with young children who have learning problems. Administering appropriately developed "time-to-learn" tests may be a helpful first approach to identifying rate of learning of the child with learning difficulties. Appropriate curriculum programming for the student may then be prescribed.

Another implication of attending to this time variable is that the teacher may determine relatively early in the school year which children require more instructional time. Resources may then be brought to bear on attempting to provide such intervention before the whole apparatus of the special education complex is brought into play. It is obvious also that the classroom organization will need to be restructured so as to factor in such intervention approaches.

Maximizing Instructional Opportunities: Regrouping Students

It is important for educators and psychologists to note the range and extent of instructional options that may be used with kindergarten and first-grade children to improve academic performance. It also must be recognized that there is no *one* approach that will miraculously "pay off" in improved learning for all students. However, there are a number of helpful suggestions that can be considered by school personnel who are in charge of early childhood education programs within a school district.

Grouping on the basis of ability or achievement performance has been common in schools for the past 60 years and is found in both elementary and secondary schools (Slavin, 1987a). Underlying grouping as a concept is the idea that the instruction of the child can proceed best by deemphasizing the grade placement of students. A first-grade classroom may include children whose reading performance ranges from the preprimer level through the second-grade level. Organizing instructional units within a school in order to reduce this wide range of performance differences is at the heart of the grouping process. It is reported that one fourth of first-grade classrooms in Pennsylvania are organized in this way (Colditron, Braddock, & McPartland, 1987).

A special form of regrouping, which has been demonstrated to have merit, is known as the Joplin Plan (Floyd, 1954; Franseth & Koury, 1966). Students remain in their regular heterogeneous classes for most of the day but are regrouped for reading across grades. Slavin (1987a) points out that many nongraded programs are similar to the Joplin form of grouping.

The Joplin plan has been described as a method that organizes the students into reading classes in which all the children are working either at the same reading level or where the range does not exceed two reading levels (Slavin, 1987a). Many studies of the efficacy of the Joplin plan have investigated the progress of children in the intermediate grades (i.e., grades 4 to 6). However, in one study of children in grades 1 to 3, Ingram (1960) followed their progress after they had been assigned to nine reading levels. At the end of 3 years, students in this nongraded program were achieving at a level 7 months higher than the performance of students in the school before the grouping plan had been introduced (Slavin, 1987a). Education-ally significant gains also were found in another study of a nongraded primary program that was similar to the Joplin plan. First-grade children in the nongraded exceeded regular first-grade classes by 9-month grade units (Halliwell, 1968; Slavin, 1987a).

However, simply to regroup children into a unit that reduces the range of performance is insufficient. Several features that are found in any successful grouping plan and will be critical to success are described below. They include the following:

(a) frequent and careful assessment of the performance of the student;
(b) use of educational materials that are appropriate to the student's performance level regardless of the grade level of the student;
(c) instruction that is closely tailored to the level of performance of the students;
(d) use of regrouping of the children only for reading and/or mathematics. The remainder of the students' time is spent in the heterogeneous homeroom class, which continues to be the children's primary reference group.

When children are carefully grouped and classes become sufficiently homo-geneous, students will have an opportunity to receive a greater amount of instructional time from the teacher than if the class is divided into three reading groups. The latter form of grouping results in many students being relegated to just seatwork activities (Slavin, 1987a, pp. 321–326).

Time Devoted to Instruction: A Case Study

Another factor that has been all but ignored by educational personnel is the amount of time allocated in the classroom for actual instruction in reading and math. Research studies have shown a wide variability in the amount of instructional time given to reading and language arts (Canady & Hotchkiss, 1985). In observing fifth-grade teachers, Canady and Hotchkiss discovered that one teacher spent 68 minutes daily for instruction in reading and language arts while another teacher allocated 137 minutes. In one second grade, a teacher spent 47 minutes a day on the above two subject areas while another second-grade teacher allocated 118 minutes (Berliner, 1984).

Researchers of the classroom instructional process also have shown that elementary school teachers spend more time in the instruction of children in high-achieving reading groups than those in low-performance reading groups. In one study investigating this phenomenon, Clauset and Gaynor (1982), followed the teachers for a 6-year period. They found that teachers spent the equivalent of 2 additional years in direct instruction with high achievers as opposed to those who were low achievers.

Researching the Classroom Day

A specific example of how low-achieving students have been helped is provided by Canady and Hotchkiss (1985). They concur with the statement that in the traditional school setting low-achieving students are often allocated less time for instruction than high-achieving students. In addition, they state that too much time is wasted in the traditional classroom because children are given too many seatwork tasks along with too little instructional supervision. The regular class-room is also subjected to many interruptions in the course of the day. Canady and Hotchkiss propose a new scheduling format for the elementary grades whereby teachers would have large blocks of uninterrupted time with their students.

This new format involved introducing the concept of parallel scheduling with emphasis on instruction in reading and math. To illustrate how such scheduling might work with children in the primary grades, a reading block for 100 students and four teachers is described. School personnel first establish the instructional level for each child; then the students are assigned to reading groups based on the results of the screening process. After the instructional assessment has been completed, the group of 100 students is divided into eight subgroups that will reflect a range of reading competency levels from very low to superior. Each teacher is assigned two groups of children, one low instructional reading group and one middle or high-level reading group. Each group contains about 13 students and is provided 70 minutes of direct reading instruction per day. Then two groups at different levels of reading competency are combined to form a heterogeneous class group. This new group then works together on various language arts activities such as writing and spelling (Canady & Hotchkiss, 1985, pp. 349–351). "Extension center" time is also provided wherein the student can engage in various enrichment activities. If the child needs support services, these can be provided at this time.

Such an organizational structure provides not only more teaching time but also involves very careful grouping of children at specific levels of performance in the subject matter area with each group composed of only a small number of students (Canady & Hotchkiss, 1985, pp. 348–350). In effect, all the conditions that are a part of the successful Joplin plan and other preventive and remediation programs previously mentioned by Slavin (1987a) and Slavin and Madden (1989) are fulfilled. In the data reported by Canady and Hotchkiss, average percentile scores in reading improved from the 27th percentile level in 1975 to the 55th percentile level in 1983.

As the authors state, this sophisticated form of grouping is effective for several reasons. Principals and teachers are learning to communicate in a more effective manner; an *equal* amount of instructional time is now provided to low-achieving students, and the teacher has a smaller group of children to work with at any one time; there is less unsupervised seatwork; and a larger amount of teacher-directed instruction without interruption is provided (p. 355).

Goal Structure of the Classroom

Recent research into the reactions of children to achievement tasks indicates that the perceived goal structure of the classroom is one important factor (Ames & Archer, 1988; Dweck, 1989; Elliott & Dweck, 1988; Jagacinski & Nicholls, 1987). Two types of classroom goal structure has been identified. One is a learning or mastery goal structure and the other is a performance or ego-involved goal structure.

Characteristics of learning-oriented classrooms include flexible instructional groups, frequent group projects, encouragement of peer assistance, and assignments varied according to student skill levels (Stipek & Daniels, 1988). The environment also may be described as informational (Deci & Ryan, 1985). The classroom emphasizes autonomy, enhances the child's learning strategies, and also acknowledges ambivalent feelings that may arise in the learning setting.

The performance-oriented classroom, in contrast, typically maintains stable (rather than flexible) learning groups for at least one subject, written assignments are graded, and only "A" or almost perfect papers are placed on bulletin boards (Stipek & Daniels, 1988). Children take tests that are graded, and letter grades are sent home to parents on report cards. Such an environment is referred to as "controlling" by Deci and Ryan (1985) because the child is under pressure to feel and behave in certain ways. Excessive evaluation of children's performance, overemphasis on grades, and the too frequent use of rewards as a means of motivating the child to learn are all factors that may be interpreted by the child as controlling influences and lead to a detriment in learning.

The importance of these two goal orientations is the effect on student learning strategies and motivational patterns. In one group of 176 secondary school students, mastery-oriented students reported positive attitudes toward class, using different learning strategies, and a preference for challenging tasks in contrast to their performance-oriented counterparts (Ames & Archer, 1988).

The focus in the performance goal orientation is to validate one's ability as compared to others (M. Gredler, 1992). Social comparison information is the yardstick for personal judgments of ability. In contrast, the focus in the learning or task-involved orientation is to learn to master new skills. The yardstick for judging ability is prior learning and subsequent improvement and progress. When classroom goals consistently emphasize social comparison, the win–loss nature of the situation generates evaluation anxiety and lowered self-esteem (Dweck, 1989).

For example, Stipek and Daniels (1988) found that children in several perfor-mance-oriented kindergartens rated their competence lower than children in learning-oriented kindergartens. In competitive goal structures, failure often is detrimental even for children with high self-concepts. Increased self-criticism and lowered perceptions of their own abilities occur (Ames & Archer, 1988).

Instructional and Remediation Options for Learning Problems in Young Children: A Summary

From the preceding discussion it has been determined that there are many factors that must be considered in order to organize and implement effective instructional and remedial intervention programs. Several instructional models have been suggested at one time or another for use within the schools. Each model has its adherents with the result that educational personnel often are confused as to what intervention approaches are of most value.

Several problems in remediation research were identified in this chapter. One major problem that has been found to be almost completely neglected by psychologists and educators is that of the Hawthorne effect. Many "new" approaches to intervention and/or remediation programs work just because of the increased attention given to the students.

The field of intervention/remediation has also been subject to several fads. Discussions in this area will emphasize one method of intervention as being of great value with no attention given to the fact that many intervention programs are of worth.

A number of intervention/remediation programs that have been shown to produce beneficial effects on students' academic performance have been discussed. These include programs that emphasize processing strategies; those that stress behavioral facets to those that blend motivational variables with a sophisticated analysis of learning strategies such as is found in the Reading Recovery Program to those that emphasize computer-assisted instruction.

It is also important to note that providing appropriate instruction to children in first grade also involves making sure that the classroom schedule is appropriately organized to provide adequate instructional time in the first place. Additionally, it has been demonstrated that careful grouping of children according to their instructional needs has paid off in improved levels of academic performance. And, last, it is important to remember that how educational goals are structured within the classroom will help improve the learning performance of the students.

12

ISSUES AFFECTING EARLY CHILDHOOD EDUCATION

The organization of early childhood education (i.e., preschool and kindergarten) and the type of curriculum to be implemented in the next several years depend on a variety of factors. Discussed in this chapter are some of the factors involved in the debate about the objectives of early childhood education. This chapter also examines some of the social forces impinging on education that affect for better or worse how we as a people attempt to educate our children. Fifty years ago, most public schools did not have kindergarten programs. Today the kindergarten is an accepted part of the school program in most school districts in the United States.

Sources of Concern

One source of concern in the education of young children is the increasing conflict over what are to be the goals of the kindergarten program.

The Kindergarten Curriculum: Dimensions of the Debate

The primary objectives of the kindergarten year have been subjected to several cyclic changes in the past 25 years, according to Katz, Raths, and Torres (1987). At times emphasis has been placed on the importance of the role of play in the lives of young children. At other times the formality of the curriculum and the primacy of academic skills have been considered more important.

This conflict over the educational objectives and goals in early childhood education is reflected in the many diverse points of view found among educators. (See Elkind, 1989; Glazer, 1988; Katz et al., 1987.)

Those opposed to formal instruction in kindergarten believe that such an emphasis fosters dependence in children at a time when children should be developing more self-reliance (Glazer, 1988). Weikart questioned this type of teaching and stated, "it is much better to have a six-year-old who is curious about the world than a kid who knows his ABC's and isn't curious" (cited in Glazer, 1988, p. 60). Elkind considered that a good education is the same for all children and believed that instructional activities "instill in children more rote, dependent learning styles, which are hard to get out later" (in Glazer, 1988, p. 60).

According to Glazer (1988) there is a "battle raging over the correct philosophy of education for four to five-year-olds" (p. 54). Glazer states that some groups seek an increasing academic curriculum for kindergarten while opposing groups charge that such a curriculum leads to anxiety about possible failure and diminished interest in school at a later age. While Glazer states that most nursery schools will offer a play-oriented experience to 3- to 4-year-olds, some educators support the introduction of academics for 4-year-olds. Glazer believes that current kindergartens all offer some academic studies, and for her the question is whether the curriculum should simply consist of prereading programs or whether there should be a full-fledged reading curriculum (p. 55).

According to Glazer the dispute is considered to be nothing more than a continuation of the feud between developmentalists such as Elkind, who emphasizes a curriculum based on Piagetian principles and learning through concrete experiences, and the behaviorists, who believe that young children have the ability to learn specific bits of information directly from the teacher. This latter view is reflected in the work of Bereiter and Engleman, who used the "direct instruction" technique to teach academic material to low-income children in Operation Headstart (Glazer, p. 56).

Advocates of the maturational school of readiness, with its emphasis on postponement, state that their approach to schooling is consistent with increased educational expectations found in some of the school districts. Although a few parents want their children to enter school as early as possible and begin a reading program, currently a number of middle-class parents take to heart the doctrine of postponement of school entrance as formulated by the Gesellians. It was as if the message was: "Since school is now going to be a rat race, I want to make sure my child is definitely ready for the arduous journey. Therefore I am going to keep my child out of school for another year. I am also going to make certain my child will be a 'leader'; I believe I can ensure that by delaying my child's entrance to school."

Pressures on the Kindergarten: What Kind of Curriculum?

The diversity of viewpoints about the kindergarten program can be seen in current educational statements. It is stated by Walsh (1989) that kindergarten has become the center of increased scrutiny due to a number of factors. One factor is the increased concern about public education in general that is reflected in the 32 reports issued over a 5-year time span. Increasing evidence that early schooling (in the form of such programs as Operation Headstart) has been effective is another factor that has brought increased attention to the kindergarten year (Walsh, 1989). Both Walsh and Glazer (1988) consider that yet another important issue is which educational group is going to "control" the kindergarten curriculum. While Glazer contends that the battle is between the Piagetians and the behaviorists, Walsh provides a somewhat different analysis. He contends that one group of educators focuses on efficiency in schooling (i.e., "the school effectiveness position"). For this group the emphasis is on academic goals, high standards, and time on task. It is probable that these educators are similar to the behaviorists that Glazer pinpoints. Walsh states that another group is composed of those who consider themselves developmentalists and follow Piagetian tenets. Although there are those who interpret Piagetian tenets "correctly" and understand the broad implications of a Piagetian curriculum, Walsh states there is another group that has gained influence. He emphasizes that many educators really follow a "vulgar-Piagetian" theory. Such a theory "uses Piagetian terminology and emphasizes the child's movement through invariant stages, but the mechanism for developmental change is not the equilibration of self-regulatory process, as Piaget argued, but biological maturation" (Walsh, 1989, p. 387). In essence the vulgar-Piagetians are those educators who are maturationalists in disguise.

Walsh considers that neither theory is helpful for present-day education. For him the real problem is that a number of students are not doing well in school. He states that the schools define the problem in inadequate ways: "The 'problem' of the late birthday child; the problem of the immature child." Walsh makes an important point when he says "school failure will never be solved by redefining it away" (Walsh, 1989, p. 388). The fact that so many personnel in the schools perceive the problem in vulgar-Piagetian terms is troubling for the future of early childhood education.

Certain school districts, faced with increased accountability demands from school administrators and politicians, have added academic requirements to the kindergarten and first-grade curriculum. In certain schools in both Texas and Florida, parents complained of the imposition of requirements for higher levels of achievement by school administrators even in excess of what has been requested by the state board of education. In interviews with school personnel conducted by the author, educators in two southeastern school districts acknowledged that the school superintendent imposed increased curriculum demands on kindergarten and first-grade children to ensure that students would perform "adequately" on standardized tests mandated to be administered in grades 3, 4, and 5.

At the same time it is generally acknowledged that young children today have had more varied experiences prior to entering kindergarten. Many children have attended some form of preschool for up to 2 years before entering kindergarten. The traditional role of the kindergarten in helping children become accustomed to being away from home is perceived as less important than it once was. However, learning to work and play together as a cohesive group is considered just as important by a number of educators (Katz et al., 1987).

In a recent analysis of kindergarten practices in the state of Virginia, Walsh (1989) remarks that the kindergarten is losing its identity and protected status. "As the elementary school changes so does the kindergarten" (p. 379). The cutoff age to enter kindergarten in Virginia was changed from December 31 in 1985 to September 30 in 1988. Walsh commented on the number of teachers who perceived children as unable to perform successfully in kindergarten. Yet it should be remembered that for the past 40 years educators have *always* emphasized that there is a group of children "too young" for kindergarten and first grade, *regardless* of the fact that the entrance age has steadily increased over that time period.

Walsh states that retention of kindergarten children in Virginia schools has increased at an alarming rate. In one school district he notes that 39% of the kindergarten children were not promoted to first grade; in another district, 48% of eligible first-grade children were retained. Just as Payton (1990) ascertained from her survey of Texas primary programs, Walsh also discovered that the decision as to who was to be retained was flawed. A variety of different criteria were used by Virginia teachers to make a decision as to who should be held back.

According to Walsh, many kindergarten teachers emphasized that the kindergarten curriculum was now "more demanding." Yet from the studies reported previously (Carrington, 1982; Dockery, 1985), it is seen that in a number of school districts kindergarten children currently are making a successful adjustment to school. It would appear that several school districts do not make impossible demands on their young students.

The Contributions of Kindergarten in American Society: A Diversity of Approaches

An excellent example is provided by Hannah (1984) of how a project during the kindergarten year helped children adapt to school and improved their "readiness" for more formal schooling in the first grade. She investigated the value of an experimental kindergarten project where primary emphasis was on the teaching of language. Selected children attended four special sessions a week of 75 minutes each during which time a specific program of language activities was implemented. Hannah was able to show a considerable reduction in children scoring below the 40th percentile on the Metropolitan Readiness Test at the conclusion of the program. For the years prior to the introduction of the specialized curriculum unit, 35% of the children scored in the lowest 40% of the kindergarten population. During the intervention year this percentage was reduced to 21% of the kindergarten population. This is one example of how intervention during the kindergarten year was helpful to the children.

Another example is the study by Rosenthal (1969). She describes the contribution of a kindergarten program in a northeastern school district. She measured the growth in readiness of kindergarten children categorized into older and younger groups. Administering the Lee Clark readiness test, she found a significant increase in readiness for both the older and younger children during their year in kindergarten. Although the older group obtained a pretest score that was significantly higher than the younger group of children, the situation changed on the posttest. The younger children's rate of gain was much greater than that of the older group with the result that the posttest readiness scores of the two groups did not differ at the end of kindergarten.

Rosenthal's study is an important one for it reminds us again of what can be accomplished during the kindergarten year and of the educational value of that year's schooling. In this study, the carefully designed curriculum to which the children were exposed resulted in considerable improvement in readiness scores.

An example of a developmentally appropriate kindergarten program that embraces the whole day has been ably presented by Bryant, Clifford, and Peisner (1989). Such a classroom features many examples of children's creative work. Children are allowed to choose from many center activities during the week. These centers contain many active learning materials such as puzzles and art materials, tapes or records. The environment is relaxed, and a cooperative atmosphere exists. John Martin's Writing to Read Program is used during 1 hour of the $6\frac{1}{2}$-hour kindergarten day. Children can choose with whom to sit during the day. Recess is incorporated into the daily routine. There is a group session where a story is read or an upcoming field trip is discussed. At holiday times there is a discussion of safety rules and children draw pictures to illustrate a rule they have selected. Notes are sent home each day to a few parents marking learning activities enjoyed by the child (Bryant et al., 1989, Appendix M).

Such a kindergarten program is worlds away from the "kindergarten reinforcement" program in operation for disadvantaged students in the Cleveland, Ohio, schools (Garvey, 1983). This project emphasizes the development of basic learning skills in inner-city schoolchildren. Serving almost 6,000 children in 84 public schools, the project has been in operation for 16 years and utilizes a staff of 50 to work with kindergarten teachers. The program centers around improving the language development of the children. Although no mention is made in the report as to the amount of time given over to such instructional activities, it obviously involves a considerable portion of the kindergarten day. Garvey notes that 85% of the children who scored below average on the prereading skills section of the Metropolitan Reading Test scored at the average or above-average level on the posttest given in the spring of the year.

Although the Cleveland program would appear to have been a worthwhile project for these inner-city children who need concentrated help with prereading skill development, the question is whether such a curriculum should be common for children in all kindergartens and whether some of this curriculum emphasis could just as easily be moved to first grade.

The Denver, Colorado, Kindergarten Project

It is also helpful to look back at an important reading project introduced into kindergarten in the 1960s. Over a quarter of a century ago the Denver public schools mounted a massive program of providing reading instruction to 4,000 kindergarten children (Burmeister, 1983; McKee & Brzeinski, 1966). It should also be noted that this group of kindergarten children were *younger* in age than current entrants to kindergarten. Instructional activities in reading were limited to 20 minutes a day throughout the kindergarten year. McKee and Brzeinski concluded that (1) beginning reading skills could be taught effectively to typical kindergarten children; (2) that the relative permanence of reading gains made in kindergarten depended upon adjustments in the educational programs made in later grades; (3) gains were made in reading comprehension, vocabulary, and speed; and (4) the number of books read independently increased. There was no evidence that this early instruction in beginning reading produced deleterious effects on vision or that it created any problems in school adjustment or produced negative attitudes toward reading (pp. 87–88).

It is recommended that present-day educators and psychologists reread this monumental study that certainly took a more relaxed approach to the teaching of reading than is found in today's applications of the "direct instruction" approach.

Curriculum Objectives in Other Societies

The many concerns of American parents have led to questions about how other societies view early childhood education and consideration of their educational practices. It might be fruitful to inquire how other societies approach the education of young children within the context of this controversy over the objectives of kindergarten education.

In a comparison of early childhood education in different cultures, Tobin, Wu, and Davidson (1989) mention that in "most Japanese preschools there is surprisingly little emphasis on academic instruction" (p. 191). These researchers found that only 2% of Japanese respondents considered that a primary reason for preschool was "to give a child a good start academically" (p. 191). However, 51% of American respondents chose this statement as one of the most important reasons for children to attend preschool.

Although the official age of entry to school is 6 years for both Japan and the United States, at age 13 achievement in math is considerably higher for Japanese students than for American students (Austin & Postlewaite, 1974). It can be legitimately concluded that *how* the curriculum is structured during the elementary and middle school years, the quality of teaching, and the motivational environment that is present are the factors that contribute important variables to produce this differential achievement rate. It would appear that stressing an academic environment in both preschool and kindergarten in the American schools is *not* a major factor that is required to produce a higher level of academic performance.

Austin and Postlewaite also reported that the reading comprehension scores of Swedish students were considerably higher than those of American students when tested at age 10. At first glance this might appear to be due to the fact that the official age of entry to school for Swedish children is 7 compared to the entry age of 6 for American children. However, such a conclusion would appear to be false since Italian children earned the same high score in reading comprehension as the Swedish students, yet they begin school at age 6. Once again it would seem that the important variable is *how* the school experience is structured during the elementary and high school years. The attention to entrance age has become an overriding concern with some American educators, psychologists, and politicians. Such a concern has deflected attention away from more important factors within the educational environment that exert a greater influence in determining academic achievement.

Early Childhood Education in Texas: A Case Study

A number of Texas parents have become child advocates opposed to those who follow the vulgar-Piagetian point of view described earlier in this chapter. This section discusses some historical facets of public education in Texas and their importance in understanding today's concerns about the education of the young child.

In 1930 the legal age for entrance to Texas schools was lowered from 7 to 6. This was followed by an expansion of required schooling from 11 to 12 years' duration. As a consequence, educators believed this would result in a positive payoff especially for children in elementary school. "In some instances traditional first grade work was [now] delayed as much as a half year" (Devault et al., 1957, p. 15). "The work in the first six grades has [now] been reorganized providing for an easier beginning for the 6-year-old child in the first grade" (Rogers, 1940, in Devault et al., p. 16).

Devault et al. noted in 1957 that there was a "problem" in the schools with underaged students, yet he and his staff acknowledged that whatever the chronological age set for admission there would always be children, within any age group admitted, who were less mature than the other children.

Although transition room or readiness room programs were discussed in 1957 by Devault et al. as one approach to "helping" the underage child, these researchers recommended the establishment of public school kindergarten for all students who became 5 by September 1. "This seems to be the best way to meet the problems associated with underage enrollees" (p. 128). Thus over one third of a century previously, Texas educators were discussing the lack of readiness of children to begin the first grade in Texas schools. Note the response: expansion of the length of schooling to 12 years and the introduction of kindergarten into the schools.

Today many Texas educators are insisting that only with the establishment of prekindergarten, retaining children in kindergarten, or the placement of children in pre-first grade classes (i.e., transition rooms) can pertinent educational objectives be reached.

Retention Problems in Texas Schools

It is also important to note the increased use of retention within the Texas school system over the years. In a study of retention rates of Whites, Blacks, and Mexican-American students, Casavantes (1974) demonstrated the dramatic differences that existed between the school systems of Texas and California. For each of 100 Anglos who failed first grade in California, 130 Anglos were failed in Texas. For every 100 Blacks failed in California, 367 Blacks were failed in Texas. And for every 100 Mexican-Americans failed in California, 228 were failed in Texas. Once again such findings indicate the high retention rate for first-grade students that existed in 1968 when these data were collected.

This brief history of earlier events in Texas education would indicate once again that the "problem" of underage students along with the extensive use of retention as a remedial device are long-standing issues. Over a time span of 34 to 50 years, Texas educators have worried about first-graders not being "ready" for school. In the 1940s public school was extended another year, and it was recommended that kindergarten also be added to help children get "ready" for first grade. Now in 1992 Texas educators again want to extend the length of schooling by requiring an additional year either by retaining the child in kindergarten or adding a pre-first grade. The same arguments are presented today as they were 50 years ago: that

(a) many children are underaged and can not compete successfully in school or (b) the children are immature and extra time will allow them to mature.

The real questions that must be asked are: (1) What are the limits of the school sorting process? (2) How long can we actually ask children to remain in school? and (3) Are there no ways that we can restructure the curriculum and require the educational establishment to reach important educational goals without further time extensions?

As will be noted in Chapter 13, on parent concerns, parents have definitely lost patience with many in the educational sector and do not consider further screening or extension of school an adequate answer for the education of their children. Truly an educational crisis in early childhood education exists!

The Resolution of Diverse Viewpoints: Some Factors to Consider

It is obvious there are a number of different points of view about childhood education being expressed by educators and psychologists. These expressions of opinion reflect the somewhat chaotic state of early childhood education today. However, there are several kindergarten programs that currently reflect important educational objectives.

Which Educational Model to Follow?

It would appear that important principles of childhood education are being overlooked in the current controversy over educational objectives. Unfortunately a number of early childhood education specialists believe that the kindergarten curriculum must follow completely one educational model or another. Although it is stated that most kindergarten programs today emphasize academic work (Glazer, 1988), the Educational Research Service (1986) reports that only 18% of kindergartens are in that category whereas 50% of kindergartens are said to engage in "some" academic preparation. And, as stated previously, forgotten in all of this controversy is the fact that children entering kindergarten today are older chronologically and perhaps should be able to handle a more advanced curriculum.

The conflict perhaps can best be resolved by embracing the viewpoint of Katz, who states that the ideal kindergarten setting should provide an opportunity for the child to pursue spontaneous play and at the same time offer the child an introduction to basic skills "on a very low-key, low pressure level" (Glazer, 1988, p. 56). Katz et al. (1987) also mention important conditions that should be considered in the teaching of prereading and reading skills in kindergarten: "If prereading and reading instruction are presented in a formal way, *using a single methodology,* experience suggests that some (perhaps as many as one third) of the class will fail" (p. 36). It is the contention of these educators that most schools do adopt a single method of instruction and implement it with some form of ability grouping. When ability grouping is introduced it is obvious that the amount of screening and testing of children will increase. As has been stated previously, many parents and educators today decry the emphasis on academics that is found in some kindergarten programs. A significant percentage of the population has believed that the school must increase the emphasis on academics at an early age to meet the competitive demands emanating from other nations such as Germany and Japan. Pressure to emphasize academics and to make sure kindergarten children are "ready" for first grade became the rallying point for a number of educators and politicians during the 1970s and 1980s. The renewed emphasis on academic activities for inner-city children in Operation Headstart fueled the demand for an increased academic curriculum for children in all kindergartens.

This report from the National Association of State Boards of Education (NASBE, 1988) sums up the current educational scene by arguing against defining education as simply a competitive struggle:

> If education is seen as a contest that pits children against their peers, or a race against our foreign competitors, we risk teaching very young children the wrong academic tasks in an inappropriate fashion before they are ready. (p. 3)

The NASBE also called for establishment of an early childhood unit within the school system that would attempt to implement a curriculum that is appropriate to the development of children with the age range of 4 to 8 years. However, it should be mentioned that some larger school districts currently have such a unit but the personnel in charge hold a maturational (i.e., Gesellian) philosophy which translates into heavy use of holding students back and frequent use of pre-kindergarten and pre-first placement programs. It is therefore important to note that organizational restructuring of early childhood education will only work successfully if the educators in charge of such a unit have an enlightened philosophy of education.

The task force of the NASBE comments that "developmentally appropriate" programs should provide an intellectually stimulating environment "that helps children extend their knowledge and skills within an atmosphere that fosters sense of belonging" (p. 12). Providing such a learning environment will require quality teaching of the highest order.

The NASBE task force also recommends increased attempts by schools to reach out to parents and says that the schools had not done enough in this area. The determined efforts of school personnel in Texas to reverse the ban on kindergarten retention and transition programs indicates that parents' concerns are still not being heard, understood, and accepted. The reader only needs to refer to Chapters 13 and

14, on the perceptions of parents and legal aspects of the readiness problem, to understand the concerns of parents over misuse of readiness testing and the use of ill-conceived placement options for kindergarten and first-grade children.

Educators vs. Parents: A Need for Cooperation

The attitude among some educators is that there has been an overemphasis on parental rights in conjunction with special education programs. Evans (1990) believes that "mainstreaming legislation is weighted toward parental rights and against professional prerogatives" (p. 73). However, analysis of the parental concerns and complaints discussed in Chapter 13 would indicate that aggrieved parents frequently find it difficult to obtain a response from school personnel or the board of education *until* they bring a lawsuit in an attempt to have their legitimate complaints considered.

Analysis of several appeals cases of special education children undertaken by the author indicates that the appeals process does help to clarify important dimensions of the assessment and placement process. Judgments in many of these cases have clarified the rights of parents in the education process (Gredler, 1991). The final question to ask is how can the crisis be solved? The resolution of so many opposing points of view concerning the "proper" education of young children, arriving at a consensus of goals and objectives for the kindergarten and first grade, will be difficult to achieve. However, there are hopeful signs on the horizon and these are discussed in the following section.

Some Hopeful Signs

It would appear that those individuals who emphasize full-scale academics in kindergarten and want an increased entrance age are actually in retreat. By emphasizing *appropriate* educational practices that are truly developmental, educators who hold this point of view are saying that readiness screening has been overemphasized; that prekindergarten and transition rooms are an unneeded impediment to a quality education; and that current retention practices are unacceptable (Bredekamp & Shepard, 1989; Gredler, 1978).

The latter part of the 1980s saw a change in attitudes about early childhood education and a definite backlash that has been led by a number of parent groups, a small group of psychologists and educators, and several professional childhood education organizations. These individuals have exerted leadership in helping to set proper curriculum objectives for kindergarten and first grade and have reemphasized the multiple and varied goals of the kindergarten curriculum.

Based on extensive interviews with parents in Tennessee, Florida, Pennsylvania, California, Texas, South Carolina, and New Hampshire, a majority of parents interviewed believe that a more relaxed setting in kindergarten is needed and that educators should leave a more formalized approach to reading for the first grade.

Understanding these limitations has brought a rare consensus among a number of important professional education groups such as the National Association of School Boards of Education and the National Association of Education for Young Children. Such groups, along with the active leadership of educators in such states as New Hampshire and Massachusetts and parent groups such as those formed in Texas, Florida, and Tennessee, indicate that a number of organizations and individuals now understand that a real crisis exists and are attempting to find a solution. The success of their efforts will be seen over the next several years as the schools introduce more individualized instruction and as there is an increase in the monitoring of schools to ascertain if their retention rates have actually declined. Continued review of early childhood education curricula and increased in-depth supervision of teaching personnel who are assigned to kindergarten and first-grade classes will undoubtedly help to improve educational practice.

However, perhaps the most important aspect in resolving the current educational crisis is whether our society can regain its confidence in directing and managing its future as a nation. If confidence is regained, perhaps the "crisis mentality" in early childhood education will abate and a greater consensus as to educational objectives and goals will be achieved.

Summary

This chapter has considered many dimensions of the controversy over early childhood education. Diverse points of view abound as to how best to educate our young children. The reader will note how the flavor of the argument has remained the same over the last generation, as witness the brief discussion of historical aspects of Texas education. However, it would seem that a watershed concerning educational practices for the young child has now been reached. This is due to the fact that retention rates have been on a steady increase. Although many educators, psychologists, and parents consider retention rates to have been unacceptably high in the 1960s, 1970s, and 1980s, these rates continue to climb in many school districts.

It has also been shown in this chapter how the same solutions have been used over a time span of 30 to 50 years (i.e., retention; readiness room placement) and still the controversy over readiness practice and curriculum objectives continues. It would seem that a solution may well be forced on the schools in the near future because (a) a number of parents have begun to lose patience and (b) there is a limit to which school time can be lengthened for the child.

SECTION **IV**

Related Issues

13

THE REACTIONS OF PARENTS

In recent years parents have become knowledgeable about the research literature on transition rooms and other forms of retention. Their reactions have ranged from sharing their concerns with each other to that of forming active groups to change school policies.

Parental Concerns

The parental concerns presented in this section were expressed in group and individual interviews with parents in Florida, New Hampshire, Tennessee, and Texas. The parents' goal is not to accelerate the progress of their children in school. Instead, their focus is on the adequacy of the school experience for all children. The range of their concerns includes (1) the lack of defensible criteria for retention decisions, (2) questions about assessment practices, (3) the focus on "late" birthdays to the exclusion of other factors which indicate competence to begin school, (4) legal issues, (5) social effects of retention, and (6) the nature of the curriculum.

The Lack of Defensible Criteria for Retention Decisions

Observations made by parents include the lack of documentation in some schools for placement decisions. One parent noted that, "In some schools no documentation is offered except that of teacher opinions about children recommended for retention." Another noted, "We have been told that the school never retains children for academic reasons; only for social reasons. What are their criteria? We are never told of the specific reasons." A third parent expressed her concern about "retention of my child for 'emotional maturity.' What do they mean?"

One parent described the situation in which "the school principal, when discussing one student, stated that the student had '80% of the knowledge he needed to be passed on to the first grade.' If this is true, why take a year of this child's educational life to teach him the 15% to 20% that he needs? Why not have a summer class instead of placing him in a transition class for a year?"

Also of concern are the different failure rates in different kindergarten classes. "Why did 50% of Mrs. X's class fail to pass to the first grade?" asked one parent. "Is it normal for any class to have a 50% failure rate? What are the criteria for 'success' in kindergarten?"

Ambiguity and contradictions in many retention decisions also are a problem. One parent reported that "on the school's final evaluation record, a number of records had 'TRANS or First' by their names. When the principal was asked that this meant, she stated that these students could have been placed in either the transition or first-grade class. What was the determining factor for the grade placement of these students?"

A similar contradiction in another school occurred when, 2 weeks before school was out, a note was sent home informing the parents that their child would not be passed to the first grade. However, up to that point, all reports indicated that the child was doing excellent work, with remarks on the report such as "student is doing great." When questioned about these remarks, the teacher stated that "great did not mean *great* sometimes."

In contrast, others reported that the school informed them very quickly that their children would undoubtedly be in the transition room the following year. "How can they know that will be the best placement when my child has been in kindergarten only 6 weeks?" asked one parent.

The lack of a definitive rationale for transition room placement is further indicated by the different placement decisions made by public and private schools. For example, one of the children slated to go to the transition room in one school district was accepted by both a private and another public school district to attend first grade. After review of the student's school records, including report cards and final test results from the state and school, the parent stated, "they had no problem accepting him in their first-grade classes." Another parent noted that "we have learned that large numbers of children have left the public school system for a private school because the parents disagree with the label of 'emotionally immature' or 'developmentally young.' "

The anxiety experienced by parents when faced with lack of definitive criteria is reflected in the following statement by a parent in a Florida community:

> The teacher can't make up her mind about why my child needs to be placed in a transition room for next year. First, she said he should be there because he had a low Gesell developmental age in October [test administered during the kindergarten year]. But when he took [the test] again in April, he was right on target [i.e., developmental age of 6-0]. But she still said he should be in the transition room and cited some classroom incidents which she said indicated "a lack of persistence" and therefore he was "immature." I disagree with her opinion but what am I to do? The teacher called me at home and said the test results were on the borderline. What does this mean? What do I do next? The school says to be on the "safe" side my child should be in the transition room next year.

The ambiguity about placement decisions as an issue is coupled with the lack of data on the effects of retention decisions, another parental concern. Typical parental comments addressed possible differences between retained and non-retained students in later years. For example, parents in a Tennessee community asked: "Do other students who passed to the first grade score higher on the state achievement test than the students who were held back in the transition class?" Similarly, "What is the failure rate from kindergarten to the first grade over the past 2 years or since the transition class was implemented? Is the passing rate any better?" School personnel had no data available to answer her questions.

Another parent from a Tennessee school district noted that

> They [school personnel] say that transition room children don't need to repeat, but I think that is due to the school policy that says no transition room child will be considered for retention after 1 year in that class. I want to see achievement test scores on these kids. But you know what? The school doesn't give any achievement tests to these children. All we get are comments on how wonderful the children are doing now [since they attended the transition room].

Questions About Assessment Practices

The development of questionable instruments, the methods of testing, and the Gesell test in particular were all of concern to parents. For example, one parent noted, "In our school district children are assigned to the transition room program based in part on a rating scale administered in April of the kindergarten year. Children were rated on behavioral dimensions such as being able to tie shoes, catch a ball, and the extent of difficulty our child showed in 'sitting still,' 'standing still,' and 'remembering.' " The 32-item scale was devised locally by the school psychologist and teachers; as far as could be determined, no validity or reliability data were obtained.

Similarly, "The school placed my child in the transition room program based on rating scales that school personnel made up. They never showed me the scales until I demanded them. I can't understand how they arrived at the cutoff score for placement in the transition room."

Parents also were concerned about decisions made as to the emotional maturity of their children on the basis of observations only. In other words, input from parents would seem to be important. Furthermore, in at least one school district, parents indicated a lack of opportunity to discuss Gesell test scores that result in a label of "emotionally immature." Also of concern was that "No input is allowed from 'outside' professional opinions, whether from physicians or private psychologists. One Florida parent said there had been a refusal to listen to 'outside' professionals because school personnel state 'they have been paid to give an opinion.' "

Number of teeth was an important criterion in another school. "Children are checked, either by asking the children, or by visual inspection, on their number of teeth. One boy, in a New Hampshire school, who was required to have several teeth pulled by the orthodontist, was in excellent shape 'developmentally' because of the loss!"

Another concern was the extent of testing. In one Florida school district, a parent reported that the school gave her child four readiness tests during the year—a Gesell and the Metropolitan in October, and the same tests again in April. In her view, that was too much testing.

Concern about the heavy reliance on the Gesell was expressed by several parents. Comments included, "We are concerned about when the Gesell should be administered. We consider it has been given at inappropriate times and under improper conditions." Another parent said, "An inordinate emphasis is placed on the results of the Gesell to the exclusion of other factors." Parents in Florida, New York, New Hampshire, and Texas all made similar comments about the use of the Gesell.

Competence of test administrators also was an issue. For example, "The teacher [in Florida] who tested my child is called a 'developmental examiner.' I don't think she has any real testing background. She had a 4-hour workshop to learn how to give and score the test and that's all."

The effects of the use of the test, in one New Hampshire parent's view, are not positive. Instead, "My son lost a year of his life based on these tests." Also, parents in Florida and New Hampshire noted that a logical negative effect is a higher dropout rate for students who have been retained than that of those kept with their age group.

Parents in one school district in New Hampshire compiled information from the professional literature on weaknesses of the Gesell and presented a document of recommendations to the school board. This document is discussed later in this chapter in the section, "Parent Advocacy Activities."

The "Late Birthday" Child

Parents in a New Hampshire school district stated that too much emphasis is placed on the child's chronological age. "When I have a conference with the teacher, she's always bringing up the fact that my child has a 'late' birthday. The teachers are obsessed with the birthdays of our children. Isn't anything else important?" asked one parent. Similarly, "The first-grade teachers point out that too many of our children are 'immature.' We don't hear about what they are doing right." Also, "Is 'young' chronological age as the 'cause' of children's learning problems the only thing they're taught in their university classes?"

Other parents in a New York State school district reported that they asked that the child's birthday not be revealed to the developmental testers. However, the parents indicated that it is the first item asked for, even before the child's name.

The reliance on birthdate was reported by one family who moved to New Hampshire from another state. The child had been kept out of school the year before the move. However when the child was tested after the move, the placement decision was pre-first. When the parents questioned the decision, school personnel asked, "Wasn't he born in 1981?" When the parents indicated that 1980 was the birth year, the answer from school personnel was that an error had been made about his birthdate and that he was now considered to be "normal."

Another New Hampshire mother described her son's entry into school. Although he was reading before the age of 5 and calculating number problems in his head, he was placed in a pre-first class because of "young characteristics." The boy later was enrolled in a private school. In the seventh grade, his math teachers reported that he was sufficiently gifted that they had difficulty providing a challenging curriculum for him. In a school district that did not rely on the Gesell for placement, the mother believes that the delayed placement would not have occurred.

Legal Questions Raised by Parents

The frustration experienced by parents at the use of transition rooms is indicated by their exploration of the legality of such actions. For example, parents in Tennessee and New Hampshire all asked, "Can children who are being placed in the transition class legally attend instead the first grade since the transition class is not required by the state?"

Others noted that the parents are not allowed to review school records such as procedures letters, policy letters, and school board minutes that address the establishment and administration of the transition class. More important, parents also indicated that the school should have in place appeal procedures that may be implemented when parents disagree with the decision of the school personnel. Also, retention decisions are sometimes made by the teachers without any consultation with the school psychologist. Parents also are not informed about their rights concerning additional assessment or review by the school psychologist.

Social Effects

Several possible social and emotional outcomes of retention decisions were discussed by Florida and New Hampshire parents. Several New Hampshire parents posed the question of the class mix in eighth grade of different age groups. That is, some children are retained as much as 2 years prior to first grade (pre-kindergarten, kindergarten, and transition room). The long-range outcome is that the eighth grade includes 13-year-old girls and 15-year-old boys. The parents wondered if this was appropriate from a developmental perspective.

Immediate social effects, however, are the reactions of other children. New Hampshire parents of children who were placed in a transition class reported that "our children were subjected to ridicule. They were told they were in the 'dummy class,' and 'the retard class.' They were also called 'retards' by the others."

Another expressed concern was the emotional growth of the retained children. In other words, if children are retained for up to 2 years and are interacting with children who are essentially 2 years younger, how can their emotional growth keep pace with their chronological age?

Parental Advocacy Activities

Parents often stated in individual interviews that they felt they were the only individuals who had concerns about readiness screening and placement decisions made by school personnel. However, as these parents began exchanging information with others in the community, they learned they shared common concerns and questions. As a result, parental advocacy groups have begun to be formed in a number of school districts throughout the United States. The response of these groups to school readiness policies has varied considerably. Activities range from meetings where parents simply share common concerns to groups that present petitions to school boards to organizing in order to change local school policies or to lobbying for change in readiness policies at the state level.

Parents frequently commented that they were listened to politely by school personnel and board members when they presented their concerns about readiness screening and placement decisions. However, few, if any, policies ever actually changed. This conclusion was the common reaction of parent groups in Florida and in Tennessee.

Once established, some parental groups develop and change in regard to their goals and objectives. Others, however, seem to be satisfied with meeting in coffee klatches to discuss what they consider to be misguided readiness and placement policies. These parents find it helpful to be able to vent their frustrations, but shrink from any other course of action because of the demands that will be made on them in time and organizational efforts.

Two New Hampshire Advocacy Efforts

In one New Hampshire community, parents whose children where all supposedly slated to go to first grade the next year banded together and informed the principal and teachers in their small school that, despite whatever the results of the Gesell test showed, all their children were going to be placed in first grade in the fall. The parents monitored the school personnel closely and made certain that the following September all children were in first grade. One of the results of their action was that the transition room teacher was reassigned to other duties. At a subsequent follow-up of these children, it was determined that all the children were making satisfactory progress in the first grade.

Parents in another small New Hampshire community formed a group to consider readiness practices in their school district. They contacted officials in the State Department of Education and also obtained information from professional sources. Members of the group prepared a petition that described some of their concerns. An abridged summary of the petition presented to the local school board is given below:

> For several years, our school system has come under scrutiny for its practice of screening first-grade applicants. Parents of first graders find themselves bewildered by the appropriateness of the screening procedure, contrasted with the excellent reputation of the school district. ...
>
> We [the parents] offer below a review of the current literature on readiness testing and the implications it has on screening in our town. In addition, we seek to answer the following questions:
>
> a. Does the Gesell School Readiness Screening Test [sic] provide reliable data in determining readiness of first graders?

b. Is there quantifiable educational value in providing "transition" programs?

c. What are the implications for our town? ...

A number of researchers have concluded that the readiness test used in our town (the Gesell) does not meet the requirements of the American Psychological Association for validity, reliability, or normative information. In addition, the National Association for the Education of Young Children has specifically disqualified the GSRST for screening due to concerns arising from the adequacy of the predictive validity. ...

Very little research has been conducted supporting the view of Gesellian educators or offering validity of their claims. ...

Since little statistical evidence can be found supporting GSRST it is recommended that our school system endorse the NAEYC position paper on standardized testing. In doing so, it would acknowledge the Standards for Educational and Psychological Testing which require standardized tests to comply with the joint committee's technical standards for test construction and evaluation. It would also require that no standardized test be used for screening, diagnosis or assessment unless the test has published statistically acceptable reliability and validity data. ...

Our school system has been moving toward an evaluation system which would require the input of various measures regarding the readiness of the child. In the coming year, first-grade applicants will be required to submit recommendation from kindergarten teachers along with formal letters from parents and a parental questionnaire. These documents, along with 2 days of teacher observations, will go a long way in authorizing the decision to hold back a first grader. The school system will continue use of the GSRST and the Metropolitan Test. It is unclear as to the percentage of weight to be given each of the input measures. If continued emphasis is placed on the GSRST, then serious questions will arise based on the findings in this position paper.

However, it appeared that little change in school policies resulted from submission of the petition. The leader of the group, who now had another child ready to enter school, became so discouraged at the lack of any change, that he felt he could not face the continued conflict over the school system's readiness policies. He therefore removed both his children from the public school system and placed them in a private school. Such a reaction is a common pattern in a number of school districts where parents become frustrated by the continued rigid kindergarten and first-grade classifications and placement policies of the school system. However, the option of leaving a school district is obviously restricted to those parents who can afford to pay the costs of private school tuition. And it is these parents, almost all middle class, who in the past have given loyal support to the public school system.

Advocacy Efforts in a Tennessee Town

In a Tennessee community, parents disturbed about the establishment of a transition program organized and presented a document to the school board about the transition room program. This document stated in part:

> Our final conclusion, as concerned parents, is that part of our children's educational career is being sacrificed so that school districts can have a transition class for reasons we do not fully understand. For school personnel to tell us that our child is too little or too immature is an insufficient answer. How large and/or how mature should a 5 or 6-year-old child be?
>
> The results of students of all grades on Basic Skills Achievement Tests and the Stanford Achievement Tests show that our children scored low compared to the state and national averages. [These results were published in the local newspaper.] As concerned parents, we believe that the children do not have a lower intelligence level than other children in this State or in any other State. However, we do believe that the problem for such low results by our children could lie with those people in leadership positions in the school system and the failure of our school board to provide proper guidance to those in leadership positions. ...
>
> We believe that when parents go to the school board with such a problem as this, the school board should investigate and notify parents of their findings, or at least show interest in some way, and make an investigation to determine if the transition class is accomplishing its goal.

The parent group in this community organized meetings and brought in a psychologist to discuss the lack of value of transition room programs. The lack of a clear explanation as to the reasons for placement of their children in a transition class brought forth angry comments from several parents whose children were slated to attend the transition class. One parent stated: "We were told our kids were being sent to the stopover class because of behavioral problems, not because they couldn't learn."

These parents were not successful in changing the school board's policies. As a result, several parents removed their children from the local school and sent them to a neighboring public school across the county line. The neighboring school district had no transition class and all the children were placed in the first grade.

From Group Meetings to Political Action: The Denver City, Texas, Case

An example of the concern about readiness practices in one school district is found in the parental opposition to readiness policies in Denver City, Texas. The conflict between parents and school personnel is described in some detail because it provides an excellent illustration of the successful organization of an active group of parents who were able to influence the educational policies of a specific school district. The parents from this district presented their case to the state board of education for Texas and were able to obtain support from this agency which in turn resulted in a ban on the use of prekindergarten programs and transition rooms throughout the state of Texas (Cohen, 1990).

Parental concerns were first expressed in 1988 in Denver City when the school trustees revised the entrance policy to kindergarten. At that time the trustees mandated that each child entering school must be screened using a "developmental assessment" instrument (i.e., the Gesell) and added that "proper placement is a privilege not a penalty." It was also stated that first-grade placement required "80%" mastery of an academic checklist and mandated that developmental first-grade placement (i.e., a transition room program) would be in order if the child obtained "less than 80% of 'behavior growth' skills consistently observed" even though the child showed 80% mastery on the academic checklist ("School policy revised . . . ," 1988).

School personnel distributed educational materials to parents that reflected the maturational philosophy of the Gesell Institute. The bulletin emphasized that children *must* be placed on the basis of a developmental age score and that the Gesell readiness test differed from all other readiness tests in the information it could provide about the child. Mention also was made of the harm of "over-placement" of children and that such overplacement was a common occurrence in schools.

One of the bulletins sent to parents mentioned that one psychologist had stated that the Gesell was an excellent predictor of achievement but neglected to mention that he had used an objective form of the Gesell. That form was different from the one in use in the Denver City system, therefore the comparison was not valid. (Refer to Chapter 5 for a description of the objective version.) Material given to the parents also stated that there was only one program that helped children entering school and this was "developmental placement." No other intervention program was discussed.

Parents who opposed this readiness policy organized in 1988. Representatives of the group then contacted the complaints and legal sections of the Texas Education Agency in Austin. In their presentation to this agency the parents made several points. First, the results of only one test were used in making placement decisions about children entering school. Second, children who tested "below 5" developmentally were not receiving the same quality of education as those who tested over 5.

The parents also asked if segregation of the developmentally immature was necessary and asked if better ways to assess children were available. They also questioned whether it was the best policy to test young children for placement 4 to 5 months before they entered school for the first time.

At a board meeting in April, 1989, the parent group again stated their concerns about the developmental program. By that time the group had compiled a book of material that provided evidence of the inadequacies of the Gesell School Readiness Test and the lack of value of a transition room program.

The local board of education appointed a committee composed of pro-transition and anti-transition program members. Reporting in July, 1989, the board accepted the committee's recommendations which included continuation of use of the Gesell as an instrument for kindergarten placement but added other methods such as observations by teachers and parents. Rather than screening 4 to 5 months before kindergarten began in the fall, screening was to be moved up to August. Some parents continued to speak against the use of the Gesell. It is of interest to note how school board members responded to the conflict in views about the transition room program. One board member stated: "We've got to work together" and cited "communications as the problem for past misunderstandings." Another board member said that "interested parties should 'get on the side of children' " ("Kindergarten placement policy okayed . . . ," 1989), completely avoiding the real issues.

It should also be noted that the Denver City school system remained committed to the transition room program, with the superintendent stating that the program was successful. However, the statement was made that "we're going to look at it every year. We will make changes that we feel like [sic] need to be made" (Fritze, 1990, p. A-20).

During 1989 each group (i.e., the parents opposed to the transition room program and the school board who were pro-transition room) brought in outside speakers to argue their particular point of view about transition rooms. However, the Denver City parent group was not satisfied with the changes made in the school program for kindergarten children. They then took their case to officials at the state board of education in Austin.

Denver City parents were also interviewed by reporters for the *New York Times* and *Dallas Times Herald.* Three of the concerned parents appeared on the CBS "Donahue" program in May, 1989. Some Denver City citizens were angry with what they considered to be the "negative" attitude portrayed about their school system and circulated a list of sponsors of the "Donahue" show in order that individuals could contact them and voice their displeasure. In addition, pro Gesellian educational personnel distributed a two-page handout which purported to show that the Gesell was a valid and reliable developmental measure.

Denver City parents who opposed the transition room program stated they were tired of hearing all the stock phrases about kindergarten and first-grade children such as "our little clock inside says we're not ready" or "we want these children to feel good about themselves." The parents replied with the statement: "Don't give us rhetoric, teach our children!" ("Kindergarten placement policy okayed . . . ," 1989). Parents also noted that the teachers in the local school system did not meet the requirements to be Gesell examiners.

As a result of the organized opposition to the transition room program of the Denver City schools, 67% of the parents of children recommended for kindergarten retention or the developmental first said "no" to placement in the transition class. Instead these parents placed their children in first grade.

Meetings with these concerned parents in Denver City resulted in members of the state board of education researching the issues involved in the readiness question. In 1990 they voted unanimously to bar school districts from retaining students in prekindergarten and kindergarten. The state board mentioned that transitional classes were adding an extra year to children's schooling before first grade and were in effect retaining the child (Cohen, 1990).

One board member mentioned that Texas state law permits 6-year-old children to enter first grade. Thus kindergarten retention or transition room placement violated that educational regulation.

The Response of the Texas Education Agency to the Use of Prekindergarten; Kindergarten Retentions and Use of Transition Rooms (A Discussion of 19TAC75.195, Texas Education Agency, 1990)

In the controversy in Texas schools about kindergarten retention and the use of transition rooms, the leadership role of the Texas Education Agency (i.e., state board of education) proved to be crucial. This state unit, at the time under the leadership of W. N. Kirby, Commissioner, provided each school district with answers to a number of issues raised by the abolishment of kindergarten retention and placement of young children in alternative programs instead of regular first grade. These issues are briefly described below.

1. Students in prekindergarten and kindergarten may *not* be retained. Kirby stated categorically that there was no need for an extra-year program for children

prior to entrance to first grade if the regular instructional program proved adequate to meet the educational needs of the children.

2. Children may *not* be placed in extra-year transition room programs either because school personnel believe or results of test measures state they are "immature," "developmentally young," or "not ready for first grade." Promotion/retention decisions are to be based on a student's *educational needs,* rather than "psychological" or "physical" needs.

3. Although use of a transition room program is not banned, if a child is placed in a transition room program this counts as the single-year retention that is permissible during grades 1 to 4.

4. A student 6 years of age on September 1 is to be enrolled in first grade "from which promotion is made to second grade."

5. The state board encouraged the schools to develop children's academic competence by the end of the third grade. Schools were urged to consider the establishment of a nongraded primary unit to include kindergarten and the first and second grades.

6. The state board of education at Austin removed criterion-referenced testing of first-grade children and also stated that numerical grading of children is not required below grade 2.

7. The state board also instituted a system of monitoring and evaluating the appropriateness of prekindergarten programs.

8. In order to eliminate the "need" for retention or transition placements, the Texas Board of Education described the following steps that should be considered:

(a) Schools should provide programs for children aged 3-8 that are "developmentally appropriate." [However it should be noted that school personnel would probably need help in providing such programs because many consider that prekindergarten and transition programs are the only way to provide developmentally appropriate education.]

(b) Schools are to avoid using numerical grades when evaluating the progress of students in prekindergarten, kindergarten, *and* first grade.

(c) Schools are to avoid establishment of rigorous academic standards that far exceed the standards required by the state. The state board of education specifically stated that school districts had implemented academic activities for young children that were artificially high.

(d) Schools should explore the use of available instructional alternatives to address the range of individual differences. [Once again it is important to mention that school personnel must not be wedded to *one* instructional approach but should consider a multitude of approaches. Readers are referred to

Chapter 2 to the discussion of Gates's research that demonstrated how the use of different instructional methods made
a considerable difference in the percentage of students who
were able to be successful in first grade.] (Kirby, 1990;
Texas State Board of Education Committee on Students,
1990)

Reaction of the Pro–Transition Room Group

Insisting that prekindergarten and transition room programs are a "must" for
Texas schools, advocates for transition rooms struck back and asked for consideration of a rule allowing that *with parental consent,* 6-year-old students who
were determined by the school to be not developmentally ready for first grade could
be "assigned to a pre-first, transitional or other grade as deemed appropriate by the
school." It was also stated that retention could still be possible in prekindergarten
and kindergarten because the Texas rule only stated, "no student can be retained
more than one time in grades one–four and one time in grades five–eight" (Texas
State Board of Education Committee on Students, 1990, p. V-63).

It should be noted how difficult it is to change the attitudes and beliefs of a
substantial number of school personnel as to the use of early retention and
placement in readiness rooms. This group of educators is insisting that only by
delay in entering students and by placement in prekindergarten and pre-first will
children be able to perform satisfactorily. No consideration is given to the
possibility of lack of suitable instructional practices that might be found in the
kindergarten and first-grade classroom or to the educational objectives of the
first-grade curriculum.

A number of Texas parents responded to these new developments by raising still
further questions about Texas educational practices. These include the following
statements.

When did "immaturity" become a condition with a fixed
prescription for making a child well?

Children, through no fault of their own, may pay the price for
an adult's view of "readiness."

All the phraseology and terminology leads one to believe
"immaturity" can be treated with an extra year, preferably
between kindergarten and first grade.

We think that special education guidelines should be used for
that kind of special placement. No teacher evaluation, or assessment measure, by itself is valid enough for that type of decision

(i.e., kindergarten retention; prekindergarten or pre-first placement).

The inappropriate curriculum of [Texas] primary grades is the underlying problem.

The Texas board asked to look at other options. Keep the focus on changes in the curriculum.

Who is going to be responsible for the decision of determining "ready"? and what qualifications will this person possess?

How will "grade as deemed appropriate" or "pre-first" be funded? Will monies be taken from "regular" classrooms?

How will academic redshirting be prevented or the dumping of minorities into these classes?

What reactions [from school personnel] will come from opting out of the extra-year program?

Will their decisions show on my child's record?

Because of the arbitrary and nebulous use of readiness terms there can be no specific guidelines set forth. Therefore what criteria can be met? There is no test or assessment which can reliably determine this "readiness" state.

Will guidelines prohibit retention for any reason other than academic failure? (Which is currently the rule?)

How does placement (in prekindergarten and pre-first) relate to P.L. 94-142? Does not such placement constitute special placement? *All* students are guaranteed education in the least restrictive environment. Any other placement falls under federal guidelines.

The above issues as found by Texas parents are quite pertinent and should be answered by the members of the Texas state board of education. It is predicted that many other state departments of education will be involved in the same controversy in the 1990s.

Summary

This chapter has documented the many concerns of parents about the labeling and placement of their children entering school.

Frequently, educators and psychologists state that it is parents who are insisting on early reading instruction or who want to make sure their children will be equipped to "make it" in our society (Elkind, 1987). Such comments leave a false impression that most parents are espousing such opinions. The concerns documented in this chapter leave a much different impression. The evidence indicates that the great majority of parents interviewed were seeking a positive introduction to schooling for their children. They sought a helpful kindergarten program, not one where reading instruction was to be emphasized. These parents were interested in the school providing an instructional program appropriate for the age of their child and they were appalled at the emphasis on screening and testing programs found in many schools.

The experiences of several parents described in this chapter should give pause to school psychologists and educators as to the real meaning of parent–school cooperation. The lengths to which parents had to go to have their message heard indicate that school personnel must redouble their efforts to understand parents' concerns about their important questions.

Without doubt the 1990s will see an increase in litigation against the schools on behalf of the "normal" child, who is being provided dubious placement options, separate from the regular class, with little or no evidence that such alternative programming is of any value.

14

ETHICAL AND LEGAL ISSUES IN THE EDUCATIONAL PLACEMENT OF CHILDREN

Introduction: Questions to Consider

Few questions have been raised concerning the legal and ethical considerations about grouping practices of kindergarten and first-grade children. Until recently the legal challenges to grouping and teaching of students have occurred in situations in which (1) grouping practices resulted in identifiable racial groups or (2) special education students were automatically segregated from their peers (Oakes, 1983).

However, within the last 15 years, alternative education programs for young children who have been deemed to be unready for the regular kindergarten and/or first-grade curriculum have proliferated in the public school system. As described in Chapter 9, prekindergarten classes have been established for children considered to lack maturity for regular kindergarten, and pre-first or readiness/transition rooms have been added in several school systems for children considered to lack the necessary "maturity" to begin first grade.

Furthermore, such programs have become a regular part of the primary school organization, and the great majority of parents whose children are recommended for such classes by education personnel accede to the school's choice of placement.

Parental rights concerning the assessment and placement of children who have been categorized as mentally retarded, learning disabled, orthopedically handicapped, or behaviorally disordered are well known and firmly established in federal and state educational regulations (Goldberg, 1982; Gredler, 1991; Weatherly, 1979). However, questions currently are being raised as to the rights and prerogatives of both school and parent in regard to (1) the placement of young children as they enter kindergarten and first grade and (2) the school's general authority in the sorting and assignment of mainstream children who attend the public schools (Friedman & Sugarman, 1988).

Topics discussed in this chapter include the need for the school system to justify special placement and the particular legal and ethical issues involved in the grouping and placement of children for regular education as well as those children entering kindergarten and first grade. The rights of parents in the school placement of their children and examples of some current practices within the schools also are reviewed.

State Efforts to Consider Parental Rights

Two states, Pennsylvania and Michigan, have, in different ways, incorporated parental rights into school entrance policies.

The Pennsylvania Law

The Commonwealth of Pennsylvania is one of the few states that has specifically encoded into law regulations to help ensure certain educational rights to the parents of kindergarten and first-grade children. The regulations, which are reproduced in part below, specify that children of a specific age must be enrolled in a particular grade and cannot be placed instead in a prekindergarten or kept out of regular first grade without the express approval of the parents.

If a child is coming to school for the first time and is between 4 and 6 years of age, the child *may* be placed in kindergarten. However, a child 6 years of age, who is entering school for the first time, must be placed in the first grade. Commonwealth law provides that the only exception is a parental request that the child be placed in kindergarten even though she or he has reached the entrance age to begin first grade (Wall, 1988).

Pennsylvania regulations also state that a child cannot be required to repeat kindergarten. Even more important is this definitive statement concerning placement in alternative classes:

> The board of directors . . . may not require the child to attend
> a kindergarten prefirst grade, transitional class or other grade or
> class that is not regular first grade without parental consent.
> (Wall, 1988, p. A-33)

These regulations are much more explicit about placement of children as they enter school than those that were in force in Pennsylvania in 1972; they mirror the new emphasis by the schools on using alternative classes to regular first grade. In one respect the Pennsylvania state regulations bow to the demand that the child should be older when entering first grade by providing a chronological range of 5 years 7 months to 6 years 0 months as an acceptable age for entrance to school. In 1968 children were allowed to enter first grade if they were 5 years 7 months before September 1. A number of school districts have since changed their entrance policy to admit only children who are 6 years of age.

However, a few school districts in Pennsylvania appear to have defied the state regulations. In the 1960s and 1970s one school district imposed a different entrance age than specified by Pennsylvania law at that time (Gredler, 1975). Similarly, Springfield Township schools currently require a higher entrance age for boys beginning school. (See Chapter 7, on entrance age, for further discussion of this situation.) It would seem that parents in this school district could refuse assignment of their children to a transition room. That is, by citing the Pennsylvania rules and regulations, they could demand placement of their male child in first grade at the age at which girls are accepted.

The Michigan Decision

That the field of early childhood education is facing confrontation and challenge on many sides is also seen in the state of Michigan. A number of schools in that state have added "developmental" kindergartens to their school program. A typical program can be described by outlining the changes in the organizational structure undertaken in two elementary schools in Berrien, Michigan (Jennings, Burge, & Sitek, 1987).

Educators in this school system followed a Gesellian model of child development in establishing a six-tier curriculum structure. Jennings et al. state that if children who are 5 by December 1 show a 6- to 12-month delay developmentally, they are not ready for kindergarten. Therefore, they added a grade before kindergarten that was to be named a "primary class." The next step was kindergarten, to be followed by a Primary I class (i.e., transition room) for children who had completed kindergarten but who were not developmentally ready for first grade.

The next level in the "curriculum ladder" was a regular first grade followed by a Primary II class. This latter class was for children who had completed first grade but were not developmentally ready for second grade. In effect, three more grades had now been added to the elementary school time period. Children were to be placed in the prekindergarten based on their score from the Gesell School Readiness Test. Primary I and II placement was to be based on teacher recommendations: "The teachers would evaluate the student socially, emotionally, physically, and intellectually, and base their recommendation on these factors" (p. 24).

Jennings et al. report "enthusiastic acceptance by the teachers of this new organization." The authors state: "We are able to give more individual help to students" and can "concentrate on problem areas without the pressure of attaining goals and objectives [for children who] are not ready for first grade" (p. 24).

That a number of parents in Michigan do not accept this educational philosophy can be seen by the fact that the attorney general of the state of Michigan has rendered a judgment about prekindergarten placement that not only questions the placement of children in a prekindergarten but obligates the school to accept children into the regular kindergarten at age 5.

In response to a letter from Lewis Dodak, a state representative, Frank Kelly, attorney general for the state of Michigan, said that the legislature has provided that a school district must admit into the kindergarten program any child who is qualified by age and residence. Such a regulation supersedes any recommendation of school personnel to the effect that the child should instead attend a developmental kindergarten program. The attorney general specifically states that if the child meets the entrance age requirement, the school district is obligated to accept the enrollment of the child in kindergarten even though school personnel may have recommended that the child attend a developmental kindergarten program (Kelly, 1987).

Legal Factors of Importance in Grouping Children

Several legal factors are important in grouping children in the school system. Included are sex, the need for role models for at-risk children, the importance of justifying the need for special placement, and the classification and sorting of students throughout their school years. The majority of children placed in transition room programs are boys (Gredler, 1984). If a transition room program results in separation of the sexes for a lengthy period of time (i.e., 1 year), such a program might be considered questionable from a legal point of view. It would seem that integration of the sexes should be considered just as desirable as integration of racial groups within the school system. Separation of the sexes is one potential legal issue yet to be addressed by schools.

Another factor of importance to be considered before any grouping practice is implemented is the availability of adequate role models for children. There is less opportunity for at-risk children to interact with children who are performing adequately when the former are segregated in a transition room program. To the extent that a readiness room program is considered by school personnel to be a less-favorable teaching assignment, the possibility also exists that less-experienced teachers will be assigned to these less-preferred groupings (Gredler, 1984; Oakes, 1983).

The Role of the School: Justifying the Need for Special Placement

The burden of proof falls on the school system to justify special class placement for children who are eligible for kindergarten or first grade. One important factor with legal implications is whether the classification system used for placement of at-risk children is a valid and reliable one. Specific questions concerning validity and reliability have been addressed in Chapter 3, on screening and assessment. The issue here is whether the school system can provide sufficient credible data on the efficacy of special-class placement of children in a prekindergarten and/or transition room program. It would seem that the repetition of first grade or kindergarten or transition room placement can not automatically meet the requirement of an appropriate education for a child with special needs. Thus, data must be provided that indicate substantial progress resulting from such placement as compared to that of children who are provided other alternatives. However, the equivocal progress of children placed in a transition room, as described in Chapter 9, indicates that, in many cases, children placed in such programs do not show improved achievement. Such data raise considerable doubt as to the legality of the continued use of this type of placement program (Gredler, 1991; Shepard & Smith, 1986).

Related to the efficacy of special placement for at-risk children is the nature of the label that results in such placement. For example, classification labels such as "slow" or "remedial" are open to question when utilized with beginning kindergarten or first-grade children. As has been stated in previous chapters, the screening and labeling of children at this age period is subject to much more error than at later age levels. When children are labeled either before kindergarten entrance or during the kindergarten year, they have not been involved in any extended period of formal learning.

A similar problem occurs with the labels "mature" and "immature" obtained on the Gesell test. O'Donnell (1968) demonstrated that the Gesell labels of "immature" and "mature" learner did not correlate at all with the academic progress made by two groups of children in first grade who had been so categorized from Gesell test results. Indeed it was determined that children labeled "immature" performed as well as "mature" children on the criterion readiness measure after exposure to a conceptual language program in kindergarten. Thus the labeling and placement of children as either "immature" or lacking in readiness skills is truly a speculative exercise and raises serious questions as to its legality as well as its educational value.

Age also is a questionable criterion for special class placement from the perspective of defensibility. As indicated in Chapter 8, on entrance age, a number of studies indicate that younger children can perform at a level similar to that of older children at the end of the first or second grade or can catch up by the end of the third grade (Gredler, 1991).

Other school practices related to special class placement also have legal implications for the school system. One is the relative permanency of the decision. Children assigned to a prekindergarten or pre-first class invariably remain in the class for an entire year. Moreover, in some suburban school systems, readiness room placement has continued for 2 or 3 years beyond kindergarten (Bell, 1972; Glennon, 1978).

Another practice that is open to question is that of interviewing parents of school-entry children about details of the mother's pregnancy, birth weight of the child, and other personal health information. As indicated in Chapter 7, low birth weight, prolonged labor, and Caesarean birth may be essentially unrelated to later school performance.

Statements about these birth factors are certain to generate anxiety and concern in parents. Two ethical issues related to this practice are (1) To what extent is such personal health information an invasion of privacy (particularly when the information does not predict later school performance)? and (2) In what ways does the school interpret such information in decisions about the child?

A final issue in the discussion of ethics related to early screening is the length of the procedure and the stress on the child. One screening program used in an Illinois school district to "waive" entrance-age cutoffs is a 2-day endurance test for the child (Correll, 1990) described below.

When the cutoff date for school entry was changed from December 1 to September 1, children who turned 5 in October and November were eligible to be examined by school personnel to ascertain if they qualified for "early" entrance to kindergarten. The eligibility examination required a period of 2 days. The first day consists of a mock kindergarten day during which the child is observed for "interaction" during the half-day session. The second day involves individual assessment of the child and the taking of a social history by a social worker. However, before this examination is scheduled, the school principal interviews the child's parents; a questionnaire must be completed by the parents; then comes a final recommendation from the principal for the child to be screened. According to Correll, the process requires a team composed of a school psychologist, a social worker, a kindergarten teacher, and a speech pathologist.

If the child passes this 2-day ordeal and is accepted into kindergarten, this acceptance is only provisional:

> an additional provision for acceptance is demonstrated by the child during a trial period of six weeks in the kindergarten classroom that he/she possesses the intellectual and emotional advancement required to adjust to an older group of children. (p. 3)

Note should be made of the extraordinary number of steps in this process. Should young children be subjected to such an elaborate screening procedure? The whole assessment process is weighted in favor of the school. School personnel also are the ultimate arbiters of whether the child will remain in kindergarten. Parents should note that no consideration is given to the quality of kindergarten teaching and the type of curriculum being used. The time period from initial screening to the end of the provisional kindergarten period covers 4 months. For many parents this will seem to be a too lengthy period to be under stress. It is doubtful that children at this age level should be subjected to such stress over such a length of time.

In the 1960s and 1970s, court cases in Pennsylvania and Massachusetts concerning learning-disabled children and appropriate assessment procedures led to the enactment of Public Law 94-142. That law prescribes the model for procedures for the placement and monitoring for exceptional children. First the parents must grant permission for a psychological assessment of their child, then information is obtained from observation of the child in the classroom; the classwork of the child is reviewed; detailed input is sought from the parents; and a formal assessment using a teacher rating scale is obtained. Finally, the parents must sign an IEP (i.e., Individualized Education Plan) before a proposed remediation/intervention plan is implemented.

The contrast with transition room placement is dramatic. Often only a brief readiness test is administered. In one county school system in Florida, for example, a 20-minute Gesell readiness test is administered and a decision then is made about placement of the child (Sincere, 1987).

Courts likely will begin to examine retention decisions that are based either on (1) the application of a single criterion applied mechanically (i.e., low score on a readiness test) or (2) a teacher's statement that a child is immature, which leads to a recommendation for placement in a prekindergarten or transition room class.

It is quite possible that a due process hearing will be considered necessary before a child's educational status can be changed from a regular class setting. And, if the program carries a label that the class is for "slow" learners, questions also may be legitimately raised as to whether the program offers equal educational opportunity.

The Need for Clarification of Policy Decisions in the Placement of School Entrants

A number of school districts have no formal policy as to ability/achievement grouping (Oakes, 1983); in some districts decisions regarding retention and placement of kindergarten and first-grade children are left completely to educational personnel. The variety and extent of differences in school practices with young children are indicated by the following examples of classification practices:

1. *School district A.* Children are administered a Gesell readiness test prior to kindergarten entrance, a Metropolitan readiness test in the fall of kindergarten, and another Metropolitan and Gesell test in the spring to assess progress in readiness.

Why is it necessary to subject the child to four readiness tests within a 1-year time span?

2. *School district B.* Kindergarten children are rated on a behavior rating scale that emphasizes motor activities. A low score results in placement in a transition room instead of first grade. No appeal mechanism is provided for the parents.

3. *School district C.* A school teacher agonizes over the promotion of a student in her kindergarten. She notes that the child is able to handle academic material "but I don't think she should go on to first grade because she is 'immature.' " She alone will make the decision, without input from other school personnel.

4. *School district D.* Children are screened using the Gesell readiness test. Kindergarten teachers also check the teething development of their children to determine whether a child's second teeth have erupted. Teething status plays a prominent role in final determination of the child's school placement the following year.

5. *School district E.* One elementary school in the district has organized a transition room program. Children are assigned to this classroom based on their scores occurring below a certain cutoff on a standardized skills assessment battery. Teacher nominations are not considered nor is parental permission sought before placement in the transition program is made. Students so placed are not told that theirs is a transition class. However, they will certainly become aware of the different status when they are promoted to the first grade the following year. They will then begin to question why most of their classmates are now in the second grade.

6. *School district F.* The screening procedure used in this district for transition room placement resulted in categorizing 25% of an *above-average* group of kindergarten children as being at risk for failure in first grade. Parents knew nothing of these results, which were not discussed by school personnel (Talmadge, 1981).

The main question to be raised by such ill-defined practices is, What are the rights of parents in making the decision about the placement of their children as they enter school?

Court Cases Involving Readiness Status of School Entrants

Two court cases, one in Pennsylvania and one in New York state, indicate the problems that can arise from poorly articulated readiness policies.

The Vincent P. Readiness Case

A case that dealt with a child's readiness for school has important implications for the need of well-defined administrative and assessment procedures. Vincent P.

entered kindergarten at age 5 in a Montgomery County, Pennsylvania, school system. Near the end of the year, his mother was informed that school personnel had recommended that Vincent repeat kindergarten instead of going on to the first grade. School administrators stated that although the kindergarten teacher considered Vincent to be a very bright boy, he "was not ready for the first-grade experience." The mother objected to this recommendation, but the child was not placed in first grade. When the child did not appear for kindergarten a criminal complaint was filed by the school district charging the mother with violation of the compulsory education law. Subsequently, the mother was found guilty and fined by the local court (Commonwealth of Pennsylvania vs. Margaret Pasceri, 1974).

The case then came before an appeals court. This court determined that because kindergarten was not mandatory, a school could not compel a child to repeat kindergarten before he entered first grade. As the judge very aptly put it: "When a child cannot be made to attend kindergarten once, he clearly cannot be made to attend twice." Pennsylvania public school code stated at the time that a school could refuse to accept or retain a child who had not reached a mental age of 5 years as determined by a school psychologist. The court noted that no determination had been made as to whether or not the child had the requisite mental age. The judge mentioned that although the school said the child was not ready for first grade, the kindergarten teacher described the child as "very bright."

The court went further and said that even if Vincent had been shown to have had a mental age below 5-0, he could not have been compelled to repeat kindergarten because kindergarten attendance in Pennsylvania was not mandatory. It was also noted that whereas Vincent was absent a total of 59 days in kindergarten, the school district never enforced the compulsory attendance requirement; as the judge stated, "Only after the appellant opposed the school recommendation did the school district suddenly remember its duty" (p. 5).

The school also stated that Vincent was administered a screening test when he began kindergarten and the test results "indicated he was not ready for kindergarten." After the mother protested, he was admitted in spite of reservations of school officials. It was stated that at the end of the year the child lacked "developmental readiness" to advance to first grade. The final chapter in this unusual case occurred when Vincent's mother won a suit against the school officials for denial of due process of law because the reasons for his kindergarten retention had never been explained to her. The federal court jury said Vincent's constitutional rights had been violated by his kindergarten teacher, principal, director of elementary education, and the school superintendent. The school officials settled out of court in the amount of $6,000 (Commonwealth of Pennsylvania vs. Margaret Pasceri, 1974; "Vindication for Vincent," 1977).

This situation is one in which a properly trained school psychologist should have been able to offer consultation and a suitable plan of action. One of the main errors in judgment included making a decision about a child from a screening test administered prior to kindergarten and also the fact that no psychological examination was administered at the end of kindergarten to help determine future placement. The court decision raised serious questions as to the use of kindergarten attendance in Pennsylvania as a remedial device for children who were considered developmentally unready. The court in fact said that because kindergarten attendance was not mandatory, children could not be retained in kindergarten.

In the past few years a number of states have attempted to introduce procedures that would identify and help children who are legitimately at risk. Chapter 766 of the Comprehensive Special Education law of Massachusetts is one such attempt (Weatherly, 1979). The regulations provide that all school-aged children should be continuously screened after entry to kindergarten and that difficulties in the cognitive, social, and emotional areas should be noted. School psychologists would have a large part in such programs, because this is one of the major areas of concentration in their program preparation.

The Norwood–Norfolk, New York, School Readiness Case

In 1987 a class action suit was brought against the New York State Department of Education concerning the placement of children in a developmental kindergarten in the Norwood–Norfolk Central school district (State of New York Department of Education, 1987).

The issue was brought to a head by the decision of the school to send 61 of the 99 entering kindergarten children to a developmental kindergarten class. This judgment was based on the children's scores on a single test—the Gesell School Readiness Test. Eligibility for admission to kindergarten required that a child be age 5 by December 1 for the year he or she was to begin school. A number of parents rejected assignment to the developmental kindergarten and placed their children in regular kindergarten classes in private schools. No parent was permitted the option of rejecting the placement of his or her child in the developmental kindergarten class or of being allowed to enter the child in the regular kindergarten class instead.

The petitioners in this court suit were a family whose daughter was one of the 61 children placed in the developmental kindergarten class. The child was tested in June prior to the beginning of school in September. The letter from the school did not mention the consequences for not appearing to take the test nor did it indicate that the family could appeal the decision to test the child. When the 5-year-old child was tested, her mother was present as were two kindergarten teachers. It was noted in the court appeal that neither teacher was trained or certified as a psychologist. However, both teachers had attended a Gesell testing workshop which can vary from 1 to 5 days in length.

Testing time was 15 minutes. The questions asked the child were given in a rapid manner and none was repeated. At the beginning of the examination the child paused and asked her mother if she should answer the teacher's questions. To the mother this was not unusual, as her daughter had not attended preschool and had been taught not to speak to strangers. One of the teachers present said later to the mother that such a question was a sign of "immaturity." At the end of the examination one of the teachers stated, when asked, that the child had done "pretty well."

Within 3 weeks after testing of the child the family received a letter informing them that their daughter had been placed in a developmental kindergarten as a result of her performance on the Gesell test. The school principal, when asked by the mother about this placement, stated that the child was a "borderline $4\frac{1}{2}$-year-old" and that the developmental kindergarten placement would mean she would have "more success in life" and would be better prepared for school. The mother requested a retest, but the principal said it should wait until the beginning of the school year.

However, the school principal never contacted the mother subsequently for a rescreening. The mother then requested an interview with the school super-intendent. The child's mother and another parent with the same concerns attended this meeting. The superintendent stated that if the child was retested, all the children placed in the developmental class would also have to be retested. Finally, the mother received a written reply from the superintendent. The letter stated that, if after 10 to 20 weeks in developmental kindergarten a child shows progress "beyond whatever anticipated, we can reevaluate and move a child into a regular kindergarten" (p. 9).

The parents then requested a hearing with the board of education members. The president said the board would contact the parents after discussing the issue among themselves. However, no further word was received from the board. The parents then met with the superintendent again. At this time he specifically stated that the mother must wait 10 weeks after school began to retest her child because the child would remember too much of the test if tested sooner (8 weeks had now passed since the first test administration). The mother asked the school to use an alternative test and to administer it before school began. Although the superintendent stated he would "look into it," no subsequent contact was made by his office to the parents. It was then that the family sought representation from legal services. In the meantime the child began school in the developmental kindergarten. Ten weeks after class began, no retesting had occurred. The mother also attempted to obtain testing outside of the school system, but the local mental health clinic rejected her request. The clinic's rationale was that her child had had "too many tests already" and also that she wasn't having any problems to justify further assessment (p. 12).

The staff of the legal aid society obtained background data on the organization and implementation of the developmental readiness program in the Norfolk and Norwood schools. These data indicated that in 1986, the first year of the program, 65 of 151 children were placed in prekindergarten or 43% of the total number of kindergarten-age children. In 1987, as previously mentioned, 61 of 99 children (or 62%) were recommended and placed in the prekindergarten program. The children were completely segregated from students in regular kindergarten, including separate schedules for physical education, library, and art instruction. No more than one or two children had been promoted from the developmental kindergarten to regular first grade. Thus, almost all students would have to attend a 2-year kindergarten before entering first grade. It was also determined that no midyear transfers were considered by school personnel. In addition, some students also repeated first grade, thus not entering second grade until 8 years of age, with high school graduation not occurring until age 20.

The following important points were made in the legal brief submitted to the court:

(1) The developmental kindergarten was not a true kindergarten program but instead was a prekindergarten program.

(2) Placement of children in a developmental kindergarten deprived them of regular kindergarten entry at age 5 which is provided for in New York state education law.

(3) Placement in the developmental kindergarten was based solely on the results of the GSRT and thus deprived children placed in the developmental kindergarten of their rights to equal protection of the law under the 14th Amendment of the U.S. Constitution.

(4) Placement of 61% of the entering kindergarten class into a developmental kindergarten was arbitrary and capricious and violated the parents' rights to due process.

(5) The GSRT did not meet professional standards of reliability or validity. Placement of a child on the basis of this instrument resulted in a 1-year delay in entering regular kindergarten and thus violated the child's right to an appropriate education under New York state constitutional law.

(6) Children placed in the developmental kindergarten could be considered to have impairments as defined under Section 504 of the Rehabilitation Act of 1973, having been segregated from regular kindergarten students. They were then entitled to the protections of this Act.

(7) By placing children in the developmental program the school had violated the provisions of the Act in the following ways:

(a) The school failed to place the students in a regular educational environment, without demonstrating with regard to the individual child that education in the regular environment could not be satisfactorily achieved.

(b) The school did not evaluate the students individually with tests that were "tailored to assess specific areas of educational need" and which should have been validated for the specific purpose administered.

(c) The school failed to evaluate the students properly *prior* to making placement in the prekindergarten by failing to (1) "draw upon information from a variety of sources, including aptitude and achievement tests, teacher recommendations, physical condition, social or cultural background, and adaptive behavior"; (2) document and consider information from all such sources; and (3) make sure that the placement decision was made "by persons knowledgeable about the child and the meaning of the evaluation data" (p. 18).

(d) The school also failed to provide notice of the proposed placement decision in prekindergarten; an outline of procedural guidelines concerning the protections afforded the child; the opportunity for the parents to examine the records on the child, to provide for an impartial hearing, and representation by counsel and a review procedure.

(8) The school failed to ensure that developmental kindergarten students were educated within the mainstream of regular kindergarten programming. In the legal brief it was also mentioned that children could not be placed in separate classes, with separate educational programming, and removed from the regular school environment "without first demonstrating that such children possess handicapping conditions, the nature and severity of which precludes regular placement . . . " (State of New York Department of Education, 1987, p. 19).

(9) The school should have referred the students who were suspected of possible problems based on the results on the Gesell tests to a committee on special education for an individual diagnostic examination.

(10) The school did not attempt to remediate the developmental kindergarten children in the regular kindergarten before placing the students in the segregated setting.

(11) The school failed to involve the parents concerning placement decisions prior to the actual placement in the developmental kindergarten and failed to inform the parents, in advance of the administration of the Gesell, of how the results would be used.

(12) The Gesell School Readiness Test was not validated for the purpose it served, i.e., segregated kindergarten placement, and also was not an instrument that was tailored to "assess specific areas of educational need" (p. 20). Such an action was considered to be in violation of specific New York educational statutes.

(13) The school used only two kindergarten teachers in the evaluation process. No other specialists were involved in the testing evaluation and placement process. The children should have been referred to a multidisciplinary team.

(14) The school failed to heed the rights of the students by evaluating them for placement prior to the beginning of the school year. The children had the right to be evaluated in "their current educational setting" (p. 21).

(15) No individualized education program was developed for these children.

(16) The parents were not informed of their right to have an alternative assessment or of the names of psychologists and agencies who undertook such assessment. Also, they were not told of their right to withhold consent for the evaluation and placement and the right to have a review of the decision made in an important hearing.

The result of the appeal filed by the North County Legal Society provided for the following:

(1) An agreement that the child in question would be transferred to a regular kindergarten class;

(2) That subsequently no kindergarten-age child would be placed by the school in a developmental kindergarten program without the written consent of the child's parents;

(3) That the school would provide the parents with the information upon which the child's placement recommendation was made; the specific test measures that were used; a statement that the developmental kindergarten program results in an extra year of schooling which then could be followed by a year of regular kindergarten and a year of pre-first grade.

> Also the school must provide a statement that the parents can accept or reject the school's recommendation for developmental kindergarten placement. If the parents reject the prekindergarten placement option, the child is to be placed in a regular kindergarten.

The results of this legal decision will have an effect on many school districts other than the Norwood–Norfolk, New York, system. School districts faced with the possibility of litigation because they have not met the standards of the law may well consider restructuring their kindergarten through first grade program so as to meet the legal guidelines.

The decision is important because it will help provide a more comprehensive observation of children who are beginning their school life. It is hoped that brief screening programs such as the one in use in the Norfolk–Norwood school district will become a matter of the past.

Although the Gesell test was the instrument involved in this particular case, the questions raised are pertinent no matter which test measures or teacher rating scales are used. Children considered by the school to be too young or immature for school will have the same rights afforded them as any child categorized as a special need child. On the basis of this court decision, children entering school will be allowed to enter a regular kindergarten and be observed and assessed during the kindergarten school year *if* such a procedure is found to be necessary.

It is quite possible that a number of children will make suitable progress during the kindergarten year so that no formal assessment examination will be required. The author is reminded of the Cooper and Farran (1988) study, which demonstrated that a considerable number of children made definite progress in developing appropriate kindergarten skills during the spring semester of kindergarten. Parents will certainly have a more positive attitude toward the school when they note that provision is being made to monitor and assess their child over a period of time instead of in a 15- to 20-minute session prior to the beginning of school.

Summary

In this discussion of legal and ethical issues, serious concerns have been raised about the grouping practices involving kindergarten and first-grade children. The increased use of placement options to regular kindergarten and first grade has led to laws in some states explicitly requiring school districts to accept children into kindergarten or first grade if they have reached the entrance age mandated by state law.

The burden of proof falls on the school system to justify special class placement for children eligible for kindergarten or first grade. From the discussion of various court cases it seems that school personnel will have to have definitive justification for placement of children in programs other than regular kindergarten or first grade.

The various legal and ethical issues mentioned in this chapter indicate the rising degree of concern about early childhood education practices that are linked with school entry and that currently exist in many school districts. Many of these practices will now be challenged by parents based on the legal cases and rulings from the offices of the state attorneys general or state departments of education. School personnel will have an opportunity to devise new educational programs that will meet the ethical and legal objections mentioned in this chapter.

15

A RECAPITULATION: SOME FINAL ISSUES TO CONSIDER

A number of topics concerning school readiness have been reviewed in the previous chapters. However, there are many issues about educational philosophy and school practices in early childhood education that need further discussion, clarification, and resolution. These concerns and issues are reviewed and summarized in this chapter.

The Anxieties and Concerns of Parents: Growth of the Parent Movement

As was noted in Chapter 13, parents are asking many questions about how the schools organize and structure early childhood education. Serious questions have been raised about whether kindergarten screening is needed, and the direction it is taking; the excessive use of retention in kindergarten, and the frequent placement of children in transition/readiness room programs.

One parent questions the continual use of retention by school personnel and mentions that educators often overwhelm parents by stating that it is in the child's "best interest" and will help to further the child's academic and social development (Merrow, 1989).

Merrow emphasizes that there is a need for a more flexible curriculum for grades K–3 and states that within these first years of school educational goals should be more general with less age segregation. He then states:

> When 300,000 kindergartners are forced to repeat what's supposed to be an enjoyable, socializing year, that's *not* their failure. That's the school system's failure, and ours. (p. 80)

A similar message is given by Conroy (1988), who categorically describes educational practices that don't work for kindergarten children and warns parents to beware of the following school techniques and programs: kindergarten screening, 2 years of kindergarten, transition rooms, and raising the entry age to school.

Conroy states to parents: "Exercise your rights. Children who meet the age cutoff have a legal right to attend kindergarten. Even if you're advised to wait a year, you still have the right to enroll your child" (p. 48). Such comments herald a new militancy among parents and indicate that school personnel will need to spend more time in designing and justifying appropriate educational programs that serve the kindergarten to third-grade population in their school districts.

Assessment Practices: The Need for Appropriate Monitoring and the Need for Change

As noted in Chapter 3, screening and assessment practices must be carefully planned to avoid errors in diagnosis and placement. Screening programs undertaken with young children are truly a speculative device and must be approached cautiously. The passage of P.L. 94-457 now provides for screening at an even earlier age than kindergarten and thus errors in decisions about learning and/or behavior deficits will be even more prevalent.

Utilization of teacher ratings or observational methods in place of psychometric measures will not improve decision making as teachers make many errors in attempting to predict potential learning/behavioral problems. What is needed is a change in educational philosophy and practice that will in effect curb the excessive use and misinterpretation of all kinds of screening measures.

Legal and Ethical Issues About Screening Practices

A question that is quite basic to the educational scene but appears to be seldom considered by school personnel is: Should a child be screened *prior* to entering kindergarten? Should parents allow their child to be screened if the result is he or she will not be allowed to enter kindergarten? Unfortunately this question is seldom asked; many schools plunge immediately into some type of screening program without an adequate understanding of underlying educational objectives. The statement is often made that we need to identify at-risk children at an early age, "that the earlier a problem or need is identified the greater is the likelihood of maximizing a child's development" (McLoughlin & Rausch, 1990, p. 456).

However, as has been discussed in previous chapters, the main intervention resulting from early identification of young children is simply placement in either a prekindergarten or pre-first class, which is, in effect, a retention in grade.

McLoughlin and Rausch also state that there is a consensus among educational personnel as to essential skills needed by children for kindergarten: "skill at performing independently"; "age-appropriate peer interaction skills," etc. However, it has been well documented in previous chapters that many schools have an overwhelming desire to label children as "immature" on the basis of a brief screening test; therefore, the specific goals of kindergarten screening need to be described very carefully.

Previously mentioned research (Cooper & Farran, 1988) records the steady increase in positive work habits in boys during the spring semester of their kindergarten year. It is quite probable that a large number of male students would be screened out prior to fall entry into kindergarten if screening goals were misapplied. Many teachers are overly sensitive to perceiving possible signs of immaturity in boys as well as in children who have late birthdays.

Educational personnel and psychologists must be alert to the possibility of self-limiting prophecies that the screening process often engenders (Shipman, 1981). School personnel should redirect the time spent on such programs into more productive and useful programs of intervention than have been the case to date. Specifically this will mean that the results of any screening program will be used more as a *guide* in providing and tailoring programs to better meet the educational needs of the children (Shipman, 1981). It must be acknowledged that early identification programs that result only in placement in prekindergarten or a transition room for a year are inappropriate.

A main concern of all parental groups interviewed by the author was that major decisions were being made about their children on the basis of brief screening measures or poorly constructed behavior rating scales or that their children were subjected to "mock" kindergarten classes after which placement decisions were made. Often the screening process of the young child took place up to 5 months before the child actually was permitted to enter kindergarten.

Readiness tests are not considered technically accurate enough to be used in making educational decisions that will interrupt a child's normal progress in school (Shepard, 1991).

Shepard also believes that the present use of readiness testing in many schools is nothing more than the reintroduction of tracking, but at an even earlier age. The tracking is found in several different forms: 2-year placement for at-risk children, separate classrooms for at-risk children, and 2-year placement based on the Gesell (i.e., transition room programs).

Early screening can only be justified it if it can identify existent problems as a child enters school and *if* indeed it can be determined that these problems are the ones that can be legitimately linked to later school difficulties (Palfrey, 1981). The screening process, as it currently functions in many school districts, can only be regarded as a speculative exercise, as Potton (1983) has pointed out and as has been discussed in Chapter 3. "One shot" screening programs for the kindergarten and first-grade child really do not take into consideration the variability of the performance of young children in the classroom over time. Because of this variability, school personnel should review the performance of children periodically rather than accept the results of merely one assessment. Thus new efforts must be made to turn away from the emphasis on early identification and instead provide more adequate instruction, assessment, and intervention programs *during all of the early years of the child's education.*

Valid assessment can only take place when adequate information is obtained and this involves detailed assessment, observation, and a carefully planned intervention program *before* any attempt is made to remove the child permanently from the regular classroom (Morgan, 1981).

Morgan categorically states that no identification program should attempt to complete the diagnostic process within the first 2 or 3 weeks of school. "Ideally observation needs to take place over the whole kindergarten year. ... It would be better still spread over the kindergarten and grade one years ... " (Morgan, 1981, p. 53 & pp. 55–56). Thus school personnel should consider how they will revise their programs to take into account all of these factors.

It is also significant to note that when measures of cognitive abilities are utilized in a screening program they are found to be more predictive when used in the second or third grades (Tramontana, Hooper, & Selzer, 1988). According to Tramontana et al. this suggests that academic skills may not be sufficiently well developed or stable by the end of first grade for reliable assessment and/or predictive purposes.

The hazards of the early identification process will become even more evident as the provisions of new federal legislation (e.g., P.L. 99-457) are implemented. Many of the measures being utilized with this younger population of 3 through 4 years of age are the same as those in current use with the 5- to 6-year-old child. The possibility of errors in diagnostic judgments and placement decisions is greater because the school is dealing with an even younger population.

The Importance of the Instructional Climate

School support personnel, as well as teachers, should become more cognizant of the value of various instructional strategies. A recent study undertaken in the Tulsa, Oklahoma, schools illustrates this point quite dramatically. This study investigated the relationship between first-grade readiness, Gesell developmental age scores, and instructional techniques utilized in kindergarten (Zenka & Keatley, 1985).

The Metropolitan Readiness Test is administered to all kindergarten children in the Tulsa school system in the spring of the school year. School personnel have stated that a child must obtain a score at least at the 40th percentile for placement in first grade in order to make acceptable progress.

The study investigated the progress of a group of kindergarten children who were placed in a regular kindergarten program with its emphasis on nonacademic activities versus a group of kindergarten children who attended a kindergarten program that had added the Writing to Read Program (Martin & Friedberg, 1986) to the regular kindergarten curriculum.

Tulsa educators were interested in the relationship between the type of kindergarten program offered, the child's "developmental age" score on the Gesell (previously administered in kindergarten), and whether the child attained the necessary percentile score on the Metropolitan for placement in first grade.

The results of the investigation showed that 73% of the children who had been labeled "immature" on the Gesell (i.e., developmental age $4\frac{1}{2}$ years or below) also fell below the 40th percentile cutoff at the end of kindergarten. Conversely, 76% of those labeled "mature" on the Gesell (i.e., developmental age of 5 or more) scored at or above the 40th percentile. A Gesellian psychologist or educator would probably state that this was evidence of the value of the Gesell. (The reader should refer to Chapter 3 for a more extensive discussion of permissible error rates.)

However, for those children assigned to the kindergarten where the Writing to Read Program had been added to the curriculum, the results were considerably different. Dramatic changes in the number of children who reached the necessary first-grade placement cutoff were found. Instead of 73% of immature children not reaching the cutoff for first-grade placement, only 44% of the immature children in the Writing to Read kindergarten program scored below the 40th percentile cutoff—a reduction of 29%.

The Tulsa study is an excellent example of how an educational intervention method interacts with the readiness status of the child to produce an outcome different from what is found when only a child's score on a test is considered.

The large increase in the percentage of immature children (29%) who now attained the necessary cutoff score for first-grade placement reflects the importance of sophisticated instructional methods in the school program. It should also be emphasized that 13% more of the mature children were now considered eligible for first-grade placement. Thus the supplemental intervention program definitely aided the group of children already considered to be ready for first grade.

However additional questions about this study need to be considered. One important issue is whether the 40th percentile cutoff score on the Metropolitan Readiness Test is an appropriate cutoff score for first-grade placement. Such a decision also should be evaluated by an appropriate research study specifically designed to answer this question. Also, should children be required to meet a certain test score cutoff before being allowed to enter first grade? Should additional educational interventions such as the Writing to Read Program be utilized instead in first grade rather than kindergarten, as is the case in some school systems? These are some of the important topics that school personnel must consider.

The important point in this discussion is that a child's immature status, based on the Gesell test, was *not* considered a hardened fact that only could be resolved by requiring additional time in kindergarten or a pre-first program. Rather, Tulsa educators determined that a sophisticated instructional program was found to be a helpful supplement for both mature and immature children.

Needed: A Reinterpretation of Research Studies on Entrance Age

Considerable confusion has also arisen over the accurate interpretation of the research results from entrance age studies as well as studies of transition room performance. There are major problems involved in the proper interpretation of these research results. In our discussion it is necessary to consider the concepts of statistical significance, practical significance, and social significance.

Statistical Versus Practical Significance Versus Social Significance

When data are reported as statistically significant the word *significant* is often confused with its more common meaning. That is, an event labeled significant is considered important or worthy of special note (Jaccard & Becker, 1990). However, the term *statistically significant* means that the results obtained in the research investigation are highly unlikely to occur by chance. For example, when significance is established at the .05 level, it is likely that there is only one chance in 20 or less that the results obtained could be due to sampling errors (Shavelson, 1988). Lykken (1968) notes that "the finding of statistical significance is perhaps the *least* important attribute of a good experiment; it is *never* a sufficient condition for concluding that a theory has been corroborated, that a useful confidence ... or that an experimental report ought to be published" (pp. 158–159; p. 172).

Further, if the size of the sample participating in a study is quite large, small differences between groups can easily be statistically significant at the .05 level. This means, as previously stated, that the small difference obtained is likely to have occurred by chance only once in 20 times. However, one cannot reason from such results that the difference obtained is important or worthy of special note within the educational environment, or that it provides evidence for the merit of a particular method or educational approach. For example, in one large-scale study of two different first-grade reading programs, a statistically significant difference favoring Program A over Program B was found. That is, a statistically significant difference in the mean scores of a reading comprehension test was obtained. However, analysis of the test responses indicated that Program A children correctly answered on the average only two more questions on the 200-item test than did Program B children (Borg, 1987). Such a small difference, while statistically significant, is of little *practical* significance. Thus, recommending the use of

Program A as the more effective method of teaching reading, although the mean group difference was statistically significant, is not supported by the data.

Such results have led researchers and educators to the concept of *educational* or *practical* significance. Concern about the practical importance of research studies has brought about the introduction of techniques that utilize units of measurement called effect sizes. In the entrance age and readiness research, effect sizes are defined as the difference between an experimental group and a control group in standard deviation units. For example the performance of an older group is compared with a young group or a retained group is compared with a regular class group. The differences between the means of two groups (group averages) are then divided by the pooled standard deviation of the two groups. The resulting score can then be considered as to its educational significance (Shepard & Smith, 1985). If the score is .50 or higher, the difference between the two groups is considered to have practical significance (Borg, 1987; Rossi & Wright, 1977).

The importance of practical significance can be seen in the study of the academic achievement of over 17,000 five- and six-year-old children attending Kentucky schools (Davis, Trimble, & Vincent, 1980). The thrust of the article is that 6-year-old children will perform better in school than 5-year-olds. Statistically significant differences between the two age groups were found in reading, math, and language at the end of first grade (mean reading score of 6-year-olds = 55.0; mean reading score of 5-year-olds = 51.6; difference = 3.4 points). The difference in achievement means between the 5- and 6-year-olds was found to be statistically significant at the .01 level in favor of the 6-year-olds. However, the question that should have been asked was whether the 3.4 score point difference was really of practical significance.

When the effect size formula is utilized (see Borg, 1987, or Shepard & Smith, 1987, for specific formulae to be used), a score value of .18 is obtained. However, a value of .50 or higher is required for the difference in average achievement to be of educational significance. Therefore, the mean difference between 5- and 6-year-olds obtained on the reading tests can be discounted; it is not worthy of special note and a change in entrance age definitely should not be considered for Kentucky schools based on such findings. To obtain an effect size of .50 or higher would have required at least a 9-point difference between the achievement mean scores of the two age groups.

Retention Procedures: A Need for Clarification

A number of different suggestions have been made by various educators and psychologists to change the retention policies of individual school districts. Although it is important to have more than one individual involved in making a retention decision, it is unfortunate that the school psychologist is often brought in only near the end of the school year to assess the performance of the first-grade child and consult with parents and teachers. At that time the focus of the retention decision is generally on the characteristics shown by the child, such as ability level and current achievement, rather than on the total school situation. If the school psychologist is expected to help plan appropriate instructional programs only for the following year, then the opportunity to help during the first year of school is lost. A number of school districts warn the parents by the end of the second month of school that their child may be in "danger" of being retained. If this is the case, then the child alone should not be the focus of attention; there must be a total appraisal of the classroom learning environment, with appropriate suggestions also being made to the teacher and specific intervention approaches instituted. However, few schools operate in this manner.

A first-grade teacher recently reported to this school psychologist that she had planned to recommend two of her male students for retention. She had informed the parents of this possibility in a conference held in early fall. However at that particular school, the Writing to Read Program was in use. First-grade students were introduced to the program in November of the school year and were involved with Writing to Read labs each day for 1 hour of instruction. The teacher stated that by March these two students had made sufficient progress in reading that she no longer considered that either one had to be retained.

School support personnel as well as teachers should spend more time helping to plan appropriate instructional strategies for use in the first grade. For a school psychologist merely to summarize the research on retention and state to school teachers that there is little evidence that retention helps over the long term is of little value when retention as a policy has always been the traditional method of handling learning problems in schools.

The Entrance Age Debate

The current emphasis on raising the age of entry to school is part of a controversy that has been ongoing within American education for the past 60 years. Despite the amassing of considerable knowledge about child development and the availability of appropriate curriculum methods, there is still little consensus as to the most effective ways to proceed to educate young children.

Parents continue to be subjected to a confusing number of statements and recommendations if their child is entering school at a young age. Many psychologists and parents agree with Conroy (1988), who urges parents to start early to investigate the school district's kindergartens. She recommends that parents shop around for kindergartens among both private and public schools. She stresses that it also might be helpful to enroll the child in a preschool and then later place the child directly in the first grade of the public school.

However, at the same time, one psychologist writes approvingly of delaying entry to school for those children who have late birthdays. Rosemond (1990a) states that in the last 2 years kindergartens have become increasingly academic, with most kindergartens saddled with the "push down" curriculum. He states that young children are at risk in such a program. If the kindergarten is of a developmental type, Rosemond feels nothing is gained by delaying the child's entry.

Rosemond in effect makes a good case for the nongraded organization for the first 3 years when he mentions that children who are slightly delayed developmentally "stand a good chance of catching up by the end of the year" (p. J3). But, at the same time, Rosemond endorses retention in kindergarten as well as transitional classes, stating about the latter, "a tip of the hat to those innovative systems" (p. J3).

This facile endorsement of retention for the young child once again indicates the difficulty many adults have in understanding the anxieties and concerns of those held back—and, as the research shows, with no improvement in performance the following year.

Rosemond does admonish parents who want to delay their child's enrollment because they hope the child will be at the top of the class the following year. Unfortunately, as Rosemond states, the child may have been quite ready for school and will be very bored with kindergarten if enrollment is delayed.

Rosemond does concede that if delayed enrollment of young-for-age children (i.e., those who turn 5 after June 1) becomes the norm, then all we have done is create a new late birthday group—those children with birthdays after March 1. There still would be 11 months' difference between these children and the oldest children. Rosemond (1989, 1990a, 1990b), a confirmed exponent of the maturational school, sees many positive benefits in retaining young children. However, he recognizes that the continual insistence on only enrolling children into school who are older becomes a ridiculous charade when the entry age is continually adjusted upward by the school.

The viewpoint of this book is that continual manipulation of the entrance age does little to help children who are enrolled in kindergarten and first grade. Evidence described in the preceding chapters demonstrated that much can be gained by the use of proper instructional methods and intervention with the child who shows signs of difficulty and/or confusion, the embrace by school personnel of an appropriate positive educational philosophy, and implementation of a humane organizational structure for early childhood education. Such an educational structure would emphasize the development of children's social and academic skills within a nongraded organization.

However, it is of little help to castigate teachers for holding such negative views about the learning process, entrance age, and retention. What is needed instead is a frame of reference to help explain the reasons for teachers' continued beliefs followed by suggestions of ways to change the educational environment to reduce the use of retention. Important aids in understanding such perceptions are social psychological constructs that help us to understand the dysfunctional as well as functional aspects of educational organizations.

Understanding the Organization of the School

One factor of importance that must be considered is the nature of the school as an organization. In the phraseology of Carlson (1964), the school can be called a "domesticated organization," meaning it is an organization that does not compete with other organizations for "clients." In fact, just the opposite occurs—there is a continual stream of individuals always available and ready to enter the institution. Carlson points out that this kind of organization does not have to struggle for survival and that its existence is guaranteed.

In Carlson's view, such organizations are slower to change and to adapt to the changing society they serve because of their protected status. Carlson mentions that when an organization exists that cannot control the entrance of its clients, it makes special arrangements to adapt to this flow of clients. He hypothesizes that the personnel in such an organization have certain goals (in the case of the school, graduating a person who knows how to "read," "do math," etc.) they hold as worthwhile objectives and which they feel cannot be realized adequately through the presence of completely unselected clients. Personnel in charge of such an organization will *constantly* look for ways and means of reducing the disruptive effect of having completely unselected "clients" (i.e., students). One reason, therefore, for the extreme emphasis by teachers on the entrance age factor and the frequent use of retention is an attempt to reduce the size and scope of their unselected group of students. Although the problem of unselected clientele is an important one, the main question is whether an increase in the entrance age results in sufficient reduction in the variability of the clients. Such a philosophy also is antithetical to a democratic viewpoint that *all* children have the right to attend school, and provisions should be made to help them to learn *after* they enter.

In the current educational climate, once children enter the school system, the agents of the system, i.e., teachers, often continue to be preoccupied with reasons why they need to further "select out" those who will not "make it" due to the unselected clientele sent to them. With such a philosophy in place in the traditional school, it follows that retention will be a frequently used tool to control the flow of clients. In addition, raising the entrance age and increasing the retention rate are obviously easier than attempting to provide flexibility within the organizational structure to cope with the individual differences of the children.

In a situation where the teacher happens to be minimally competent to handle the diversity of pupils' needs within the classroom, concurrent with the lack of support personnel and programs to help improve the performance of students, there will be an increased tendency to minimize teacher responsibility concerning a child's difficulties within the class. Thus develops what can be called *procedural displacement* wherein school personnel will emphasize methods that channel the student with a problem away from the regular classroom. Such an atmosphere also fosters a belief that only with the manipulation of variables outside of the classroom environment (i.e., changing the entrance age) will the teacher be able to do a successful job with her first-grade students.

The Role of the School Psychologist in Assessment and Intervention

The school psychologist's function in planning and carrying out a screening program for kindergarten and first-grade children is an important one. Analyses of the activities of school psychologists in regard to use of screening and diagnostic measures reflect a wide range and variety of practices. These practices range all the way from the use of the Gesell for making placement decisions to organizing and implementing screening programs that also include regular consultation with school personnel on the progress of kindergarten and first-grade children. A few school psychologists have taken leadership in implementing educational programs that utilize sophisticated intervention methods such as Reading Recovery and Writing to Read, or perceptual remediation programs similar to the one implemented by professionals at Ohio State School of Medicine (Arnold et al., 1977). However, more information is needed on the specific activities of school psychologists in regard to readiness practices. For example, one school psychology organization, the California Association of School Psychologists, has organized readiness workshops and programs on a regular basis for their members for the past 5 years.

In a recent school psychology publication, McLoughlin and Rausch (1990) take note of the controversy over kindergarten screening and the lack of accepted standards. However, they unfortunately add to the controversy by repeating statements about young children that have little or no evidence to support them. They state, for example, (1) that the academic problems of young children often continue through their school career and into adulthood; (2) that "premature" entrance into school can cause suicide at a later age; and (3) that behavior age should determine time of school entrance and promotion (p. 465).

There is no evidence that children who enter school at a young age will automatically have difficulty in adulthood. The linking of suicides to "youngness" of age has already been discussed at length in Chapter 6. It has been demonstrated that *no* such linkage can be made. The flaws in the Ohio study (Uphoff & Gilmore, 1984) have been discussed at length in this book. Attempting to relate the adjustment problems and concerns of youth up to age 25 with the age they enter kindergarten or first grade requires a leap in logic that just cannot be made. Once again such statements reflect the misconception by many American educators and psychologists that, with the change of the entrance age, learning problems will disappear.

"Behavior age," that is, a thorough assessment of the child as outlined in Chapter 3, on assessment, may help to better understand a child as he or she enters school. However, there never has been, nor is there currently, any measure that can accurately pinpoint *all* children who are at risk, and all who will succeed in school, *without* incurring substantial error.

The Importance of Child Advocates

School psychologists have long considered that they have a broad role to provide psychological services to all children. This role usually encompasses assessment and instructional activities as well as child advocacy activities. Most school psychologists are familiar with child advocacy functions that stem from P.L. 94-142 legislation. However, in recent years there has been a distinct broadening of the child advocacy movement to include children other than those covered by legislation for the handicapped. One main concern of advocates today is the provision of quality education for children beginning kindergarten and first grade. Before entering into meaningful social, political, or legal action on behalf of these children, there must be a core of ideas and philosophies that will provide a springboard or impetus for further actions on behalf of children. Described below are some of the individuals and organizations that (a) have been prime contributors of important ideas in the betterment of education of young children and (b) have attempted to incorporate these ideas into specific actions to benefit children.

As has been mentioned in prior chapters, two educational researchers, Lorrie Shepard and Mary Lee Smith (1989a,b), have provided us with the most up-to-date ideas on the effect of retention on children. They vividly portray the negative results of kindergarten retention and the lack of academic progress of those who have been retained. Smith (1986) also has pointed out the high cost of retaining children in kindergarten. In Boulder, Colorado, she found that this additional expense amounted to $3,000 per child in the late 1980s with no gain in academic performance or social maturity. The cost of the transition room program in the Ft. Wayne, Indiana, schools has been estimated as in excess of 2 million dollars (Mossburg, 1987).

The concerns expressed by Shepard and Smith (1989a,b) also have been expounded on by the National Association of Early Childhood Specialists in state departments of education (1987). In a monograph published under the title *Unacceptable Trends in Kindergarten Entry and Placement,* this group has been quite successful in increasing public awareness about educational policies that can adversely affect young children. This position paper emphasizes several important points. Included are (a) the need for an appropriate kindergarten curriculum; (b) children's enrollment in kindergarten must be based on their legal right to enter; (c) families should not be counseled or pressured to delay entrance to school by keeping children at home or enrolling them in preschool; (d) retention is not a viable option for young children; (e) tests used in kindergarten should be reliable and valid; and (f) children are not to be segregated into extra-year performance programs prior to or following regular kindergarten.

A group of early childhood educators led by Lillian Katz has published a monograph entitled *A Place Called Kindergarten* (Katz, Raths, & Torres, 1988) that provides the reader with an intimate view of a kindergarten program in one school system. Professionals as well as parents will benefit from reading this comprehensive analysis because it provides a viable example of how the consultation process works and how improvements in a kindergarten program can be made.

The California State Department of Education document *Here They Come: Ready or Not* (1988) is a report of a school readiness task force appointed by the superintendent of public instruction, William Honig. Co-chaired by Carolee Howes and Carla Sanger, the report recommends a drastic overhaul of early childhood education programs in California. The members found that many children in the age range of 4 to 6 were receiving inappropriate instruction, were subjected to assessment tests of dubious value, and were beginning their school experience by being tracked and labeled. The committee recommended that classes be nongraded up to age 7.

The role of the school psychologist in California will be drastically changed when the California plan is implemented. School psychologists will not be routinely testing children to make retention decisions for kindergarten and first grade as the committee recommends that such practices be eliminated.

Right from the Start, a report on early childhood education from the National Association of State Boards of Education (1988), has received wide distribution in the public schools. Among the many suggestions made, major ones include emphasis on improved assessment practices. The report emphatically rejects the use of readiness tests to determine classroom placement of young children.

Other groups also have been active as advocates on a regional basis. The Atlantic Center for Research in Education and the North Carolina Association for the Education of Young Children worked 5 years to convince legislators in that state to ban standardized testing of children in the first and second grades. The ban was enacted over intense opposition from the division of testing and research and the office of the state superintendent (Fair Test Examiner, 1988).

Last, but certainly not least, is the role that parents have been playing as advocates of positive childhood education practices. These various parent groups have not been completely successful in reaching their goals. Nevertheless, they have made major strides in gaining the attention of educators and have forced a number of school systems to begin a dialogue with parents about controversial childhood education practices.

Perhaps the most influential of all parent groups has been the one formed by parents in Denver City, Texas. Over a period of 3 years this group (Kids, Education, and You [KEY], N.D.) has not only educated parents within the local school system about the deficiencies in the Gesell screening program and placement options for children entering school but has been able to influence the state board of education in its policies. Based largely on the efforts of this small group of parents, the Texas Education Agency voted to phase out the use of prekindergarten and transition room placement within all the schools in the state of Texas beginning in 1991.

Further, the Maryland State Department of Education (1987) is to be congratulated for recently refusing to be pressured into raising the entry age to school. They maintain that this approach is no real answer to providing for individual differences within the classroom.

What is important and central to all of these examples is that there are a large number of individuals and groups who are involved in trying to provide better educational opportunities for young children, to improve assessment practices, and to provide suitable educational interventions. A number of these groups have been able to have their viewpoint considered seriously by boards of education as well as to help implement new program ideas for the education of young children. It is hoped that, with such leadership springing from these many sources, the quality and structure of early childhood education will change for the better.

REFERENCES

Abidin, R. R., Galloway, W. M., & Howerton, A. L. (1971). Elementary school retention: An unjustifiable, discriminatory and noxious educational policy. *Journal of School Psychology, 9,* 410–417.

Abramson, G. W. (1990). Writing to Read Program. *Educational Leadership, 48,* 93.

Achenbach, T. M., & Edelbrock, C. (1983). *Manual for the Child Behavior Checklist and Revised Child Behavior Profile.* Burlington, VT: Department of Psychiatry, University of Vermont.

Adelman, H., & Fishbach, S. (1975, April). *Early identification of children with learning problems: Some methological and ethical concerns.* Paper presented at conference of the Society for Research in Child Development, Denver, CO.

Ames, C., & Archer, J. (1988). Achievement goals in the classroom: Students' learning strategies and motivational processes. *Journal of Experimental Psychology, 80,* 260–267.

Ames, L. B. (1967). *Is your child in the wrong grade?* New York: Harper & Row.

Ames, L. B., & Gillespie, C. (1970). The cure for overplacement. *Instructor, 52,* 81–83.

Andreas, V. J. (1972). *School entrance age and subsequent progress.* Unpublished master's thesis, University of Northern Colorado, Greeley.

Annelli, C. M. (1977). *Computer assisted instruction and reading achievement of urban third and fourth grades.* Unpublished doctoral dissertation, Rutgers University, New Brunswick.

Argyros, R. N., & Rusch, R. R. (1974). Trimodal programmed instruction in reading. *Journal of Experimental Education, 42,* 1–5.

Arnold, L. E., Barnebey, N., McManus, J., Smeltzer, D. J., Conrad, A., Winer, G., & Desgranges, L. (1977). Prevention by specific perceptual remediation for vulnerable first-graders. *Archives of General Psychiatry, 34,* 1279–1294.

Arter, J. A., & Jenkins, J. R. (1979). Differential diagnosis-prescriptive teaching: A critical appraisal. *Review of Educational Research, 49,* 517–55.

Asher, S. R., Singleton, L. C., Tinsley, B. R., & Hymel, S. (1979). A reliable sociometric measure for preschool children. *Developmental Psychology, 15,* 443–444.

Atkinson, R. C. (1974). Teaching children to read using a computer. *American Psychologist, 29,* 169–178.

Austin, G. R., & Postlewaite, T. N. (1974). Cognitive results based on different ages of entry to school: A comparative study. *Journal of Educational Psychology, 66,* 857–863.

Ausubel, D. P. (1962). *Theory and problems of child development.* New York: Grune & Stratton.

Ausubel, D. P., & Robinson, F. G. (1969). *School learning: An introduction to educational psychology.* New York: Holt, Rinehart & Winston.

Ausubel, D. P., & Sullivan, E. V. (1970). *Theory and problems of child development* (2nd ed.). New York: Grune & Stratton.

Ayres, L. P. (1909). *Laggards in our schools.* New York: Survey Associates.

Baer, C. J. (1957). *The school progress and adjustment of underage and overage students.* Unpublished doctoral dissertation, University of Kansas, Lawrence.

Baer, C. J. (1958). The school progress and adjustment of underage and overage students. *Journal of Educational Psychology, 49,* 17–19.

Bailey, T., & Rogers, C. (1979). Screening, diagnosis and prescription: An infant check. *Association of Educational Psychologists Journal, 5,* 47–55.

Bale, P. (1981). Prenatal factors and backwardness in reading. *Educational Research, 23,* 134–143.

Barnes, K. E. (1982). *Preschool screening: The measurement and prediction of children at-risk.* Chicago: Charles C. Thomas.

Bell, M. (1972). *A study of the readiness room program in a small school district in suburban Detroit, Michigan.* Unpublished doctoral dissertation, Wayne State University, Detroit.

Berger, J. (1990, May 13). Is flunking a grade ever for a pupil's own good? *New York Times,* p. 20.

Berk, L. E. (1989). *Child development.* Boston: Allyn & Bacon.

Berliner, D. C. (1984). The half-hour glass: A review of research on teaching. In P. Hosford (Ed.), *Using what we know about teaching* (pp. 51–77). Alexandria, VA: Association for Supervision & Curriculum Development.

Bieger, G. R. (1985). Review of Metropolitan Readiness Tests. In D. J. Keyser & R. C. Sweetland (Eds.), *Test critiques: Volume II* (pp. 463–471). Kansas City, MO: Test Corporation of America.

Bigelow, E. B. (1934). School progress of under age children. *The Elementary School Journal, 35,* 186–191.

Bird, J. A. (1987). *Relationships between physical maturity, as measured by maturation of teeth and academic competence.* Unpublished doctoral dissertation, University of Utah, Salt Lake City.

Bloom, B. S. (1968). *Learning for mastery.* Evaluation Comment, *1*(2), Los Angeles Center for the Study of Evaluation of Instructional Programs, University of California.

Boehm, A. (1971). *Boehm test of basic concepts: Manual.* New York: The Psychological Corporation.

Bohl, N. (1984). A gift of time: The transition year. *Early Years, 14,* 14.

Bookbinder, G. (1978, December). Meddling with children. *The Times Educational Supplement, 1,* 17.

Bordens, K. S., & Abbott, B. B. (1988). *Research design and methods: A process approach.* Mountain View, CA: Mayfield.

Borg, W. R. (1987). *Applying educational research* (2nd ed.). New York: Longmans.

Bradley, R. H. (1985). Review of Gesell Preschool Test. In J. V. Mitchell (Ed.), *Ninth mental measurements yearbook* (pp. 609–610). Lincoln, NE: Buros Institute of Mental Measurements.

Braymen, R. K. F. (1988). *Early and young kindergarten entrants: Academic and school outcomes in high school.* Unpublished doctoral dissertation, University of Nebraska, Lincoln.

Braymen, R. K. F., & Piersel, W. C. (1987). The early entrance option: Academic and social/emotional outcomes. *Psychology in the Schools, 24,* 179–189.

Bredekamp, S., & Shepard, L. (1989). How best to protect children from inappropriate school expectations, practices, and policies. *Young Children, 44,* 14–24.

Brocato, F. (1988). Multi-variable approach solution to placement in kindergarten programs. *Oklahoma Educator, 18,* 4–5 & 18–19.

Broward County Public Schools. (1987). *Early childhood report: Impact of Prefirst Program on peer acceptance.* Ft. Lauderdale, FL: School Board of Broward County.

Brownell, W. A. (1938). A critique of the committee of seven's investigation on the grade placement of arithmetic topics. *Elementary School Journal, 38,* 495–508.

Bruner, J. S. (1966). *Toward a theory of instruction.* Cambridge, MA: Harvard University Press.

Bryant, D. M., Clifford, R. M., & Peisner, E. S. (1989). *Best practices for beginners: Quality programs for kindergartners.* Chapel Hill: Frank Porter Graham Child Development Center, University of North Carolina.

Bucko, R. L. (1986). Elementary grade retention: Making the decision. *ERS Spectrum, 4,* 9–13.

Burkart, J. E. (1988). *The effects of a developmental kindergarten on promotion to first and second grades.* Unpublished doctoral dissertation, University of Minnesota, Minneapolis.

Burkholder, R. B. (1968). *The improvement of reading ability through the development of specific underlying or associated mental abilities.* Unpublished doctoral dissertation, University of Arizona, Tucson.

Burmeister, L. E. (1983). *Foundations and strategies for teaching children to read.* Reading, MA: Addison-Wesley.

Buswell, G. T. (1938). Deferred arithmetic. *Mathematics Teacher, 31,* 195–200.

Butler, S. R., Marsh, H. W., Sheppard, M. J., & Sheppard, J. L. (1982). Early prediction of reading achievement with the Sheppard School Entry Screening Test: A four-year longitudinal study. *Journal of Educational Psychology, 74,* 280–290.

Byrd, E. (1951). A study of validity and constancy of choice in a sociometric test. *Sociometry, 14,* 175–181.

Byrnes, D. A. (1989). Attitudes of students, parents, and educators toward repeating a grade. In L. A. Shepard & M. E. Smith (Eds.), *Flunking grades: Research and policies on retention* (pp. 108–131). Philadelphia, PA: The Falmer Press.

Cadman, D., Chambers, L. W., Walter, S., Feldman, W., Smith, K., & Ferguson, R. (1984). The usefulness of the Denver Developmental Screening test to predict kindergarten problems in a general community population. *American Journal of Public Health, 74,* 1093, 1096.

Caggiano, J. A. (1984). *A study of the effectiveness of transitional first grade in a suburban school district.* Unpublished doctoral dissertation, Temple University, Philadelphia.

California State Department of Education. (1988, February). *Here they come: ready or not.* Sacramento: The School Readiness Task Force.

Campbell, S. M. (1984). *Kindergarten entry age as a factor in a school failure.* Unpublished doctoral dissertation, University of Virginia, Charlottesville.

Canady, R. L., & Hotchkiss, P. R. (1985). Scheduling practices and policies associated with increased achievement for low achieving students. *Journal of Negro Education, 54,* 344–355.

Cannella, G. S., & Reiff, J. C. (1989, April). *Mandating early childhood entrance/retention assessment: Practices in the 50 states.* Paper presented at American Educational Research Association, San Francisco.

Cantrell, V. L., & Prinz, R. J. (1985). Multiple perspectives of rejected, neglected, and accepted children: Relation between sociometric status and behavioral characteristics. *Journal of Consulting and Clinical Psychology, 53,* 884–889.

Carlson, R. D. (1985). The Gesell Preschool Test and the Gesell School Readiness Test. In D. J. Keyser & R. C. Sweetland (Eds.), *Test critiques* (Vol. 2, pp. 310–318). Kansas City, MO: Test Corporation of America.

Carlson, R. O. (1964). Environmental constraints and organizational consequency: The public school and its clients. In D. E. Griffith (Ed.), *Behavioral science and educational administration, 63rd Yearbook, National Society for Study of Education, Part II* (pp. 262–276). Chicago: University of Chicago Press.

Carrington, M. A. (1982). *The effect of school entrance age on achievement and adjustment.* Unpublished doctoral dissertation, Rutgers University, New Brunswick.

Carroll, J. B. (1963). A model of school learning. *Teachers College Record, 64,* 723–733.

Carson, M. R. (1969). *A descriptive study of roles: Elementary school counselors, psychologists and social workers.* Unpublished doctoral dissertation, University of Washington, Seattle.

Carter, H. L. J., & McGinnis, D. J. (1970). *Diagnosis and treatment of the disabled reader.* London: Macmillan.

Casavantes, E. (1974). *Reading achievement and in-grade retention rate differentials for Mexican-American and Black students in selected states of the Southwest.* Unpublished doctoral dissertation, University of Southern California, Los Angeles.

Chang, L. (1989, February). *An evaluation of Writing to Read.* Paper presented at meeting of South Carolina Educators for Practical Use of Research, Columbia, South Carolina.

Chase, J. A. (1970). *Differential behavioral characteristics of nonpromoted children.* Unpublished doctoral dissertation, University of Maine, Orono.

Clark, W. W. (1959, March). Boys and girls—Are there significant ability and achievement differences? *Phi Delta Kappan, 41,* 73–76.

Clauset, K. H., & Gaynor, A. K. (1982, March). *Improving schools for low achieving children: A system dynamic policy study.* Paper presented at the annual meeting of the American Educational Research Association, New York.

Clay, M. M. (1979). *The early detection of reading difficulties.* Exeter, NH: Heinemann.

Clay, M. M. (1987). Implementing reading recovery: Systematic adaptations to an educational innovation. *New Zealand Journal of Educational Studies, 22*, 35–38.

Cohen, D. L. (1989, October). Gesell Institute is facing uncertain future in wake of budget woes, testing questions. *Education Week, 9*, pp. 1, 13.

Cohen, D. L. (1990, August 1). Texas board votes to forbid retention before the first grade. *Education Week, 9*, pp. 1 & 15.

Cohen, S. E., Parmelee, A. H., Sigman, M., & Beckwith, L. (1988). Antecedents of school problems in children born preterm. *Journal of Pediatric Psychology, 13*, 493–508.

Coie, J. D., & Dodge, K. A. (1983). Continuities and changes in children's social status: A five year longitudinal study. *Merrill-Palmer Quarterly, 29*, 261–281.

Colditron, J. R., Braddock, J. H., & McPartland, J. M. (1987, April). *A description of school structures and classroom practices in elementary, middle, and secondary schools.* Paper presented at annual American Educational Research Association Conference, Washington, DC.

Commonwealth of Pennsylvania vs. Margaret Pasceri. (1974). Court of Common Pleas of Montgomery County, PA, No. 377.

Conroy, M. (1988, April). Kindergarten strategies for today: How to make sure your child gets a good start in school. *Better Homes and Gardens, 66*, pp. 46–48.

Cooper, D. H., & Farran, D. C. (1988). Behavioral risk factors in kindergarten. *Early Childhood Research Quarterly, 3*, 1–19.

Cooper, J. D. (1969). *A study of the learning modalities of good and poor first grade readers.* Unpublished doctoral dissertation, Indiana University, Bloomington.

Correll, J. H. (1990, March). *Early kindergarten entrance: How do children really do?* Paper presented at conference of The National Association of School Psychologists, San Francisco, CA.

Davie, R., Butler, N., & Goldstein, H. (1972). *From birth to seven.* London: Longmans.

Davis, B. G., Trimble, C. S., & Vincent, D. R. (1980). Does age of entrance affect school achievement? *Elementary School Journal, 80*, 133–144.

Day, M. J. (1986). *Effectiveness of a transitional first grade program.* Unpublished doctoral dissertation, North Texas State University, Denton.

Deci, E. L., & Ryan, R. M. (1985). *Intrinsic motivation and self-determination in human behavior.* New York: Plenum Press.

Dennebaum, J. M. (1991). *Kindergarten retention and transition classrooms: Their relationship to achievement.* Unpublished master's thesis, University of Rhode Island, Kingston.

Dennler, J. S. (1987). *Behavioral characteristics associated with primary grade retention.* Unpublished doctoral dissertation, University of Toledo, Toledo.

Devault, M. V., Ellis, E. C., Vodicka, E. M., & Otto, H. J. (1957). *Underage first grade enrollees: Their achievement and personal and social adjustment.* Austin: University of Texas Press.

DeWitt, B. F. (1961). *An analysis of the effect of chronological age as a factor in achievement in the elementary school.* Unpublished doctoral dissertation, University of Iowa, Iowa City.

Diamond, K. E. (1990). Effectiveness of the Revised Denver Developmental Screening Test in identifying children at risk for learning problems. *Journal of Educational Research, 83*, 152–157.

Dickson, V. E. (1923). *Mental tests and the classroom teacher.* Yonkers-on-Hudson, NY: World Book.

Dietz, C., & Wilson, B. (1985). Beginning school age and academic achievement. *Psychology in the Schools, 22*, 93–94.

DiPasquale, G. W., Moule, A. D., & Flewelling, R. W. (1980). The birthdate effect. *Journal of Learning Disabilities, 13*(5), 234–238.

Dockery, K. A. (1985). *The effects of IQ, sex, and school entrance age on the achievement and self-esteem of ten- to eleven-year-old students.* Unpublished doctoral dissertation, Temple University, Philadelphia.

Dodge, K. A. (1983). Behavioral antecedents of peer social status. *Child Development, 54*, 1386–1399.

Dolan, L. (1982). A follow-up evaluation of a transition room program for children with school and learning readiness problems. *The Exceptional Child, 29*, 101–110.

Donofrio, A. F. (1977). Grade repetition: Therapy of choice. *Journal of Learning Disabilities, 10*, 349–351.

Downing, J. (1973). *Comparative reading: Cross-national studies of behavior and processes in reading and writing.* New York: Macmillan.

Duffey, J. B., & Fedner, M. L. (1978). Educational diagnosis with instructional use, *Exceptional Children, 44*, 246–251.

Dweck, C. S. (1989). Motivation. In R. Glaser & A. Lesgold (Eds.), *The handbook of psychology and education* (Vol. 1, pp. 187–239). Hillsdale, NJ: Lawrence Erlbaum.

Dyer, C. A. (1973). Sex differences in reading: An evaluation and a critique of current theories. *Review of Educational Research, 43*, 455–467.

Edwards, J., Norton, S., Taylor, S., Weiss, M., & Dusseldorf, R. (1975). How effective is CAI? A review of the research. *Educational Leadership, 33*, 147–153.

Elkind, D. (1987). *Miseducation: Preschoolers at risk.* New York: Alfred A. Knopf.

Elkind, D. (1989). Developmentally appropriate practice; Philosophical and practical implications. *Phi Delta Kappan, 71*, 113–117.

Elliott, E. E., & Dweck, C. S. (1988). Goals: An approach to motivation and achievement. *Journal of Personality and Social Psychology, 54*(1), 5–12.

Evans, R. (1990). Making mainstreaming work through prereferral consultation. *Educational Leadership, 48*, 73–77.

Faerber, K., & Van Dusseldorp, R. (1984). *Attitudes toward elementary school student retention.* Anchorage, AK: University of Alaska. (ERIC Document Reproduction Service No. ED 250 109)

Fletcher, J. D., & Atkinson, R. C. (1972). Evaluation of the Stanford CAI program in initial reading. *Journal of Educational Psychology, 63*, 597–602.

Floyd, C. (1954). Meeting children's reading needs in the middle grades: A preliminary report. *Elementary School Journal, 55*, 100–103.

Frankenburg, W. K. (1985). The concept of screening revisited. In W. K. Frankenburg, R. W. Emde, & J. W. Sullivan (Eds.), *Early identification of children at risk* (pp. 3–17). New York: Plenum Press.

Frankenburg, W., Dodds, J., Fandal, A., Kazuk, E., & Cohrs, M. (1975). *Denver Developmental Screening Test.* (Reference manual, rev. ed.) Denver: LADOCA Project & Publishing Foundation.

Franseth, J., & Koury, R. (1966). *Survey of research on grouping as related to pupil learning.* Dept. of Health, Education, & Welfare. Washington, DC: U.S. Government Printing Office (Publication # OE20089).

Freyd, P., & Lytle, J. H. (1990). A corporate approach to the 2 R's: A critique of IBM's Writing to Read program. *Educational Leadership, 47,* 83–89.

Frick, R. (1986). In support of academic redshirting. *Young Children, 41*(2), 9–10.

Fricklas, R., & Rusch, R. (1974). Trimodal reading instruction with inefficient learners. *The Slow Learning Child, 21,* 44–52.

Friedman, L. S., & Sugarman, S. D. (1988). School sorting and disclosure: Disclosure to families as a school reform strategy. Part I: Existing practices and the social interacts in school information disclosure. *Journal of Law and Education, 17,* 53–89.

Fritze, D. (1990, March 4). Kindergarten policy becomes a big issue in small town. *Dallas Times Herald,* A-20.

Frymier, J. (1989). *A study of students at risk: Collaborating to do research.* Bloomington, IN: Phi Delta Kappa Educational Foundation.

Funk, S. G., Sturner, R. A., & Green, J. A. (1986). Preschool prediction of early school performance: Relationship of McCarthy scales of children's abilities prior to school entry to achievement in kindergarten, first, and second grades. *Journal of School Psychology, 24,* 181–194.

Gagné, R. M. (1962). Military training and principles of learning. *American Psychologist, 17,* 83–91.

Gagné, R. M. (1968). Contributions of learning to human development. *Psychological Review, 75*(3), 177–191.

Gagné, R. M. (1977). *The conditions of learning* (3rd ed.) New York: Holt, Rinehart, & Winston.

Gagné, R. M. (1985). *The conditions of learning* (4th ed.) New York: Holt, Rinehart, & Winston.

Gagné, R. M. (1987). Peaks and valleys of educational psychology. In J. A. Glover & R. A. Ronning (Eds.), *Historical foundations of educational psychology* (pp. 395–402). New York: Plenum.

Garrett, W. (1956). *Factors relating to school entrance age.* Warren, OH: Warren City Schools.

Garvey, R. (1983). *Kindergarten reinforcement. Disadvantaged pupil program fund. Evaluation report 1982–1983.* Cleveland, OH: Cleveland Public Schools, Department of Research and Analysis. (ERIC Document Reproduction Service No. ED 236-289)

Gates, A. I. (1937). The necessary mental age for beginning reading. *Elementary School Journal, 8,* 497–508.

Gates, A. I., & Bond, G. L. (1936). Reading readiness: A study of factors determining success and failure in beginning reading. *Teachers College Record, 37,* 679–685.

Gesell, A. (1954). The ontogenesis of infant behavior. In L. Carmichael (Ed.), *Manual of child psychology* (pp. 355–356). New York: John Wiley & Sons.

Gettinger, M. (1978). *Is time-to-learn or measured intelligence a stronger correlate of school learning?* Unpublished doctoral dissertation, Columbia University, New York.

Glazer, S. (1988). Preschool: Too much too soon? *Editorial Research Reports, Feb. 5*, Library of Congress Catalogue No. 39-924. Washington, DC: Congressional Quarterly.

Glennon, A. J. (1978). *Field study involving use of the Gesell Developmental Examination: An ex-post facto analysis.* Unpublished doctoral dissertation, University of Pittsburgh, Pittsburgh, PA.

Goldberg, S. D. (1982). *Special education law: A guide for parents, advocates and educators.* New York: Plenum.

Good, R. H., Kaminski, R., Schwarz, I., & Doyle, C. (1990, March). *Identifying at-risk kindergarten students using the slope of pupil progress: A pilot study.* Paper presented at National Association of School Psychologists Convention, San Francisco.

Gott, M. E. (1963). The effect of age differences at kindergarten entrance on achievement and adjustment in elementary school. Unpublished doctoral dissertation, University of Colorado, Boulder.

Gourevitch, V. (1965). *Statistical methods: A problem-solving approach*, Boston, MA: Allyn & Bacon.

Grant, J. (1989). Theory is reality. *School Success Network*, Fall, pp. 1 & 4.

Gray, R. (1985). *Criteria to determine entry into school: A review of research.* Springfield, IL: Illinois State Department of Education.

Gredler, G. R. (1956). *Relationship of entrance age of children and success in first grade.* Unpublished report, Canton, Ohio, Board of Education.

Gredler, G. R. (1964, February). *Dilemmas in the assessment of readiness for school.* Paper delivered at conference of kindergarten teachers, Atlanta Public Schools, Atlanta, GA.

Gredler, G. R. (1975). Ethical and legal dilemmas in assessment of readiness of children for school. In G. R. Gredler (Ed.), *Ethical and legal factors in the practice of school psychology* (pp. 196–221). Harrisburg: Pennsylvania State Department of Education.

Gredler, G. R. (1978). A look at some important factors in assessing readiness for school. *Journal of Learning Disabilities, 11*, 284–290.

Gredler, G. R. (1979). Trimodal reading instruction with disadvantaged children. *Perceptual and Motor Skills, 49*, 707–712.

Gredler, G. R. (1980). The birthdate effect: Fact or artifact? *Journal of Learning Disabilities, 13*, 239–242.

Gredler, G. R. (1984). Transition classes: A viable alternative for the at-risk child? *Psychology in the Schools, 21*, 463–470.

Gredler, G. R. (1987). Special education in the 80's: A critical analysis. *Psychology in the Schools, 25*, 92–100.

Gredler, G. R. (1990). Approaches to the remediation of learning difficulties: A current assessment. In P. M. Gupta & P. Coxhead (Eds.), *Intervention with children* (pp. 171–198). New York: Routledge.

Gredler, G. R. (1991, March). *The school readiness issue: The concerns and rights of parents.* Paper presented at the California Association of School Psychologists, Los Angeles.

Gredler, M. E. (1992). *Learning and instruction: Theory into practice* (2nd ed.). New York: Macmillan.

Green, D. R., & Simmons, S. V. (1962). Chronological age and school entrance. *Elementary School Journal, 63*, 41–47.

Gronlund, N. (1959). *Sociometry in the classroom.* New York: Harper.

Haag, G. J. (1980). *The effect of delayed kindergarten entrance on first grade achievement.* Unpublished specialist thesis. Northeast Missouri State University, Kirksville, Missouri.

Hainsworth, P. K., & Siqueland, M. L. (1969). *Early identification of children with learning disabilities: The Meeting Street School Screening Test.* Providence, RI: Crippled Children and Adults of Rhode Island.

Halliwell, J. W. (1968). Reviewing the reviews on entrance age and school success. In N. H. Noll & R. P. Noll (Eds.), *Readings in educational psychology* (pp. 55–69). New York: Macmillan.

Halliwell, J. W., & Stein, B. W. (1964). A comparison of the achievement of early and late starters in reading related and non-reading related areas in fourth and fifth grades. *Elementary English, 41,* 631–639.

Hannah, J. N. (1984). *The relationship of a kindergarten intervention program and reading readiness, language skills, and reading achievement.* Unpublished doctoral dissertation, George Peabody College of Vanderbilt University, Nashville.

Hardyck, C. D., & Petrinovich, L. S. (1969). *Introduction to statistics for the behavioral sciences.* Philadelphia, PA: Saunders.

Hargis, C. H. (1990). *Grades and grading practices: Obstacles to improving education and to helping at-risk students.* Springfield, IL: Charles C. Thomas.

Harrison, P. (1979). *Mercer's adaptive behavior inventory: The McCarthy scales and dental development as predictors of first grade achievement.* Unpublished doctoral dissertation, University of Georgia, Athens.

Hedges, W. D. (1977). *At what age should children enter first grade?* Ann Arbor, MI: University Microfilms International.

Hefferman, H. (1964). What is a good education in nursery school and kindergarten? *Childhood Education, 41,* 25–28.

Helton, G. B., Workman, E. A., & Matuszek, P. A. (1982). *Psychoeducational assessment: Integrating concepts and techniques.* New York: Grune & Stratton.

Hemphill, F. (1953). *A study of the effects of acceleration on the educational welfare of elementary school pupils.* Unpublished master's thesis, West Texas State College, Canyon.

Higgins, C. G. (1971). *Trimodal programmed instruction in reading: Background and rationale.* Albany, NY: Learning Research Center, Board of Education.

Hildreth, G. H., & Griffiths, N. L. (1949). *Metropolitan Readiness Tests.* Tarrytown on Hudson, NY: World Book.

Hindley, C. N., & Owen, C. G. (1978). The extent of individual changes in the IQ for ages between six months and seventeen years in a British longitudinal sample. *Journal of Child Psychology and Psychiatry, 19,* 329–350.

Hodapp, S. J. (1986). *Kindergarten Study I.* Defiance County, OH: Defiance County Schools.

Hodge, C. C., Jr. (1981). *Predictive study of the Meeting Street School Screening Test and academic achievement in grades two through six by race, sex and kindergarten experience.* Unpublished doctoral dissertation, University of South Carolina, Columbia.

House, E. R. (1989). Policy implications of retention research. In L. A. Shepard & M. L. Smith (Eds.), *Flunking grades: Research and policies on retention* (pp. 202–213). Philadelphia: The Falmer Press.

How North Carolina stopped testing. (1988). *Fair Test Examiner*, Spring, 2, 1–2.

Hughes, S. (1987). Metropolitan Readiness Tests: 1986 edition. In D. J. Keyser & R. C. Sweetland (Eds.), *Test critiques* (Vol. 6, pp. 341–349). Kansas City, MO: Test Corporation of America.

Hymes, J. L. (1958). *Before the child reads.* Evanston, IL: Row, Peterson.

Hymes, J. L. (1963). More pressure for early reading. *Childhood Education, 30,* 34–35.

Ilg, F. L., & Ames, L. B. (1965). *School readiness—Behavior tests used at the Gesell Institute.* New York: Harper & Row.

Ilg, F. L., & Ames, L. B. (1972). *School readiness: Behavior tests used at the Gesell Institute.* New York: Harper & Row.

Ilg, F. L., Ames, L. B., & Baker, S. M. (1981). *Child behavior from the Gesell Institute of Human Development* (rev. ed.). New York: Harper & Row.

Ilika, J. (1963). *Age of entrance into the first grade as related to rate of scholastic achievement.* Unpublished doctoral dissertation, University of Michigan, Ann Arbor.

Ingram, V. (1960). Flint evaluates its primary cycle. *Elementary School Journal, 61,* 76–80.

Jaccard, J., & Becker, M. A. (1990). *Statistics for the behavioral sciences.* Belmont, CA: Wadsworth.

Jagacinski, J. M., & Nicholls, J. G. (1987). Competence and affect in task involvement and ego involvement: The impact of social comparison information. *Journal of Educational Psychology, 79,* 107–114.

Jansky, J. J. (1978). A critical review of some developmental and predictive precursors of reading disabilities. In A. L. Benton & D. Pearl (Eds.), *Dyslexia: An appraisal of current knowledge* (pp. 313–347). New York: Oxford University Press.

Jansky, J., & DeHirsch, K. (1972). *Preventing reading failure.* New York: Harper & Row.

Jennings, G., Burge, S., & Sitek, D. (1987). Half-steps from kindergarten to second grade. *Principal, 6,* 22–25.

Johansson, B. R. (1965). *Criteria of school readiness.* Stockholm: Almquist & Wiksell.

Johnson, B. E. (1967). *Relationship of chronological age to kindergarten admission.* Unpublished specialist thesis, Western Michigan University, Kalamazoo.

Joiner, L. M. (1977). *A technical analysis of the variations in screening instruments and programs in New York State.* New York: City University of New York, New York Center for Advanced Study in Education. (ERIC Document Reproduction Service No. ED 154 596)

Jones, D. M. (1968). Practices and problems in school entrance requirements. *Education, 88,* 197–203.

Jones, R. R. (1985). *The effect of a transition program on low achieving kindergarten students when entering first grade.* Unpublished doctoral dissertation, Northern Arizona University, Flagstaff.

Katz, G. L., Raths, J. D., & Torres, R. D. (1987). *A place called kindergarten.* Urbana, IL: Clearinghouse on Elementary and Elementary Childhood Education.

Kaufman, A. S. (1971a). *Comparison of tests built from Piaget's & Gesell's tasks: An analysis of their psychometric properties and psychological meaning.* Unpublished doctoral dissertation, Columbia University, New York.

Kaufman, A. S. (1971b). Piaget and Gesell: A psychometric analysis of tests built from their tasks. *Child Development, 42,* 1341–1346.

Kaufman, A. S., & Kaufman, N. L. (1972). Tests built from Piaget's and Gesell's tasks as predictors of first-grade achievement. *Child Development, 43,* 521–533.

Kaufman, N. L. (1985). Review of Gesell Preschool Test. In J. V. Mitchell (Ed.), *Ninth mental measurements yearbook* (Vol. 1, pp. 607–608). Lincoln, NE: Buros Institute of Mental Measurements.

Kelly, F. J. (1987). *Right of child to attend kindergarten.* Office of Attorney General, Lansing, MI: Opinion #6467.

Keogh, B. K., & Becker, L. D. (1973). Early detection of learning problems: Questions, cautions, and guidelines. *Exceptional Children, 40,* 5–10.

Kids, Education, and You. (Key). (N. D.). *Everything we learned as kindergarten parents.* Brochure, P.O. Box 970, Denver City, TX 79323.

Kilby, G. A. (1982). *An ex post facto evaluation of the junior first grade program in Sioux Falls, SD.* Unpublished doctoral dissertation, University of South Dakota.

Kindergarten placement policy okayed by board. (1989, July 20). *Denver City Press,* p. 1.

King, I. B. (1955). Effect of age of entrance into grade 1 upon achievement in elementary school. *Elementary School Journal, 55,* 331–336.

Kingslake, B. J. (1981). *An experimental examination of on-entry to school screening.* Unpublished doctoral dissertation, City of Birmingham Polytechnic, Birmingham.

Kingslake, B. J. (1983). The predictive (in) accuracy of on-entry to school screening procedures when used to anticipate learning difficulties. *British Journal of Special Education, 10,* 24–26.

Kirby, W. N. (1990, October 19). *Discussion of retention in prekindergarten and kindergarten.* Memo to Committee on Students. Austin, TX: State Board of Education.

Kirk, S. A., & Kirk, W. D. (1971). *Psycholinguistic learning disabilities: Diagnosis and remediation.* Urbana: University of Illinois Press.

Koch, D. (1968). *Kindergarten entrance age as a factor in school progress in selected school districts in Camden County.* Unpublished doctoral dissertation, Teachers College, Columbia University.

Ladd, G. W., & Mars, K. T. (1986). Reliability and validity of preschoolers' perceptions of peer behavior. *Journal of Clinical Child Psychology, 15,* 16–25.

Lambert, N., & Bower, E. M. (1961). *A process for inschool screening of children with emotional handicaps: Technical report for school administrators and teachers.* Berkeley, CA: Educational Testing Service.

Larrabee, D. F. (1984). Setting the standard: Alternative policies for student promotions. *Harvard Educational Review, 54,* 67–87.

Lawrence, D. (1971). The effects of counseling on retarded readers. *Educational Research, 13,* 119–124.

Lawrence, D. (1972). Counseling of retarded readers by nonprofessionals. *Educational Research, 51,* 48–51.

Lawrence, D. (1973). *Improving reading through counseling.* London: Ward Lock Educational.

Leach, D. J. (1980). Considerations in screening for school learning difficulties: An overview of practice. *Educational Studies, 6,* 181–197.

Leach, D. J. (1981). *Early screening for school learning difficulties: Efficacy problems and alternatives.* Occasional papers, Division of Educational and Child Psychology, British Psychological Society, 5, 46–59.

Leinhardt, G. (1980). Transition rooms: Promoting maturation or reducing education? *Journal of Educational Psychology, 72,* 55–61.

Leiter, K. C. W. (1974). Ad hocing in the schools: A study of placement practices in the kindergartens of two schools. In A. V. Cicourel, K. H. Jennings, K. C. W. Leiter, R. MacKay, H. Mehan, & D. R. Roth (Eds.), *Language use and school performance* (pp. 17–75). New York: Academic Press.

Lennox, B. (1983). The editor regrets and the Hawthorne effect. *Medical Education, 17*, 347–348.

Let's give boys a break! (1959). *Phi Delta Kappan, 40*, 281–283.

Li, A. K. F. (1986). Low peer interaction in kindergarten children: An ecological perspective. *Journal of Clinical Child Psychology, 15*, 26–29.

Lichtenstein, R. (1990). Comparative validity of two preschool screening tests: Correlation and classification approaches. *Journal of Learning Disabilities, 14*, 68–72.

Lichtenstein, R., & Ireton, H. (1984). *Preschool screening: Identifying young children with developmental and educational problems.* Orlando, FL: Grune & Stratton.

Liddle, G., & Long, D. (1958). Experimental rooms for slow learners. *Elementary School Journal, 59*, 143–149.

Lieberman, L. M. (1980). A decision-making model for in-grade retention (non-promotion). *Journal of Learning Disabilities, 13*, 268–272.

Lindsay, G. (Ed.). (1984). *Screening for children with special needs.* Dover, NH: Croom Helm.

Longnecker, R. (1962). *A comparison of the academic achievement of children entering first grade at different chronological ages.* Unpublished master's thesis, Millersville State College, Millersville.

Loughlin, C. E. (1966). *First grade adjustment and achievement of early kindergarten entrants and older kindergarten entrants.* Unpublished doctoral dissertation, Rutgers University, New Brunswick.

Lykken, D. D. (1968). Statistical significance in psychological research. *Psychological Bulletin, 70*, 151–159.

Malmquist, E. (1958). *Factors related to reading disabilities in the first grade of the elementary school.* Stockholm: Almquist & Wiksell.

Mandl, H. (1976). Current views about school readiness in Germany with specific reference to their predictive validity for identifying potential failure in school. In K. Wedell & E. C. Reybould (Eds.), *The early identification of educationally at risk children* (p. 54). Birmingham: University of Birmingham.

Mantzicopoulos, P., Morrison, D. C., Hinshar, S. P., & Carte, E. T. (1989). Nonpromotion in kindergarten, achievement, socioeconomic and demographic characteristics. *AERA Journal, 26*, 107–121.

Martin, J. (1973). *Design of man-computed dialogues.* Englewood Cliffs, NJ: Prentice-Hall.

Martin, J., & Friedberg, A. (1986). *Writing to read.* New York: Warner.

Maryland State Department of Education. (1987). *Entry age report.* Baltimore, MD: Author.

Matthews, H. W. (1977). *The effect of transition education, a year of readiness, and beginning reading instruction between kindergarten and first grade.* Unpublished doctoral dissertation, St. Louis University, St. Louis.

May, D. C., & Welch, E. I. (1984). The effects of developmental placement and early retention on children: Later scores on standardized tests. *Psychology in the Schools, 21*, 381–385.

McDaid, E. W. (1950). *A study of an experimental reading readiness program in a large city school system.* Unpublished doctoral dissertation, Wayne State University, Detroit.

McDermott, P. A. (1980). Prevalence and constituency of behavioral disturbance taxonomies in the regular school population. *Journal of Abnormal Child Psychology, 8,* 523–536.

McDermott, P. A. (1981). The manifestation of problem behaviors in ten age groups of Canadian school children. *Canadian Journal of Behavioral Science, 13,* 310–319.

McDermott, P. (1983). A syndromic typology for analyzing school children's disturbed social behavior. *School Psychology Review, 12,* 250–260.

McDermott, P., & Watkins, M. W. (1983). Computerized vs. conventional remedial instruction for learning disabled pupils. *Journal of Special Education, 17,* 81–88.

McGuinness, D. (1985). *When children don't learn: Understanding the biology and psychology of learning disabilities.* New York: Basic Books.

McKee, P., & Brzeinski, J. (1966). *The effectiveness of teaching reading in kindergarten.* Colorado State Department of Education and Denver Public Schools Report. (ERIC Document Reproduction Service No. ER010 058).

McLaughlin, C. S., & Rausch, E. (1990). Best practices in kindergarten screening. In A. Thomas & A. Grimes (Eds.), *Best practices in school psychology, II* (pp. 455–468). Washington, DC: NASP.

Meeks, B. S. (1982). *A study of children in second grade who were predicted to be ready for school while in kindergarten.* Unpublished doctoral dissertation, University of Georgia, Athens.

Meisels, S. J. (1985). *Developmental screening in early childhood: A guide* (rev. ed.). Washington, DC: National Association for the Education of Young Children.

Meisels, S. J. (1989a). *Developmental screening in early childhood: A guide* (3rd ed.). Washington, DC: National Association for the Education of Young Children.

Meisels, S. J. (1989b). Can developmental screening tests identify children who are developmentally at risk? *Pediatrics, 83,* 578–585.

Merrow, J. (1989). Repeating a grade. *Children, 3,* 80.

Miller, L. C. (1984). *Louisville Behavior Checklist.* Los Angeles: Western Psychological Services.

Miller, W., & Norris, R. C. (1967). Entrance age and school success. *Journal of School Psychology, 6,* 47–60.

Moore, R. S., & Moore, D. N. (1975). *Better late than early.* New York: Reader's Digest Press.

Moore, R. S., & Moore, D. N. (1979). *School can wait.* Provo, UT: Brigham Young University Press.

Moran, J. J. (1988, Summer). Information management; aid to professional retention decisions. ERS *Spectrum 6,* pp. 31–36.

Morgan, G. (1981). Problem and promise in early identification: Children with special needs. In H. Silverman, I. F. Davidson, & L. S. Weintraub (Eds.), *Early identification and intervention* (pp. 48–69).

Morphett, M. V., & Washburne, C. (1931). When should children begin to read? *Elementary School Journal, 31,* 496–503.

Morrison, F. J. (1989, November). *School readiness, entrance age, and learning in children.* Paper presented at annual meeting of the Psychonomic Society, Atlanta, GA.

Morrison, F. J., & Smith, L. (1990). *Education and cognitive development: A natural experiment.* Project supported by National Sciences and Engineering Research Council of Canada, Ottawa.

Mossburg, J. W. (1987). *The effects of transition room placement on selected achievement variables and readiness for middle school.* Unpublished doctoral dissertation, Ball State University, Terre Haute.

Naglieri, J. A. (1985). Review of Gesell Preschool Test. In J. V. Mitchell (Ed.), *Ninth mental measurements yearbook* (Vol. 1, pp. 608–609). Lincoln, NE: Buros Institute of Mental Measurements.

National Association of Early Childhood Specialists in State Departments of Education. (1987, November 11). *Unacceptable trends in kindergarten entry and placement: A position statement.* Adopted at the association's annual meeting, Chicago, IL.

National Association of State Boards of Education. (1988). *Right from the start. Report of the NASBE task force on early childhood education.* Alexandria, VA: NASBE.

Naylor, J. G., & Pumfrey, P. D. (1983). The alleviation of psycholinguistic deficits and some effects on the reading attainments of poor readers: A sequel. *Journal of Research in Reading, 6,* 129–153.

Neale, M. D. (1958). *Neale analysis of reading ability—Manual of directions and norms.* London: Macmillan.

Neligan, G., Prudham, D., & Steiner, H. (1974). *The formative years.* Oxford, England: Oxford University Press.

Nelms, V. (1990). Not a balanced assessment: A response to Freyd & Lytle. *Educational Leadership, 47,* 89–91.

New Jersey State Department of Education. (1975). *Screening children ages 3–5.* Trenton: Bureau of Special Education and Pupil Personnel Services.

Northway, M. L. (1952). *A primer of sociometry.* Toronto: University of Toronto Press.

Norton, M. S. (1983). It's time to get tough on student promotion—or is it? *Contemporary Education, 54,* 283–286.

Nurss, J., & McGauvran, M. (1976). *Metropolitan Readiness Tests.* Teacher's manual, *Part II: Interpretation and use of test results.* New York: Harcourt, Brace & Jovanovich.

Oakes, J. (1983). Tracking and ability grouping in American schools: Some constitutional questions. *Teachers College Record, 84,* 801–819.

O'Donnell, C. M. (1968). *A comparison of the reading readiness of kindergarten pupils exposed to conceptual-language and basal reader pre-reading programs.* Maine State Department of Education Cooperative Research Project Number 7-8426, Augusta, ME.

O'Donnell, L. E. (1972). *Theoretical framework of reading retardation: After data gathering and before remedial action.* Unpublished doctoral dissertation, University of Illinois, Urbana.

Ogletree, E. J. (1975). *A review and evaluation of school readiness on the basis of the bioplasmic force theory.* (ERIC Document Reproduction Service No. ED 124 286)

Pain, K. (1981). *Grade one entrance age study.* Research report, St. Albert Protestant School District Edmonton, Alberta #6 (Education). (ERIC Document Reproduction Service No. ED 208 985)

Palfrey, J. S. (1981). Preschool screening: Ready? Set? Go! In H. Silverman, I. F. Davidson, & L. S. Weintraub (Eds.), *Early identification and intervention* (pp. 33–69). Ontario, Canada: Minister of Education.

Palincsar, A. S., & Brown, A. L. (1984). Reciprocal teaching of comprehension-fostering and comprehension-monitoring activities. *Cognition and Instruction, 2,* 117–175.

Palmer, R. (1971). *Starting school.* London: University of London Press.

Payton, M. M. (1990). *Transition classes for kindergarten students in Texas: Practices, policies, and issues.* Unpublished doctoral dissertation, University of Texas, Austin.

Pennsylvania State Department of Education. (1971). *Retention rates in Pennsylvania Schools, 1970–1971.* Unpublished report. Harrisburg, PA: Author.

Pheasant, M. (1985). *Amusville, Oregon school district's readiness program: Helping first graders succeed.* Eugene: Oregon School Study Council, University of Oregon. (ERIC Document Reproduction Service No. ED 252 967)

Piaget, J. (1970). *Genetic epistemology.* (E. Duckworth, Trans.). New York: Columbia University Press.

Piaget, J. (1972). Intellectual evolution from adolescence to adulthood. *Human Development, 15,* 1–12.

Piaget, J. (1975). Comments on mathematical education. *Contemporary Education, 47*(1), 5–10.

Pinnell, G. S., DeFord, E. E., & Lyons, C. A. (1988). *Reading Recovery: Early intervention for at risk first graders.* Arlington, VA: Educational Research Service.

Potton, A. (1983). *Screening.* London: MacMillan Education.

Preston, R. C. (1962). Reading achievement of German and American children. *School and Society, 90,* 350–354.

Prince, J. A. (1966). *A comparative study of early and late enterers into first grade.* Unpublished doctoral dissertation, University of Illinois, Urbana.

Pringle, M. L. K., Butler, N. R., & Davie, R. (1966). *11,000 seven year olds.* London: Longmans.

Pumfrey, P. D., & Naylor, J. G. (1978). The alleviation of psycholinguistic deficits and some effects on the reading attainments of poor readers. *Journal of Research in Reading, 1,* 87–107.

Quay, H. C., & Peterson, D. E. (1983). *Interim manual for the Revised Behavior Problems Checklist.* Coral Gables: University of Miami.

Rafoth, M. A. K. (1984). *Early identification of learning disabilities: The predictive validity of the Meeting Street School Screening Test.* Unpublished doctoral dissertation, University of Georgia, Athens.

Rapala, M. M. (1990, March). *Gesell School Readiness Screening Test: Measuring readiness or special needs?* Paper presented at National Association of School Psychologists Convention, San Francisco.

Raygor, B. (1972). *A five-year follow-up study comparing the school achievement and school adjustment of children retained in kindergarten and children placed in a transition class.* Unpublished doctoral dissertation, University of Minnesota, Minneapolis.

Reichmuth, M. (1983). *Evaluation of the predictive ability of four screening measures used in prekindergarten screening: A follow-up study.* Unpublished specialist thesis, University of Northern Iowa, Cedar Rapids.

Reynolds, C. R. (1979). Should we screen preschoolers? *Contemporary Educational Psychology,* 175–181.

Rie, H. E. (1974). Therapeutic tutoring for underachieving children. *Professional Psychology, 5,* 70–75.

Rodgers, W. A. (1970). Retention as a school policy. *Urban Review, 4,* 29–30.

Roethlisberger, F. J., & Dickson, W. J. (1939). *Management and the workers.* Boston, MA: Harvard University Press.

Rosemond, J. (1989, July 2). To retain or not to retain—A hot education question. *The Columbia State* (SC), p. 3-E.

Rosemond, J. (1990a, March 29). Should "late-birthday" kids delay starting kindergarten? *Orange County (CA) Register,* p. J3.

Rosemond, J. (1990b, June 10). Holding a child back in school can work out ok. *Charlotte (NC) Observer,* p. 4E.

Rosenfield, S., & Kuralt, S. K. (1990). Best practices in curriculum-based assessment. In A. Thomas & A. Grimes (Eds.), *Best practices in school psychology* (pp. 275–286). Washington, DC: National Association of School Psychologists.

Rosenthal, M. (1969). *A comparison of reading readiness achievement of kindergarten children of disparate entrance ages.* New York: Research paper, Queens College, City University of New York. (ERIC Document Reproduction Service No. ED 033 745)

Rossi, P., & Wright, S. (1977). Evaluation research: An assessment of theory, practice, and politics. *Evaluation Quarterly, 1,* 5–52.

Rotenberg, L. (1984). Booting up for reading. *Teaching and Computers, 1,* 16–19.

Roth, J. A. (1963). *Timetables: Structuring the passage of time in hospital treatment and other careers.* Indianapolis: Bobbs-Merrill.

Satz, P., & Fletcher, J. M. (1988). Early identification of learning disabled children: An age old question revisited. *Journal of Consulting and Clinical Psychology, 56,* 824–829.

Satz, P., Taylor, H. G., Friel, J., & Fletcher, J. (1977). Some developmental and predictive precursors of reading disabilities: A six year followup. In A. L. Benton & D. Pearl (Eds.), *Dyslexia: An appraisal of current knowledge* (pp. 313–347). New York: Oxford University Press.

Schiefelbein, E. (1975). Repeating: An overlooked problem of Latin American education. *Comparative Education Review, 19,* 468–487.

School policy revised for younger students. (1988, December 15). *Denver City Press,* p. 1.

School Readiness Task Force. (1988). *Here they come: Ready or not.* Sacramento, CA: State Department of Education.

Shapiro, E. S. (1990). An integrated model for curriculum-based assessment. *School Psychology Review, 19,* 331–349.

Shavelson, R. J. (1988). *Statistical reasoning for the behavioral sciences* (2nd ed.). Boston: Allyn & Bacon.

Shepard, L. A. (1989). A review of research on kindergarten retention. In L. A. Shepard & M. E. Smith (Eds.), *Flunking grades: Research and policies on retention* (pp. 64–78). Philadelphia: The Falmer Press.

Shepard, L. A. (1991). Readiness testing in local school districts: An analysis of backdoor policies. *Journal of Education Policy, 5,* 159–179.

Shepard, L. A., & Smith, M. L. (1985). *Boulder Valley kindergarten study: Retention practices and retention effects.* Boulder: University of Colorado, Laboratory of

Educational Research.

Shepard, L. A., & Smith, M. E. (1986). Synthesis of research on school readiness and kindergarten retention. *Educational Leadership*, November, 78–86.

Shepard, L. A., & Smith, M. E. (1989a). *Flunking grades: Research policies on retention.* Philadelphia: The Falmer Press.

Shepard, L. A., & Smith, M. E. (1989b). Introduction and overview. In L. A. Shepard & M. E. Smith (Eds.), *Flunking grades: Research and policies on retention* (pp. 1–15). Philadelphia: The Falmer Press.

Shilling, J. L. (1989). *Entry age report.* Baltimore, MD: Maryland State Department of Education.

Shipman, V. C. (1981). Perspectives in early identification and intervention. In H. Silverman, I. F. Davidson, & L. S. Weintraub (Eds.), *Early identification and intervention* (pp. 6–32). Ontario, Canada: Minister of Education.

Silva, P. A., McGee, R., & Williams, S. (1983). Developmental language delay from three to seven years and its significance for low intelligence and reading difficulties at age seven. *Developmental Medicine and Child Neurology, 25*, 783–792.

Silva, P. A., & Ross, B. (1980). Gross motor development and delays in development in early childhood: Assessment and significance. *Journal of Human Movement Studies, 6*, 211–226.

Simpson, C. H. (1984). *A prefirst developmental program and its effects on the achievement of children.* Unpublished doctoral dissertation, Rutgers University, New Brunswick.

Sincere, M. (1987). Prefirst: Why Broward County public schools want to retain more than a third of their kindergarten students every year. *Florida Parent*, May/June, 20–21, 28–29 & 40–42.

Skinner, B. F. (1972). *Cumulative record: A selection of papers.* New York: Appleton-Century-Crofts-Meredith.

Slavin, R. E. (1987a). Ability grouping and student achievement in elementary schools: A best evidence synthesis. *Review of Educational Research, 57*, 293–336.

Slavin, R. E. (1987b). *Mastery learning reconsidered.* Baltimore, MD: Center for Research on Elementary and Middle Schools, Johns Hopkins University.

Slavin, R. E., & Madden, M. A. (1989). What works for students at risk: A research synthesis. *Educational Leadership, 46*, 4–13.

Smead, V. S. (1977). Ability training and task analysis in diagnostic/prescriptive teaching. *Journal of Special Education, 11*, 113–125.

Smith, M. L. (1986). The whole is greater. Combining qualitative and quantitative approaches in evaluation studies. In D. D. Williams (Ed.), Naturalistic evaluation, *New directions for program evaluation, 30*, 37–54.

Smith, M. L. (1989). Teachers' beliefs about retention. In L. A. Shepard & M. L. Smith (Eds.), *Flunking grades: Research and policies on retention* (pp. 132–150). Philadelphia: The Falmer Press.

Sparrow, S. S., Blackman, B. A., & Chauncey, S. (1983). Diagnostic and prescriptive intervention in primary school education. *American Journal of Orthopsychiatry, 53*, 721–729.

Springfield, Pa. Township Schools. (1988). *Welcome to Springfield Township schools.* Springfield: Author.

Stapleford, D. C. (1982). *The effects of a second year in kindergarten on later school achievement and self-concept.* Unpublished doctoral dissertation, Michigan State University, East Lansing.

State Department of Education. (1988). *Analysis of schools with kindergartens and transition rooms.* Unpublished data. Concord, NH.

State of New York Department of Education. (1987). Appeal Case of Diane & David Liebfred, Nov. 30.

Stevenson, H. W. (1976). Predictive value of teachers' ratings of young children. *Journal of Educational Psychology, 68,* 507–517.

Stevenson, H. W., Parker, W., Wilkinson, A., Hegion, A., & Fish, E. (1976b). Longitudinal study of individual differences in cognitive development and scholastic achievement. *Journal of Educational Psychology, 68*(4), 377–400.

Stipek, D. J., & Daniels, D. H. (1988). Declining perceptions of competence: A consequence of changes in the child or in the educational environment? *Journal of Educational Psychology, 80*(3), 352–356.

Stott, D. H. (1962). *Programmed Reading Kit.* Toronto, Canada: Gage.

Stott, D. H. (1970a). *Manual for the Bristol Social Adjustment Guide.* San Diego, CA: Educational and Industrial Testing Service.

Stott, D. H. (1970b). *Programmed Reading Kit: Manual for Parts 1 & 2.* Toronto, Canada: Gage.

Stott, L. H. (1967). *Child development: An individual longitudinal approach.* New York: Holt, Rinehart & Winston.

System 80. (1977). Arlington, IL: Borg Warner Educational Systems.

Talmadge, S. J. (1981). *Descriptive and predictive relationships among family environments, cognitive characteristics, behavioral ratings, transition room placement, and early reading achievement.* Unpublished doctoral dissertation, University of Oregon, Eugene.

Taylor, R. L. (1984). *Assessment of exceptional students: Educational and psychological procedures.* Englewood Cliffs, NJ: Prentice-Hall.

Texas State Board of Education: Committee on Students. (1990, October). *Discussion of retention in prekindergarten and kindergarten by W. N. Kirby* [Memo]. Austin: Discussion items: pages V-43 through V-66.

Thackray, D. (1971). *Readiness for reading with I.T.A. and T.O.* London: Geoffrey Chapman.

Thompson, E. (1985). *The effect of the Writing to Read program on low reading ability students.* Unpublished doctoral dissertation, University of Denver, Denver.

Thompson, G. B. (1975). Sex differences in reading attainments. *Educational Research, 18,* 16–23.

Tobin, J. J., Wu, D. Y. H., & Davidson, D. H. (1989). *Preschool in three cultures: Japan, China & the United States.* New Haven, CT: Yale University Press.

Tramontana, M. G., Hooper, S. R., & Selzer, S. C. (1988). Research on the preschool prediction of later academic achievement: A review. *Developmental Review, 8,* 89–146.

Tisci, N., Lowe, T., Rice, N., & Rivard, J. J. (1984–85). Chippewa Valley Schools. (1984–85). *A Report of the Chippewa Valley Developmental Kindergarten program.* Mt. Clemens, MI: Chippewa Valley Schools.

Troidl, R. C. (1984). *Analysis of the impact of retention on kindergarten children.* Unpublished doctoral dissertation, Tennessee State University, Nashville.

Turley, C. C. (1979). *A study of elementary school children for whom a second year of kindergarten was recommended.* Unpublished doctoral dissertation, University of San Francisco, San Francisco.

Uphoff, J. K. (1988). *Changes vs. facts: Answering the critics of gift of time.* Peterborough, NH: Society for Developmental Education.

Uphoff, J. K., & Gilmore, J. E. (1984, July 26). Local research ties suicides to early school entrance stress. *Dayton Daily News,* p. 34.

Uphoff, J. K., & Gilmore, J. (1985). Pupil age at school entrance—How many are ready for success? *Educational Leadership, 43,* 86–90.

Vernon, V. E., O'Gorman, M. B., & McLellan, A. (1955). A comparative study of educational attainments in England and Scotland. *British Journal of Educational Psychology, 25,* 195–203.

Vindication for Vincent. (1977, January 10). *Newsweek,* p. 44.

Vygotsky, L. S. (1930–35/1978). *Mind in society: The development of higher psychological processes.* Cambridge, MA: Harvard University Press.

Vygotsky, L. S. (1934/1962). *Thought and language.* Cambridge, MA: Massachusetts Institute of Technology.

Wall, D. D. (1988). Rules and regulations covering the establishment and operation of kindergarten, early admission policy and admission of beginners in Pennsylvania: Harrisburg State Department of Education. *Basic Education Circulars,* #1-88, A-29 to A-34. Harrisburg: State Department of Education.

Walsh, D. J. (1989). Changes in kindergarten: Why here? Why now? *Early Childhood Research Quarterly, 4,* 377–391.

Walsh, W. B., & Betz, N. E. (1990). *Tests and assessment* (2nd ed.). Englewood Cliffs, NJ: Prentice-Hall.

Washburne, C. (1936). Ripeness. *Progressive Educators, 13,* 125–130.

Waters, E. (1985). Review of Gesell preschool test. In J. V. Mitchell (Ed.), *Ninth mental measurements yearbook* (Vol. 1, pp. 610–611), Lincoln, NE: Buros Institute of Mental Measurements.

Weatherly, R. A. (1979). *Performing special education: Policy implementation from state level to street level.* Cambridge, MA: MIT Press.

Weinstein, L. (1968). School entrance age and adjustment. *Journal of School Psychology, 7,* 20–28.

West, P. (1991, January 23). Mississippi study of 'Writing to Read' finds 'significant' gains in students' skills. *Education Week, 10,* 10.

White, B. (1990, May 6). Schools flunk when kids fail a grade, experts say. *Atlanta Journal Constitution,* pp. 1 & A-13.

Wilson, B. J., & Reichmuth, M. (1985). Early screening programs: When is predictive accuracy sufficient? *Learning Disability Quarterly, 8,* 182–188.

Wolf, J. M., & Kessler, A. L. (1987). *Entrance to kindergarten: What is the best age?* Arlington, VA: Educational Research Service.

Wonderly, B. W. (1981). *Entrance age as it relates to school adjustment.* Unpublished doctoral dissertation, Kent State University.

Wood, C., Powell, S., & Knight, R. C. (1984). Predicting school readiness: The validity of developmental age. *Journal of Learning Disabilities, 17*, 8–11.

Ypsilantis, I. N., & Bernart, E. H. (1957). Variation in age, grade school performance. *Teachers College Record, 58*, 268–277.

Zenka, L. L., & Keatley, M. J. (1985). Progress toward excellence: Tulsa's kindergarten program. *ERS Spectrum*, Fall, *3*, 3–8.

Index